Sophie Thurnham was born in 1967, and grew up in the Lake District. She is the middle member of a large, happy family with an even larger collection of animals. After leaving school, she spent three years in London, acquiring a law degree and roaming the parks with her dog Georgie. She then took a break, before going on to Bar school. This book is the story of how she filled her time during that break. She has now abandoned her law studies, and spent the summer of 1991 travelling through Romania with her donkey, Hannibal.

The Great Donkey Trek

Sophie Thurnham

HEADLINE

Copyright © 1991 Sophie Thurnham (text and drawings)

Map drawn by Mick Wolf, Oxford Illustrators Ltd

The right of Sophie Thurnham to be identified as the Author
of the Work has been asserted by her in accordance with the
Copyright, Designs and Patents Act 1988.

First published in 1991
by HEADLINE BOOK PUBLISHING PLC

First published in paperback in 1992
by HEADLINE BOOK PUBLISHING PLC

10 9 8 7 6 5 4 3 2 1

ISBN 0 7472 3743 3

Printed and bound in Great Britain by
HarperCollins Manufacturing, Glasgow

HEADLINE BOOK PUBLISHING PLC
Headline House
79 Great Titchfield Street
London W1P 7FN

For Bella and Bogey, the ones I left behind

Acknowledgements

Neither the journey nor the book would have been possible without the support and encouragement of my parents, the best in the world. Sorry, Mum, for all the worry I put you through.

I'd like to thank Mary Holland, Jane Lewis, Sarah Woodward and all at MENCAP for having such faith in me from the start, and Elisabeth Svendsen and the vets at the Donkey Sanctuary for their invaluable advice. Thanks to John Wood in Staveley for his endless enthusiasm and generosity, to Elleray School in Windermere and Casterton School for their tireless money-raising and to all the many companies and individuals who gave donations to MENCAP and helped to make it all worthwhile.

Thank you to everyone who showed me kindness on the trip itself. My editors put lines through half of you who were originally included in the book – apparently you're much too nice to make good copy – and I'd like to apologize and say that nothing will ever make me forget your smiles of encouragement. Particular thanks to the Stolloffs – I've lost your address, do get in touch – and the Palmers; to Polly, Polly and Rose; and to Peter Hindle for all he did to make the Côte d'Azur so enjoyable.

Thanks to Emu for being so brilliant at the beginning; to Clare for being mad enough to want to come out *twice*; and to Tim for that great fortnight in September. And a special thank you to Stevie for talking about that last drive out to Rome to fetch Hannibal as if it was the holiday of a lifetime.

I owe a mention to all those who helped me get my act together when I returned to England in October – to Hugh Whitworth for persuading me to chase my dreams, to Patrick Walsh for convincing me that I could write, and to Colin and Ivor in Majorca for refusing all visitors to my room while I was stuck on Chapter 1. And finally many thanks to David Clement-Davies for that exhausting week in January when we finally managed to cut the manuscript down to size.

Contents

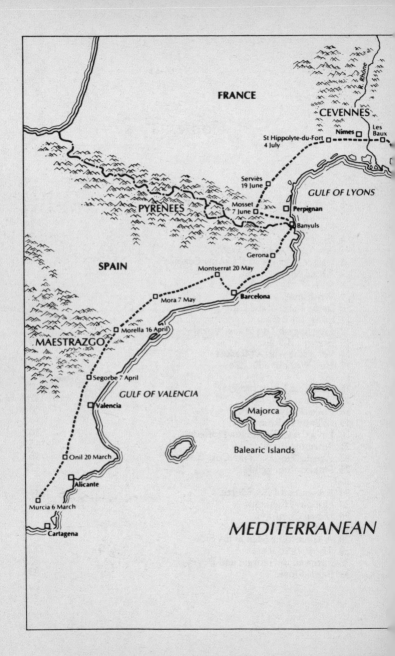

FRANCE

CEVENNES

Nîmes Les Baux

St Hippolyte-du-Fort
4 July

Serviès
19 June

GULF OF LYONS

Mosset
7 June

Perpignan

PYRENEES

Banyuls

SPAIN

Gerona

Montserrat 20 May

Barcelona

Mora 7 May

Morella 16 April

MAESTRAZGO

Segorbe 7 April

GULF OF VALENCIA

Valencia

Majorca

Onil 20 March

Balearic Islands

Alicante

Murcia 6 March

Cartagena

MEDITERRANEAN

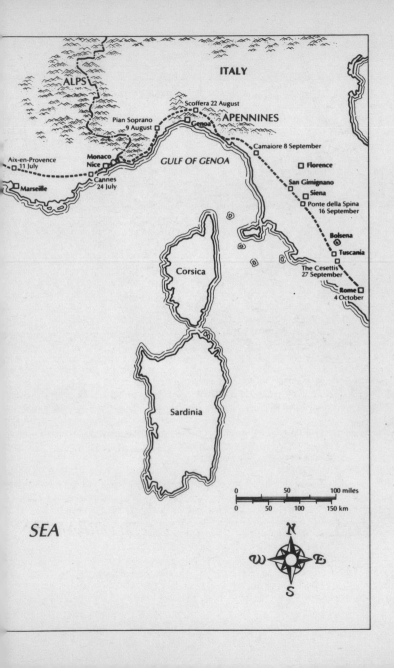

ITALY

ALPS

APENNINES

Scoffera 22 August

Pian Soprano
9 August

Genoa

GULF OF GENOA

Camaiore 8 September

Aix-en-Provence
11 July

Monaco
Nice

Florence

Marseille

Cannes
24 July

San Gimignano

Siena

Ponte della Spina
16 September

Bolsena

Tuscania

Corsica

The Cesettis
27 September

Rome
4 October

Sardinia

0   50   100 miles

0   50   100   150 km

SEA

N

W   E

S

Introduction

I have found this introduction – an attempt to explain why I went gallivanting across Europe on my own – difficult to write, for in doing so I have realized how incredibly selfish my reasons were. The fact that I raised money for charity made me a bit of a heroine in the eyes of many, and with all the publicity after my return I was beginning to believe it myself. But the initial decision to help MENCAP was in truth nothing but a last-minute 'Why not?', since I was going to be walking all that way anyway. If I'd merely wanted to boost charity funds, I can think of far better ways of going about it.

It would not be over-cynical to describe my journey as a seven-month ego trip. I wanted to test myself, mentally and physically, against unknown odds; I wanted excitement and danger; I wanted to experience what life had to offer at its most basic level.

I was twenty-one years old, middle class (as they say) and well educated, halfway to becoming the barrister I had wanted to be since I was fourteen. I come from a large, happy family and I was the luckiest person I knew. Yet I felt restless and dissatisfied. My dreams were at odds with the life I was actually creating for myself, and I was feeling 'There must be more' – the mid-life crisis twenty years early. I was aware that I was not making the most of my abilities, but I wasn't sure where I'd gone wrong.

As a child I enjoyed excelling but hated the way that, because I was clever, adults trivialized the other things I loved. I led a double life between school, where I was a sociable swot, and home, where I preferred to be alone and outside with my animals. I bred sheep and chickens, swam in the tarn and sailed my beloved dinghy all over Windermere. I wanted to be a shepherd when I grew up but the first careers adviser I met told me not to be so stupid – I had a brain, so I must use it, and leaflets on medicine, accountancy and law were thrust into my hand. I wanted to have it all and was led to believe that a career in a traditionally male-dominated sphere was the way to get it. I enjoy arguing and making an exhibition of myself, so decided I would make a good barrister. Of conventional jobs, it seemed to me to be the best – and it still does. So I ended up studying law at King's College, London. Dreams of sailing the Atlantic single-handed, of running a safari in Africa, of living in France in a gypsy caravan while writing romantic novels were all pushed to the back of my mind. There would be time enough for all that when I'd made my fortune as the best lady barrister ever to hit the Old Bailey; and anyway, didn't everyone have those dreams?

The thrill of London soon wore off and I found living without animals difficult. In a rash moment I acquired a scrawny, wonky-eared mongrel from Battersea Dogs' Home. Georgie kept me sane and happy through university; she accompanied me everywhere, attending lectures and becoming quite a college personality. I persuaded my grandmother to look after her when I worked abroad during the holidays and I prayed that I would somehow find a set of dog-loving chambers when I qualified.

After three years at university I felt in need of a break from law, so I postponed my place at Bar school for a year. I wanted a last chance to do all that was not compatible with life as a barrister. I wanted to earn spendable weekly wages in a job where refusal to kowtow to the boss would not jeopardize my entire future. I wanted to dance till dawn ten nights in a row if my stamina could take it. I wanted to be carefree and irresponsible while I was still young and pretty enough to get away with it.

So I took myself off to Tuscany to work in a rather grotty hotel and I achieved most of these superficial ambitions. I cooked for the English tourists meals whose quality depended on the seriousness of my rows with the incompetent manager. I became wonderfully brown, I had a crazy love affair with a beautiful Italian and I was bored out of my mind. I couldn't stand having my character judged by the height of my spinach souffles, and I missed my dog, so at the end of October I returned to my parents' house in Cumbria. I toyed with the idea of cooking on a charter boat in the Caribbean, but my lack of enthusiasm shone through at interviews and I was relieved not to be offered a job. I loved being at home with the animals, looking after my handicapped little brother, reading a lot of books and being gloriously anti-social. I would have been happy doing nothing else for the rest of the year, but there was still a nagging voice in the back of my head chanting, 'This is your last chance. If you don't do it now, you never will. If you can't do it, no one can.'

'What?' I screamed back.

I thought that maybe the time had come to find a serious boyfriend; then I realized that something *had* to be wrong if I was considering that old cop-out.

I was reading Laurie Lee's *As I Walked Out One Midsummer*

Morning and feeling sorry that we can't just take to the road and discover a foreign land any more. Then I read Hilaire Belloc's *Path to Rome* and I began to think, 'Why not?' When I'd worked in Spain and Italy I had discovered that traditional communities *do* still exist off the tourist trail. I had a basic knowledge of Spanish, French and Italian. I had two very strong legs and a ridiculously healthy constitution. I had some money saved and I had nine months to fill. Why not? My parents were away and I remember downing a glass of wine, sitting on the kitchen table, and making my decision. I would pack a rucksack and just wander for a while, free from the comforts and restrictions of my background and the career that I had set for myself. I would see whether I was as capable and independent as I liked to think. I would put my values and courage to a test set by myself rather than examining boards or employers. I would strip life of its trimmings and see if I could survive.

Sophie Thurnham
Cumbria, 1991

Spain

Chapter 1
Preparations

My parents accepted the news with their customary calm.

'That sounds great, poppet,' said my father, getting on with whatever he was busy doing at his desk. 'Let me know if there's anything I can do to help.'

My mother was, if anything, too approving – she decided that she wanted to come too. My friends' reactions were mixed. Some rashly promised that they would come out and join me for a while, but others, especially the ones who had travelled a lot themselves, were incredibly condescending, saying I would never last more than a week. They pointed out that they couldn't remember a day since I was fifteen when I hadn't worn make-up, that I'd never done anything like this before – I'd never been a girl guide or won a Duke of Edinburgh medal, and I'd always done my best to miss the annual Christmas fell walks at home. All this was true, but their antagonism only made me cussed and determined to prove them wrong.

Jo, my elder sister, thought that I should do it Don Quixote style and ride. I was tempted, but I soon realized that a horse would double my costs, and I didn't feel I knew enough about horses to take on the extra responsibility. However, the suggestion gave me an idea. I remembered a book that had absorbed my mother twelve years ago about the Chitty family's journey from Santiago de Compostela in Spain to Smyrna in Greece. They had taken two donkeys – one to carry their children and the other for the baggage. We'd had a donkey when I was little and my mother had recently fostered two from the Donkey Sanctuary. I knew about donkeys – mainly that they can be difficult, but also that they are hardy, strong and cheap to run. I'd be able to carry enough gear to live in a little comfort, and I would have a companion – my mind was soon made up.

Italy was where I wanted to go most, but even the south is cold until May. As the romantic wanderings of my dreams always took place under a hot sun, I decided to start in southern Spain. There I could set off as early as February, walk north away from the strengthening sun into France, then make a U-turn down into Italy.

I began searching the library for historical routes to follow, pilgrim ways and military marches that I could weave together to take me from Spain to Italy. I found a biography of Hannibal, and couldn't believe my luck – I'd always wondered why an African had crossed the French Alps to reach Italy, and now I discovered that he had journeyed all the way round from the south of Spain. Perfect! I became so carried away that for a while I decided to take an elephant instead of a donkey, until I found out how much it would eat – a ton of hay a week – and I realized that tethering it on a village green could be difficult.

I soon discovered that it would be impossible to follow Hannibal exactly. He had marched close to the coast in Spain, and if I tried to retrace his steps I'd be walking through tower blocks and discotheques. Hannibal began his campaign at Cartagena in the southeastern province of Murcia, which was perfect. But after that we'd have to part company. I'd walk up eastern Spain keeping about thirty miles from the coast. I found the map of an old pilgrim route across the eastern Pyrenees which would take me into France; then I would rejoin Hannibal at the Rhone and follow him through the Alps. In Italy he had rampaged in convoluted circles as he fought off the Roman legions, so I planned to leave him in the Po valley and make my own way directly to the capital. So the inspiration was Hannibal, but most of the itinerary was to be my own.

I agonized over what I should do about George, my dog. Mum wasn't keen to look after her and I felt I couldn't dump her on friends for long, so eventually I decided to take her with me. I visited some of the nearby quarantine kennels, and I booked her into a friendly place near the sea at Fleetwood in Lancashire.

I decided to raise money for MENCAP, the Royal Society for Mentally Handicapped Children and Adults, by being sponsored. The main reason was to give my journey a sense of purpose; it would no longer be merely the whimsical self-indulgence of a Tory MP's spoilt daughter, but something I could be proud of.

My younger brother, Stephen, is severely mentally handicapped and my family has been involved with MENCAP for some time. The charity's appeals department leapt at the idea of my collecting money for them, and had incredible faith in me, almost more than I did myself. I originally thought I'd collect just a few hundred pounds from family and friends, but MENCAP and my parents had greater plans and set a target of £10,000. Suddenly my journey took on a whole new meaning; it was the 'MENCAP Donkey Walk', and other people were depending on me. There was no going back.

By now it was Christmas. I planned to set off in late February, so I had two months to make preparations and endless lists of all I thought a professional traveller would take.

Animal Regulations

The Chitty family had taken their donkeys and their dog from Spain, through France to Italy in 1975, so I didn't anticipate any problems, but I rang all three embassies to make sure. They all confirmed that I could take a dog and a donkey across the relevant borders, provided I had evidence of the dog's anti-rabies vaccine and obtained a health certificate for the donkey from official vets at the borders. I took George to the vet in Windermere and had myself vaccinated against rabies as well, just in case I became caught up in any dog fights.

Maps

Off I went to Stanford's in London. France is well mapped, but I discovered that Spain and Italy have nothing similar to our Ordnance Survey system. After applying to the Ministry of Defence I was given permission to photocopy fourteen maps of Spain, which had been drawn to a scale of 1:100,000 by the British War Office in 1941. The contours can't have changed, I thought, and I spent the next week in the RGS library diligently copying tracks and footpaths from the more up-to-date and detailed maps on to my black and white copies. I was very proud of the results, but couldn't face doing the same for Italy so decided to wait and see what maps were available once I was there.

Equipment

Friends recommended tents, sleeping bags, boots and clothes with very impressive-sounding names, but I was flabbergasted by the prices. Instead I bought a second-hand tent for £60; I chose the YHA's cheapest sleeping bag (£25.99); and I persuaded K Shoes to give me a free pair of Brasher boots. I found an old Calor gas stove in the cellar which seemed to work, and Mum produced a set of saucepans that she'd bought for a camping holiday in Wales fifteen years ago. They fitted into each other like Russian dolls and the lids could be used as frying pans.

My one big expense was a self-inflatable 'wondermat' to sleep on. It cost a fortune, but I was completely taken in by its blurb about being a godsend on K2 expeditions. I almost treated myself to some Gore-tex waterproofs, but after seeing the price tags I decided that my old red sailing jacket and orange Peter Storm bottoms would do just as well.

Mileage

I spent hours bent over my maps and a calculator and worked out I would have to walk thirteen miles per day. Donkeys, I read, walk at 2.5 miles per hour, so that meant five hours and fifteen minutes' walking a day, six days a week. Most of my male friends scoffed at this, apparently expecting me to walk at least twenty-five miles a day, but thirteen sounded plenty to me.

Sponsorship

I traipsed around Kendal with sponsorship forms and was amazed by the generosity of the local shopkeepers; I held a goodbye party in London and poured strong drinks down my friends until they promised (in writing) to give vast sums of money upon my return. Many of the companies I wrote to paid up immediately, apparently far more convinced than I was that I would reach Rome by October.

Transport to Spain

Taking a dog abroad by air costs a fortune, so I decided to go by train and boat instead. Brittany Ferries sail from Plymouth across the Bay of Biscay to Santander in northern Spain, and I booked a passage for 28 February. From there we could catch a train to Madrid, then change to a sleeper which would take us directly to Murcia.

Donkeys

I spent a day at the Sidmouth Donkey Sanctuary in Devon learning all there is to know about donkeys. Elisabeth Svendsen, founder of the Sanctuary, wasn't the cranky old do-gooder I'd expected, and gave me the most sensible advice that I received from anyone. She showed me how to make a pack saddle, and reassured me that it was not cruel to expect a donkey to walk thirteen miles a day with a 50 lb pack on its back. Donkeys are sociable animals, she said, and as long as they are treated kindly they prefer working with people to being left on their own in a field all day. She advised me not to plan my trip too precisely, but to wait and see what my donkey was capable of.

But she was astonished to find that I had not heard about the ban on the export of donkeys from Spain. A few years ago, she told me, some zebras arrived in Madrid zoo from Morocco, bringing with them African Horse Sickness, a fatal and highly contagious disease that rapidly spread and caused havoc in the Spanish equine world. Because of this England had placed a ban on imports of equines from Spain and, as far as Mrs Svendsen knew, so had France.

My boat was due to leave England in three weeks' time. I immediately began ringing embassies and ministries to find out the exact rules, but I couldn't get a definite answer out of anyone. I was frantic with frustration and out of desperation I asked my father for help.

Dad went straight to the top and told Sir Geoffrey Howe, the then Foreign Secretary and a lifelong MENCAP supporter, of my problem. Within a few hours I had all the information I needed, but it was not good news. Not only were there no exceptions to the French ban on the import of equines from Spain, but there were also severe restrictions on the movements of equines within Spain – I would have to have a *guia*, a special veterinary certificate that must be renewed every five days.

My initial reaction was to scrap the whole idea of taking a donkey, and I tried desperately to think of another type of pack animal, going through everything from yaks to St Bernards; Mum got very excited about llamas, but a few phone calls revealed that the travel restrictions on cameloids are even more complicated than on equines.

I knew that if I were truly hearty I would carry my gear in a rucksack until I reached France, but the image of a pack-animal was by now too firmly lodged in my mind for me to give it up easily. And the stubborn side of my nature was determined not to let red tape get the better of me. I would just have to harden my heart and change donkeys at the Pyrenees.

Sir Geoffrey Howe's involvement triggered an invasion of outside interest that I would have been much happier without. The press for some reason loved the connection and were suddenly ringing me up every five minutes for the latest news of the 'Howe Donkey Saga'. Local television and radio wanted to interview me, and a barrage of hate mail began arriving from members of the public who'd jumped to extraordinary conclusions about what I was doing.

The best was the one telling me that if I wanted to raise money for charity I should spend seven months clearing dog shit from the streets of Newcastle, to 'prevent the fatuous use of an innocent donkey who at the end of the trek would be left – to what??' (She must have thought I was planning to dump it at Rome airport before flying nonchalantly home.) Clearing dog mess, she continued, 'will be much harder and much less glamorous than lolling about Spain and France on a donkey sponging free meals from all.' Quite.

I got on with my packing and last-minute plans. I sewed four yards of bright green canvas into six saddle bags, breaking poor

Mum's sewing machine in the process, and then I tried to fit into them the clothes and equipment that I had finally decided were coming with me. It was a strange mixture of vital necessities and self-indulgent luxuries that I couldn't bear to be without.

Clothes
Knickers: 3 pairs
Bras: 1 Triumph sports, 1 silk with lace trim
Thermals: 1 vest, 1 pair long johns
Trousers: 1 pair jeans, 1 pair shorts
Tops: 1 MENCAP T-shirt, 1 Liberty tana lawn blouse, 2 jumpers
Dresses: 1 dropped waist, 1 with fitted bodice and tiered skirt
Socks: 2 pairs
Waterproofs: 1 jacket, 1 pair trousers
Boots: 1 pair

Food
Fruit cake: 1
Alpen: 2 kg
Drinks: 1 tin powdered milk, 2 jars instant coffee, 100 tea bags
Soups: 24 Sainsbury's Cup-a, 12 stock cubes
Pedigree Chum: 10 tins

Equipment
Camping: 1 tent, 1 sleeping bag, 1 mat
Cooking: 1 stove, 2 pans, 2 knives, 2 forks, 2 spoons
Donkey: 1 hoof pick, 1 30 foot rope, 1 hay net
Survival: 1 torch, 1 axe, 1 pen knife
Culture: 1 box watercolours, 1 sketch book, 2 reading books
Washing: 2 towels, 1 scrubbing brush, 2 tubes travel wash
Sponge bag: 1 hairbrush, 10 hair elastics, 1 toothbrush, 1 tube toothpaste, 1 soap box, 1 flannel
First-aid kit: 1 bottle tranquillizers, 6 tubes worming mixture, 1 can flea spray, 1 can donkey's hoof spray, 50 aspirin, 20 anti-histamine, 20 diarrhoea pills, 2 tubes Germolene, 1 bottle Dettol, 2 bandages.
Female necessities: 1 tube Canesten cream, 80 Tampax, 20 sanitary towels, 168 contraceptive pills
(Having to cope with the curse every month was something I was trying not to think about, but I was at least going to make it as light and painless as possible. I also reckoned that if I were raped halfway up the Pyrenees, a morning-after pill might be pretty hard to come by. And you never know, I thought, with any luck I might meet Prince Charming and not be able to control myself.)

Emu, my younger sister, volunteered to travel out to Spain with

8

me for the start. She was due to begin work in a hotel in Majorca at the end of March and had a month free. I was extremely grateful, for I was beginning to feel nervous about the great unknown that lay ahead of me. I doubted that Emu would be much help with the practicalities of finding a donkey and organizing papers, but at least I wouldn't be alone.

Three days before we were due to leave I had the first stroke of good luck for weeks. My father met the Spanish Ambassador in London at an official dinner and told him of my plans. He promised to let the Minister of Tourism, Señor Luis Arroniz, know of my arrival in Murcia on Friday. I tried not to let myself expect too much from this, but it was reassuring to know I could turn to someone if I had any great difficulties.

Our final departure from home was chaotic. I frantically finished my packing and sewed the final straps on to the saddle bags while watching my last episode of *Neighbours* and making phone calls that should have been made weeks before – organizing Bar school and giving Mum authority over my bank account. I gave my two pregnant pet sheep a hug, kissed the cats, and said a very tearful goodbye to Rootie, my parents' old spaniel. She hadn't been well, and I felt certain that I'd never see her again.

Mum drove us to Carlisle and saw us safely aboard the sleeper to Plymouth. She gave me some Suchard chocolate eggs and told me to save them for Easter, which made me want to cry. Finally we were off and I waved out of the window until Carlisle was just a speck in the distance.

I lay on my bunk listening to the rhythm of the wheels as they hurtled southwards and for the first time I wondered what the hell I was doing. I'd talked about this journey for so long I could now hardly believe it was really beginning. I was excited and terrified at the same time. I looked at Georgie, and she wagged her tail back at me before calmly settling down to sleep. She probably thought we were on our routine journey back to London for another term at college, and half of me wished it could be true, that all I had to fear was a law exam. I must be mad, I thought, and drifted off into a strange dream in which I was the first human being ever to catch African Horse Disease.

Chapter 2
Strange Way to Find a Donkey

There are nearly four years between my younger sister and me, but it seems less because she's always been so tall. Her real name is Emma but she's been called Emu for as long as I can remember. It arose from her obsession with an emu puppet when she was little, and from a very mean trick I played on her when she was four. I put a goose egg down her bed one night, and for years she was convinced that she had laid it. Anyway, the name seems strangely appropriate. She's five feet twelve, as she prefers to put it, and very beautiful, with huge blue eyes, short spiky hair and legs that go on for ever. She's the easiest-going person I've ever known, seeming to glide through life without even noticing the trivialities that constantly vex the rest of us.

Emu has always been able to make me laugh; we share a close, French-and-Saunders type of humour, often incomprehensible to the rest of the world. Whatever horrors lay ahead of us in the next month, I hoped that somehow we'd be able to laugh our way through them.

On the ferry Emu broke my expedition rules and nearly doubled her amount of luggage by buying most of the cosmetics counter. At Carlisle station, while she was wearing my red waterproof jacket and Mum's old fell boots, she'd been mistaken for a British Rail porter and was furious. She retaliated by dolling herself up to the nines and chatting up as many of the lorry drivers as she could. I was violently seasick and spent most of the crossing in the cabin.

When the ferry reached Santander it wasn't long before my carefully scheduled plans began to go wrong. At the station I was told that there was no train until the following morning that would take dogs; I ended up shoving Georgie down my jumper and we raced on to a direct train to Madrid just as it was leaving the station. In Madrid we managed to find a dog-loving station cleaner who smuggled Georgie into our sleeping compartment; when the ticket inspector came I hid her down my bed and miraculously we reached Murcia without being found out.

We were met at the station by a beautiful girl called Carmen who said she was to be our interpreter for the next few days while a donkey was being found for us. She explained that Señor Arroniz, the minister, had set the whole tourist office to work on our donkey quest, and they were doing all they could to find a suitable animal as soon as possible. Meanwhile, we were to stay in the best hotel in town, and we would be given a guide to show us round the city.

I was stunned by all this, and couldn't work out why the minister should be going to so much trouble. As Carmen talked on, I began to understand. Murcia is the least known to foreigners of the Spanish Mediterranean regions, but Luis Arroniz is trying to put the area on the tourist map. He saw our donkey quest as a wonderful publicity opportunity, and there seemed to be a simple bargain involved: if we wooed and wowed the press, he would find us our donkey.

The next three days were a frantic round of interviews with newspaper and radio reporters, and photo sessions as we met the local matadors, tasted the regional specialities and ate strawberries and ice cream with Señor Arroniz. Our guide Maria and her boyfriend Marcello showed us round the city, which was much more beautiful than I'd expected. It has a strong Arab feel to its crooked narrow streets and intricate plasterwork on the buildings. There were fountains in almost every *plaza,* and palm trees and ornamental gardens filled every spare patch of land. It's a colourful, bustling city, with newspaper stands and lottery kiosks at every corner, and cafés spilling on to the streets and squares. The endless din of Spanish voices fascinated me, for I found the dialect almost impossible to understand, its slurring softness making the words indistinguishable.

We visited the elaborately decorated casino, where the eyes of the figures painted on the walls wouldn't leave us alone as we drank the strongest, sweetest coffee I'd ever tasted. We watched a society wedding take place at the huge old cathedral in the central square and afterwards I climbed up the bell tower and looked out over the flat Segura plain towards the mountains to the north, where I knew we would soon be walking. I gazed out at the barren grey landscape and surprised myself by feeling no fear, only a vague longing for the excitement that lay ahead.

Most beautiful of all in Murcia were the people. They were small and finely boned, with black hair, dark skin and an exotic appearance which I found incredibly attractive. The women dressed in smart, tightly fitting clothes, were apparently unaffected by the intense heat, and made Emu and me (in our jeans and fell boots) feel like a couple of ugly pink hippos. We stood out a mile, towering over most of the men, and we were stared at incessantly as we wandered along the streets.

George, on the other hand, fitted in as if she'd lived here all her life. With her street urchin looks she was very like the Spanish dogs and trotted around quite happily, unperturbed by the dramatic change of surroundings. I noticed that people were much more wary of dogs than in England and would ask whether she bit before touching her.

Saturday night was spent flamenco dancing. I loved the strong Arabic music and the erotic thrusting of hips, the clicking of heels and the flirting eyes – but Emu and I were hopeless, a pair of clod-hopping giants, and caused much amusement with our clumsy enthusiasm. Emu flirted outrageously with our teacher, a beautiful man who was the spitting image of Sazillo's sculpture of Jesus which we'd been admiring that afternoon. We kept going until after 4 a.m., and were up five hours later visiting the Santuario de la Fuensanta, a monastery up in the hills to the south of the city. (I was beginning to look forward to the start of my walk, if only as a way of having some rest!)

On Sunday evening Maria rushed over to our hotel with the news that a donkey had been found. The owner wanted £200 for it, four times as much as I'd been expecting to pay, but since we'd stayed at the hotel for nothing and dined out free all weekend, I felt it didn't matter too much. We drove out the next morning with half the tourist office to a small village on the outskirts of Murcia to have a look at it.

A tiny brown jenny was waiting. I'd been imagining something larger, like the big Andalucian donkeys; this one seemed so pathetic and small that I suddenly felt terribly guilty about what I was doing. Her backbone didn't even reach my tummy button – how could she possibly carry all my luggage?

Everyone was looking at me expectantly, so I tried to act like the hearty professional traveller they thought I was. I inspected her feet, which were good and hard, although longer than I would have liked. She had a solid roll of fat on her neck (the donkey equivalent of the camel's hump), she had no sores or lumps, her eyes were bright and clear, and her nose was clean. The owner, a fat old peasant dressed in his Sunday best, insisted that she was only six years old, but by the look of her teeth I reckoned she was more like twelve. She was fluffy-haired and a silvery brown colour; her mane had been cut off and the top of her tail shaved, which looked peculiar but apparently it's the custom. She was by no means the finest physical example of the donkey species I had laid eyes on, but there seemed to be nothing wrong with her, and she walked obediently round the yard with me.

I tried to find out what kind of work she was used to, but all the old man would say was that she would do everything, from pulling a cart to ploughing a field to carrying two people on her back. He jumped on her himself to convince me, and began telling me how I should whack her with a stick if she was stubborn. Immediately my doubts about taking her vanished – at least I'd be rescuing her from this. Yes, I said, I'll buy her.

Suddenly my hand was being shaken and the press photographers were huddling us all together around the donkey. We stared at each other, the donkey and I, and in her deep brown eyes I saw calm resignation and perhaps a little sadness. Lord knows what she saw in mine.

We went back into Murcia for the *guia,* the travel permit without which I could be fined up to half a million pesetas, and were sent on a wild goose chase around the city trying to find the right official. I'd presumed a vet would have to inspect the donkey, but I was given a health certificate just by paying the required amount of money. Thus I realized that the *guia* system was not part of a structured effort to eliminate equine disease, but merely part of the crazy red tape that Spain is so famous for. My certificate was valid for only five days, after which I must find the right official in the next province and pay for another.

Emu and I argued for half an hour over what to call the donkey. For some reason I had been expecting it to be a boy, and had earlier decided on 'Hasdrubel the Handsome', the name of the Carthaginian leader before Hannibal who had never left Spain. Now we had to think of a girl's name, but I couldn't remember what Hannibal's wife was called and there weren't really any other women directly connected with the Hannibal story. After much bickering we returned to the original idea and adjusted it slightly, christening her 'Hasdrubella the Beautiful', which was soon shortened to Bella.

We had another press photo session, with Señor Arroniz hugging the donkey, and me trying to arrange the saddle bags on her and said sad goodbyes to everyone. For three days I'd enjoyed a complete abdication of responsibility, but now it was all up to me again – no guides, no interpreters, no big names to help us, just me and my beautiful nutty sister. I waved frantically as the last car drove away, and tried to feel brave.

This was it – we were off. I felt very proud and rather strange. Everything was perfect: the donkey was walking beautifully, the sun was shining and we were on a quiet little road heading vaguely northwards. I was gloriously happy. The journey had begun.

My happiness did not last long. After just ten minutes our small road joined the main Murcia to Orihuela highway, and our voices

14

were drowned by the roar of heavy traffic. We were walking north-east, away from the city, and I prayed that we would soon leave the huge factories and grey warehouses behind. From the flat Murcian plain I gazed longingly at the mountains to the north; they looked unreal, like a cardboard backdrop and it was impossible to tell how far away they were. I didn't care, I just wanted to reach them, for *they* were what this journey of mine was all about – wild and unin-habited, dusty and bare, utterly foreign.

Meanwhile we were stuck on this busy road while lorry drivers hooted and jeered at us; the donkey was marvellous and didn't even seem to notice, but we felt miserable. We couldn't think of anything to say to each other, and walked along in silence. This was not the stuff my dreams were made of; I kept my eyes skinned for a turning, and sang *Que Sera Sera* to stop myself from crying.

Although it wasn't signposted, we took a small turning to the left a couple of miles later. As we walked through huge orange and lemon groves, my happiness returned. The buildings and the traffic disappeared and the sickening fumes were replaced by the sharp, invigorating scent of ripe lemons. The groves were shining exam-ples of efficient modern farming, exact rows of well-pruned trees stretching as far as the eye could see, with a grid of water pipes lying over the tractor-tilled soil and huge electric wire fences sur-rounding it all. Though this was welcome after the factories, it was hardly the simple peasant-toiling that I'd imagined of Spanish agri-culture. I was heartened by the sight of three old ladies in black carrying huge baskets of lemons, and I said a cheery '*Buenas tardes*' as they passed. They looked at us warily and said a curt '*adios*' before hurrying on.

We reached the hills surprisingly quickly. They were smaller than they appeared from a distance, but still formidable. The higher land was completely bare, but around us the ground was covered in a strange scrub, a network of long brown tendrils like scorched heather. They looked dead but when I tugged at them they tore back at my hands like wire. The soil was a dusty grey on top, but whitish-red below, the colour of a strawberry roan horse.

I wondered where this road of ours would lead. I couldn't find it on any of my maps, but since a bridge had been built especially for it over the motorway, I didn't doubt that it would end up some-where – even when it became little more than a dirt track. I felt much happier now that we were out in the wilds. George was in heaven; after being cooped up in boats, trains and hotels for so long, she was madly running about, chasing lizards and sniffing out rabbits.

Our track wound slowly upwards and we were soon engulfed by the grey hills, all signs of Murcia gone. The track forked, but I wasn't too worried and we took the more northerly branch, completely unprepared for its abrupt end twenty minutes later. It had been washed away by a great torrent of long-since vanished water, and a huge gully had been carved across our path. I stared down at the deep, red gash and wondered what to do. Even if Emu and I scrambled over to the other side, there was no way a laden donkey could manage the fifteen-foot drop. The gully stretched on from east to west as far as the eye could see – there seemed little point in walking along its edge. We would have to turn back and try the other track.

The light was beginning to fade and we should have found somewhere to camp hours ago. I looked round desperately, but there was nowhere flat enough to put up the tent and nothing for Bella to eat. I walked on more urgently, although I hadn't a clue what I was looking for – just some vague image of a friendly little farmstead, with smiling peasants welcoming us to safety.

After about half an hour the track petered out completely. This wasn't meant to happen. I looked at my map again, as if I could find a solution if I just stared hard enough. God knows where we were. I couldn't bear the thought of having to retrace our steps all the way to Murcia. We *must* be near a road. I suggested to Emu that we try going cross-country, and poor Emu, under the impression that I knew what I was doing, agreed.

Hasdrubella did her best walking through the scrub, but it caught at her legs continually and made her trip, which sent the saddle bags careering over her head. To escape we climbed up to rocky high ground, where she was as nimble as a goat, though Emu and I now kept losing our footing. We made slow progress but went on northwards, and I looked round desperately for somewhere to camp. I cursed myself for having been so stupid, for not having prepared my first day properly. I should have made enquiries about where we could stay before setting off. Emu hadn't said a word for ages and I could see that she was frightened.

At last I spotted a road to the west beneath us. Climbing down to it was difficult and Bella's saddle bags kept falling off as she charged down the steep slope, but I felt ridiculously happy to have found something definite and identifiable at last. If we walked along it we would soon find a house, I thought, and I'd ask if we could camp in their garden.

My elation quickly wore off. The road just seemed to be heading deeper into the mountains and brought us no sign of happy farmsteads or welcoming peasants. We saw a large monastery-like building off to the right, but the gates were firmly locked and it looked sinister in the growing darkness. We plodded on up the twisting road, our conversation drying up as we each determined

16

not to convey our fear to the other.

Emu suddenly screamed and pointed to the ground: there were hundreds of hypodermic syringes all over the sides of the road. How had they got here? My imagination went wild, and I soon convinced myself that this must be where all the junkies from the southeast of Spain came to buy their supplies. Tentatively I led the way back along the tarmac, keeping well away from the lethal edges, terrified that one of us would step on an AIDS-infected needle. The torchlight threw grotesque, dancing shadows across the nearby rocks, and in them I saw crazed men with distorted limbs waiting to leap out at us. I was convinced that we were going to be murdered on the very first night.

If there'd been a way I would gladly have given up the whole idea of this crazy journey there and then, and in my desperate, non-believing way I prayed for deliverance. Then I noticed that Emu was crying and I realized that I had to be brave, if only for her sake. It was now completely dark and I shone the torch across the surrounding hills. To the right, about a hundred yards above us, I noticed the outline of a building and I suggested that we take a look. Emu sobbed that she was too scared, so I left her with the animals while I took the torch to explore.

I found the remains of a stone house. There was no roof and most of the walls had fallen in, but it was clean and we would at least be able to hide there. There was even a fair amount of grass growing around it. I called Emu over, and we decided to spend the night in what I guessed had been the kitchen. I unloaded Bella and tethered her to what had once been the front doorway. She started to graze contentedly, and suddenly life didn't seem so bad. We made a cup of hot chocolate, and I realized I was starving, so attacked the muesli; we laid our mats out on the ground – it was too rocky to put up the tent – and snuggled into our sleeping bags – by now it was very cold. But I managed to puncture my 'wonder-mat' within five minutes and then my sleeping-bag split, the zip broken irretrievably. I tried to mend it with safety pins, but nothing seemed to keep the cold air out. I wondered what else could go wrong and apologized to Emu for making such a mess of the first day.

'It's OK,' she said, 'it could have been worse. Those things we were imagining out on the road could really have happened.' On which sombre note we said goodnight and tried to go to sleep.

Thinking it must be about midnight, I scrabbled about in the saddle bags and found the alarm clock. I shone the torch at it, then put my ear against it to make sure it was still working. It said five past eight.

Suddenly both Emu and I were doubled up with laughter. It

17

seemed ludicrous to have been so frightened when it was so early. In all my careful preparations of the previous months, I hadn't even thought to find out what time it gets dark in southern Spain in March.

It was a relief to have something to laugh about, and we sat up and shared a cigarette, noticing for the first time what a beautiful spot we were in. We were very high up, with an amazing view over Murcia. All the stars were out and Emu was trying to show me the Plough when I thought I'd better check on Bella. I got up again and walked over to the front door, found her tether and tugged at it. The end came flying back at me and I stared down in disbelief at where my knot had been. Bella had gone.

I shouted at Emu to bring the torch, but Bella was nowhere to be seen. I suddenly felt sick. We began searching the hillside, desperately calling her name and continually tripping in the scrub as we looked for hoof marks in the earth. Now it was my turn to start crying. We'd only set off five hours ago and already I'd lost my donkey. After about fifteen minutes we gave up the search, convinced that she must have run all the way back home, so we turned back towards our ruined house. There was nothing more we could do till morning.

I couldn't stop thinking of the motorway that lay between us and the farm Bella would be heading for. I was starting to imagine the most horrific accidents when suddenly, out of nowhere, there was Bella, running towards us. She stopped in front of me and nuzzled her head into my chest, wanting me to rub her brow bone. From that moment on, as I sank my face into her soft grey fur, I adored her, this gentle trusting creature who had no idea of what was in store for her. I led her back to camp and this time I tied the rope so well that it took twenty minutes in the morning to undo.

Emu and I lay down again and tried to sleep. Just as I was dozing off, Bella found the saddle bag containing our food, and before I could stop her she had finished half the muesli and taken a large chunk out of the fruit cake. I reckoned that whatever the old man had given her for good behaviour had worn off.

I kept waking in the night, freezing with cold; nothing I could do to my sleeping-bag would stop it letting in a draught somewhere, and I ended up putting on all our spare clothes. At dawn I woke to find Bella lying down beside me and I had a priceless view of 'sunrise over Murcia', framed by donkey ears. I cuddled into her back and found it was the best way to keep warm. As I dropped off to sleep again I wondered vaguely what would happen if she rolled.

Chapter 3
Donkey Under Attack

It took hours to pack up the next day. In the darkness we had spread our gear around indiscriminately and emptied all six saddle bags, as we hadn't known where to look for anything. It took three attempts to get the balance right; the bags would lurch to one side as soon as Bella began walking and then suddenly swing round under her belly. The poor donkey would peer down between her legs with a bemused expression on her face and wait patiently for me to rearrange it all. We finally reached the road by twelve, and headed northwards once more.

The sky was a cloudless blue, and it was already incredibly hot. It felt as if we were walking through a western film set; we'd reached the top of the hills and were now on a kind of plateau, with no sign of civilization. Dry scrub grew everywhere and the occasional cactus plant gripped the firmer rock.

Seeing a lorry parked at the side of the road, I decided to ask the driver where we were. I found him in the back, a fat little man of about fifty with bulbous eyes and blotchy red skin. He stank of sweat and tobacco. He said something much too quickly for me to understand, so I apologized about my bad Spanish and asked him to repeat it more slowly. I moved closer to try to catch the words.

He wanted to sleep with me. Ah. Feeling naive and embarrassed, I wished I could think of something cutting to say. I couldn't, so I just turned and made a quick exit.

'What did he say?' asked Emu, idly kicking stones at the side of the road. 'Where are we?'

'I don't know; he said he wanted to sleep with me.'

'You're kidding!' Emu thought it was hilarious. 'What did he look like?'

'Horrible!'

Emu's laughter was infectious and I wasn't upset for long. A car stopped not long afterwards and a friendly couple told us that if we turned right at the next junction we'd be on the road to Fortuna, a town about twenty kilometres to the north. So we walked on, happy to know at last where we were, enjoying the sunshine and

19

the peace of so much open space.

The backs of our necks became sore and red from the strong sun and George lost interest in the lizards, lolling along beside us with her tongue out. We sat down for lunch under the only tree we had seen all day. The road descended into a more fertile plain, and an hour later we arrived at the small village of Los Valientos. At the end of the main street, lined with simple white houses and shaded by cedar trees, we found a bar, where we gratefully downed an ice-cold beer. Half a dozen old men were gathered round the counter, and they peered at us as if they'd never seen anything like us in all their lives. I grinned back at them and introduced myself. They didn't seem to believe what I was saying, so I found one of the newspaper articles about us, which the younger man behind the bar read out loud to the rest of them. At the end of it they turned to us with huge smiles and welcomed us to their village as if we were famous explorers. The owner took us to the grassy area by the side of the bar and said we were welcome to stay. It was perfect and meant we could eat at the bar in the evening and have a good scrub in the washroom.

The entire village seemed to have heard of our arrival by the time we tried to put the tent up. I wanted to die of embarrassment as they crowded round to watch; the ground was so hard that I couldn't make the pegs go in and the tent kept collapsing. Finally someone brought me a mallet and we managed it, to loud and prolonged applause.

We gave the children donkey rides, and then spent a lovely evening in the bar. It was the social centre of the village, packed with people of all ages and the din was incredible. A girl in a wheelchair, who spoke good English, acted as interpreter for the queue of people who asked us an extraordinary assortment of questions, ranging from, 'How much did your boots cost?' to 'Do you know that you have the same name as our queen?'

Back at the tent I had a go at mending the zip on my sleeping bag, but it was a goner, so we opened both sleeping bags out like duvets, one below us and one on top. Although my tent was very clever – it folded up to the size of a Swiss roll and weighed under four pounds – it was definitely a squeeze with both Emu and me inside. We had to cuddle up and curl into each other like spoons; Georgie fitted into the remaining space, which was fine until one of us turned over.

But we slept surprisingly well. When we woke in the morning we were freezing – a thick layer of condensation had collected on the inside of the tent and the top sleeping-bag was soaking wet. Draping it over a tree to dry, we packed up and tried to think of a way to prevent it happening again.

The skies were grey and it was cold enough for jumpers. As we climbed up into the hills it began drizzling, quickly turning the earth from dusty grey to a reddy brown. We sang songs to keep our spirits up – *Cockles and Mussels* and *Early One Morning* – all the lovely old nursery songs that I hadn't sung for years because they're far too uncool to be caught even humming in your teens.

Rough tracks led off the busy road to Fortuna and I couldn't resist them for long. I persuaded a reluctant Emu to set off along one that seemed to head straight for the town and to our delight it took us the whole way: by lunchtime we'd reached the outskirts.

I'm not sure why I'd expected Fortuna to be a nice place. It was a shock to find an ugly modern town. Old stone buildings stood empty and derelict, while beside them shoddy apartment blocks had been raised, most of them covered in graffiti. Groups of boys were hanging around on mopeds and stared at us without a trace of friendliness or humour – I felt vaguely threatened.

Feeling cold and tired, we went into a bar for a hot drink, tying Bella outside, but some lads kept revving up their engines beside her to see if she would be scared, so we left and went on into the centre of town. A church of warm red stone opened on to the small, well-kept square where old men sat watching the world go by. We found a patch of grass behind what looked like a school and Emu stayed with the animals while I went to the supermarket.

At the check-out I met a lovely old man who asked if I needed any help. I explained that I wanted to find somewhere safe to camp, and he took me to a piece of waste land beside a rubbish tip. It wasn't exactly what I'd had in mind – we'd be visible to half the town and the tip was probably full of rats – but the grass was good, so I supposed it would be better than nothing.

He walked with me back to Emu. Just as I was thinking that Fortuna wasn't such a bad place after all, I noticed a great crowd gathered at the place where I'd left her. I quickened my pace and couldn't believe my eyes – Emu was surrounded by at least 100 children, none of them more than about fourteen, all throwing stones at Bella and chanting '*Burro! Burro!*' over and over again. Some were poking at her with sticks and pulling her tail. Emu was doing her best to fend them off, but she was being hit too and George was cowering in terror behind her.

I dropped my shopping and sprinted over, screaming at them to clear off, but they simply jeered and threw stones at me as well. It was terrifying, like a scene from *Lord of the Flies*. I heard the word '*gitanas*' – gypsies. They really seemed to want to hurt us, and they were enjoying it.

The old man bellowed at them and they ran off, but Emu was shaking and close to tears. She told me that soon after I had gone, the school bell had rung. First of all just a few of the smaller children had come out; they had been quiet and sweet, and she had started giving them rides on the donkey. But then the older children arrived, pulled the little ones off, and started this semi-riot. The old man tried to apologize for the *'bastardinos'* and shook his head in shame.

I thought of the *Daily Mail* articles about the donkey called Blackie and the Lenten rituals at Villanueva de la Vera. As part of the organized parish activities, the fattest man in the village rides a tiny donkey through the streets while the other villagers attack it with clubs, sticks and an onslaught of stones. The animal usually dies at the end of it.

I'd found it difficult to believe anyone could be so mindlessly vindictive towards an animal as sweet and harmless as a donkey, but now it seemed all too real. All I wanted to do was get as far away as possible from this vile town, so we set off for a camp site about four kilometres away. The old man looked ashamed and miserable as we left, and I felt depressed.

The camp site was huge, foreign flags waving at the entrance gates and neat rows of caravans stretching as far as the eye could see. It all looked far too organized and official for gypsies like us. The old couple in charge, however, were very friendly; I showed them one of the newspaper articles, and they said they would be 'honoured' if we stayed! We camped on rough ground at the far end of the site and they refused to accept a penny in payment. Bella immediately began demolishing their vegetable patch, heading straight for the broad beans, but they didn't seem to mind so we left her to it while we spent nearly an hour luxuriating under jets of hot water in the shower block. I couldn't believe how dirty I had got in just three days. Our faces were red and burnt from the sun and we both felt incredibly ugly, so we got out the make-up and had some fun, lavishly tarting ourselves up for no one's benefit but our own.

It was dark by the time we reappeared. We concocted a delicious mixture of very greasy rice with tuna, onion, garlic and herbs, which George ate too; we hadn't been able to find any dog food in Fortuna.

I woke early the next day and watched a beautiful sunrise over the mountains. A horrible German man who claimed to 'know all about horses' came up and inspected Bella's feet, announcing that she would go lame if we didn't find a blacksmith and shoe her, and that we were cruel and ignorant. Feeling guilty and worried, we sought out the name of a blacksmith in Abanilla, a town about ten kilometres away.

It was hotter than ever when we finally left. We had an amazing walk through extraordinary lunarscape country – it was just how I imagine the moon to be, with cavernous grey mountains rising up from us in the north, and flat semi-desert stretching away to the south. I would go mad if I was lost here, I thought, and was comforted by the tarmac road.

Our empty wilderness suddenly disappeared: we joined a busy main road, descended to a smelly, dry riverbed, and then saw Abanilla, a depressingly large town sitting on the hill above us. I prayed that we'd find the farrier quickly and have time to get well away before nightfall.

The blacksmith was actually '*el conde*', the foreman of a building site and he wasn't there anyway. His son said he would be back at three, so we found a patch of grassy land, unsaddled Bella and sat down to wait. There was litter everywhere, an ugly mixture of junk and household waste, and I panicked when Bella tried to roll, frantically grabbing wire and bottles from beneath her feet. Two little boys were playing nearby; I thought they were sweet until they began picking out used Durexes from the rubbish and throwing them at us, so we left and waited at the building site instead. The smith's son finally turned up at five to say his father didn't have any donkey shoes, but would maybe look at Bella's feet in the morning. I asked him if he knew of anywhere safe to camp, and he told me there was a castle above the town that would be quiet and safe. This sounded wonderfully romantic, so we walked through Abanilla to the hill above.

The town wasn't as bad as it had seemed at first; the upper part was old and rather pretty, its wide cobbled main street leading steeply up to the church at the top. We stopped at a couple of the tiny shops to buy food for supper and found an incredible range of fruit and vegetables; they were even selling strawberries, and we came out with a huge bagful.

The *castello* was a disappointment. A huge reservoir tank had been built on the remains of what hadn't been much of a castle anyway; it was very exposed, with no good place to camp and litter everywhere. We walked back down to the town, beginning to worry as the sun sank and I realized it would be dark in half an hour.

I often wonder now why I always had such trouble finding a safe camping place, why I didn't just set up the tent in the middle of nowhere, as I had imagined in my dreams. But then I think of the landscape, and I remember. There were no trees, no fences, no hedges; everywhere was exposed, there was nowhere to hide.

We headed along the road to Hondon, feeling vulnerable and fearing a repeat of Monday's wanderings in the dark. Seeing a smallholding about 100 yards off the road, I decided to ask if we could camp near the house. A very friendly lady answered the door, and said we could stay in the large field on the other side of the track; she gave us water, fruit and a lovely smile. I immediately felt calm again. (I was amazed by the suddenness of my mood swings. I could go from despair to elation and back again within minutes.)

We were in a great position, farther up the valley and hidden from Abanilla, with a stunning view over our lunarscape mountains. We frantically made camp, Emu building a fire while I put up the tent, and it turned out to be a lovely evening. We ate a delicious pepper and rice concoction of Emu's, and a disgusting pastry which she'd bought because she hadn't wanted to offend the lady in the bakery by walking away empty handed.

There was something about being on neutral territory a long way from home that had changed the relationship between Emu and me, and we talked more easily than ever in our lives. She was no longer my little sister; she was my friend. We started talking about all the things that sibling rivalry had never let out into the open before, about our family and the way we'd been brought up, about what we were going to do with our lives. We didn't go to bed until we'd run out of wood. We took some hot stones from the fire with us into the tent and hugged on to them to keep warm as we drifted off to sleep.

We slept well and woke up to a lazy, sunny morning. I realized that the *guia* needed renewing already, so I walked into town in search of both the blacksmith and a vet. The building site was deserted and I was told that the men had already gone. So much for the blacksmith.

At the town hall I was introduced to Carlos. There are various types of policeman in Spain. Carlos was part of the *Policia Municipal*, who play the role of the old-fashioned village bobby. He was rather too large for his blue and white uniform, with a big, round face, a great black beard and a deafening laugh, and when I explained my predicament he took on the search for a vet as if it were a test of national pride. Carrying a huge loudspeaker, he jumped into a very old and battered Renault 4, and set off round the town booming out of the window,

'Has anyone seen the vet? There's an English girl who needs the vet! If you can find him send him to the *Ayuntamiento*!'

Half the town turned up just to have a look at me, but there was no vet amongst them. Carlos was not one for giving up, though, and told me to get in the car: we were going to Fortuna. After a similar performance there, we found him. He was far too sexy to be a vet, young and slim and wearing nothing but a pair of jeans; he renewed the *guia* but said he wouldn't bother with it if he were me, as no one would ever ask for it.

As Carlos drove me back to the camp, he told me he'd never heard of anything so daft as two girls wandering about on their own. We'd be lucky to last out the week without being raped, or worse.

'We've got a dog,' I pleaded; but as soon as he saw George he roared with laughter.

'That little *bastardo* won't stop a child attacking you,' he said, and remembering the school the day before, I couldn't really argue.

'If you really want to continue with this madness,' he persisted, 'at least get a proper guard dog, an Alsatian or a Dobermann. And if you wear clothes like that,' he added, 'men will think you're asking for it.'

He pointed to my bare calves. Personally I didn't think my knee-length khaki green Gurka army shorts made me look very sexy at all, but from then on Emu and I lived in the long cotton dresses we'd brought for special occasions. I had a spotty blue sailor dress, Emu a flowery creation; we looked like something out of *Little House on the Prairie*, but in fact found that loose dresses were the coolest and comfiest clothes to wear when it was hot, and when no one was about we hitched the skirts up round our knickers to give our legs some sun.

It was already past one o'clock and boiling when I returned, so we checked with the lady at the house and decided to stay another night, declaring an official afternoon off. While I'd been away Emu had reorganized the saddle bags, writing the contents of each on the outside, so that we wouldn't have to rummage through the whole lot just to find an aspirin. It was brilliant, but it didn't quite match my planned image – I don't think Don Quixote would have had 'worming tablets', 'batteries' or 'dirty undies' written on the side of *his* saddle bags.

We had a lovely lazy afternoon, writing the diary and snoozing in the tent. A goatherd passed us, with about twenty very large and skinny goats. Some of the nannies were wearing bras! Hilarious cloth contraptions tied round their heavy udders and up over their hips.

In the evening Emu lit a fire and I cooked a gourmet supper: pork and ratatouille, with strawberries to follow. We got rather drunk on a bottle of the local wine; it was heavy and strong, and delicious after the first mugful.

We both slept fitfully. At about 2 a.m. we were woken by men's voices. We froze. They were right outside the tent. I looked at the flimsy unlockable zip of the tent and my legs clamped together. I looked at Emu, her huge terrified eyes staring up at me, and I desperately tried to think of something to do. George! Perhaps if they heard a dog barking they wouldn't dare attack us. I grabbed hold of her and tried to drag her to the mouth of the tent, but she just wriggled away from me. She was shaking and I realized that she was as frightened as we were.

They were coming closer. This is it, I thought, and I grabbed hold of the biggest, heaviest object I could find, the torch. Where the hell was my knife? I realized I must have left it outside by the camp fire, along with the axe and the spare tent poles – we had nothing to defend ourselves with. We held our breaths and waited.

There seemed to be at least three of them. They were speaking in gruff whispers and shining a torch over the ground. I signalled to Emu to keep dead still; perhaps if we didn't provoke them, if they thought we were asleep, they would leave us alone.

My shoulder bag! I'd left it outside! Inside were my passport, purse, cheques – all my valuables. Of course, that's what they'd be doing – stealing our gear. I cursed myself for getting so drunk and leaving everything outside, but I also felt hugely relieved that that was all they were after.

Two heads were suddenly silhouetted against the tent. I was so terrified I couldn't breathe. We lay there feeling like condemned escapees from a prison camp, not daring to move an inch, staring helplessly at each other.

The voices moved away, back on to the track towards the road. Relief flooded over me. I unzipped the tent and peered out cautiously, half expecting someone to pounce on me. My bag was still there! I crawled out to get it and saw that they had kicked stuff around, but they didn't seem to have taken anything at all.

We must have still been sozzled from the wine, because we soon dozed off again. Ten minutes later we were violently woken when the tent was completely lit up by headlights, and we heard a car zooming towards us. Convinced that it was going to run us over, we frantically unzipped the tent and scrambled out to see a car drive past us into the field. There were more headlights shining down from a larger vehicle on the road. What the hell was going on now? We stood watching in confusion, dazzled by the lights and the noise, trying to work it out.

The car had picked out the donkey in its headlights and it drew to a stop in front of her. Emu twigged before I did. 'Oh God, Soph,' she screamed. 'They're after Bella!'

I was suddenly more angry than frightened. How dare the bastards steal my donkey! Two men were getting out of the car and walking towards her. Emu ran to the house to get help while I grabbed the torch and raced over to Bella, screaming obscenities and waving my arms about to look as big and frightening as possible. The men just stood and stared at me. Feeling terrified, I grabbed hold of Bella's halter and desperately tried to untie the tethering rope; she nuzzled her head into me and a huge lump in my throat nearly choked me. I couldn't cry, not now! I fought back the tears and kept screaming hysterically at the men, making as much noise as possible. After a few seconds' hesitation they calmly returned to their car, closing the doors and switching out the lights. The vehicle on the road did the same. I finally managed to untie Bella's rope and began running with her towards the house; she came gladly, and we charged headlong into Emu coming in the other direction with the man from the house.

He was marvellous. Emu had forgotten what few words of Spanish she knew and had just banged on their door screaming for help. He had immediately grabbed his rifle and come with her, without any idea of what was wrong. I quickly tried to explain, and he took my torch and walked across the field to the car. When he was about ten yards from it, the engine started and it drove slowly away, followed seconds later by the lorry.

Emu and I were both shaking and our bare feet were covered in blood from having run through the scrub. Manuel took control of the situation, telling us to bring our valuables and come into the house. He locked Bella in his garage while we went inside and were fussed over by Gabriela, his wife. I realized that I was still wearing nothing but my pink thermal vest and long johns – no wonder those men had just stood there staring! Manuel insisted on ringing the *Guardia Civil*, who said they'd patrol the area and asked us to let them know if we had any more trouble. Gabriela wouldn't let us go back to our tent, and we were put to bed in their spare room. I've never appreciated kindness so much.

The following morning Manuel gave us a huge sackful of oranges and lemons, and directed us to Macisvenda, the next small village to the north, while Gabriela kept rushing back into the house and bringing us more and more little presents – packets of biscuits, a bottle of wine, photographs – for good luck, she said. She gave us each a big hug before we finally forced ourselves to take to the road once more.

As we walked along the quiet road up the Chicamo valley the policeman's words came back to me, and I thought about buying a guard dog. Our fierce protector George had refused to emerge from the tent at my hour of need, dispelling forever my hopes that if put to the test she would die fighting for me. Emu would be leaving soon, and I realized I wouldn't have been able to cope without her. But I was frightened of the commitment another dog would entail. I decided to wait and see how I felt in a few days' time, after the trauma of last night's escapade had worn off.

Chapter 4
Going Loco

We reached Macisvenda by 3 p.m. and headed for the bar. A white-haired old man with strange blue eyes was sitting by the door, and I asked him to keep an eye on our donkey while we bought our drinks. He didn't seem to understand and reached out with his hand, nearly jumping out of his skin when he touched Bella's rump; a younger man came out laughing and explained that the old fellow was blind and almost deaf. He shouted *'burro'* into his ear, which I thought appertained to our donkey but the old man took it to be an insult and started swiping the air at head height with his stick. We all took refuge in the bar.

The large room fell silent as we entered. It was full of young men, which surprised me until I realized that it was Saturday. Spotting a phone, we tried ringing home and got through straight away. It was wonderful hearing Mum's voice. I felt rotten faking cheerfulness but it would have been cruel to have let her know how frightened we'd been. Unfortunately Mum had some bad news for us: Rootie, our spaniel, had died three days ago. The men shuffled on their chairs and looked away in acute embarrassment as tears began pouring down my cheeks; I handed the phone over to Emu and ran outside to be alone. Emu came out a few minutes later and sat down beside me on the kerb. George licked the tears from our faces, which made me feel even sadder.

Eventually I went back inside and asked the friendly lady behind the bar if she knew of anywhere we could camp. I'd hoped she would quietly suggest somewhere to me, but to my horror she called out my request to the whole room. Suddenly the men came to life, all volunteering suggestions, and between them they decided that the best place would be Ernesto's empty house. I asked the barmaid if we would be safe there; she laughed and said yes, introducing us to a small man of about fifty, with thinning black hair and a missing bottom tooth.

I drove out with Ernesto in his car to have a look at the place. It was almost a mile off our route, but the thought of us all being behind a locked door – Ernesto said we could have the keys – was irresistible. I agreed that we would stay and went back for Emu and the animals. The walk back to the bungalow took forever; Bella was being difficult and we felt exhausted and short-tempered.

Ernesto was waiting for us when we arrived and helped us to unpack. He showed us how to use the well in the kitchen and apologized for the lack of toilet facilities. He chatted on and on; I wished he would hurry up and leave us alone, but I didn't want to appear ungrateful so I tried to nod and smile at the appropriate pauses. But then I caught the gist of what he was saying: since we were so worried about being safe, he would spend the night with us in the bungalow. I suddenly felt wide awake.

'No!' I almost screamed. 'We're OK, really, you don't have to do that.' I tried to be insistent without seeming rude.

'I've got a gun, you'll be safe if I stay with you,' he continued.

A gun! Oh God!

I desperately tried to convince him that we would be perfectly all right without his protection.

'Why?' he asked, with a horrible smile on his face. 'Why don't you want me to stay here with you? What are you frightened of?'

'We just want to be alone,' I pleaded. 'Just give us the keys, please.'

'All right,' he said, 'but they're in my house. You'll have to come back with me to get them.'

The house wasn't much more than a barn. Ernesto opened the front door into a long, dark room; it took a while for my eyes to adjust and it was the smell that hit me first – the stench of rotting dung. After a few seconds I saw that the walls were lined with caged birds; their droppings were encrusted on the floor. It couldn't have been cleaned for years.

Ernesto disappeared into his kitchen and Emu and I wandered round the room, morbidly fascinated by the junk and filth.

'Jesus Christ!' Emu gasped from the other side of the room. 'Come and have a look at this!'

She pointed to one of the pictures. I rubbed at the dusty glass and squinted at it, and suddenly realized what it was: a tiny man with a huge phallus fucking the daylights out of a giant rabbit. I have to admit that it was quite funny at first, until we looked at the other pictures. They depicted every conceivable type of bestiality – sheep, horses, men, women, groups . . . I felt that same cold, sickening fear of the night before come creeping back. There was no way we would stay now. I called out to Ernesto that we'd changed our minds and were leaving.

'You won't find anywhere as safe as this!' he shouted as we left. 'There are lots of dangerous men out there who'll want to hurt you and you won't have me to protect you from them!'

We walked back towards the village feeling utterly miserable. We were so in need of a safe haven, yet so useless at finding it. It was already five o'clock, and we wouldn't have time to reach the next village before dark. Between us and it lay deserted, open scrubland. I wanted to cry.

The old part of Macisvenda formed a semicircle round a large central plaza which had been made into a children's playground. The western side dropped steeply, with a stunning view of open country and the setting sun. I looked at the grassy patch at the open edge of the plaza, and thought what a perfect camp it would make. We'd have no privacy but it would be completely safe.

A crowd gathered as we made camp. They became friendly once we began talking to them, even the children, and an old man offered me the use of his stable for Bella, just twenty yards from our camp. I was still paranoid that the men with the lorry would make a second attempt to steal her, so I accepted. He gave her hay and fussed over her, and it cheered me to see that at least some Spaniards were fond of animals. I asked him where I could find a farrier, but when he looked at her feet he said I'd be mad to shoe her. Her hooves were beautifully hard naturally, he said, and shoes could make her lame if she wasn't used to them. I thought of that pompous German man at the camp site and mentally shot him.

Later I spread the maps out on the ground and found that we were still depressingly close to Murcia. It was only forty kilometres away; we should have walked that distance in two days, but it had taken us five. We would have to start walking much earlier in the morning.

Just as Emu was putting the spaghetti in the pan, the farce with the old ladies began. They came up to us one by one, bearing gifts and offering help, as if there was a competition to see who could be the most hospitable. We were presented with eggs, fruit and tomatoes, and invited to use five different water supplies, three different telephones and a hair dryer. We tried to explain to them what we were doing, but it was difficult since they couldn't read, so our usual method of passing round a newspaper article failed. Anyway they seemed much more interested in whether we were married than where we were going.

When I told them that I was raising money for the handicapped, they were confused. They seemed to have no idea of a national, organized charity that wasn't connected with the Church. 'But there's nothing wrong with you!' one of them said. 'You shouldn't have to beg!'

They were kind, though, and most concerned for our safety, saying we could knock on their doors in the night if we had any trouble. Maybe the Spanish weren't so bad after all.

We slept badly, however, haunted by nightmares and panicking whenever we heard a car drive past. We'd kept our clothes on, just in case, and I'd organized a collection of arms beside us, with a planned method of defence:

1. Torch, to dazzle
2. Fly repellent, to spray into eyes, nose and mouth
3. Knife, to plunge into private parts
4. Axe, to thrash indiscriminately until victory was ours.

Consequently, half my nightmares were about what would happen if I actually killed someone. Meanwhile, Emu, who had a broken Tic-Tac box in her back pocket, thrashed about all night dreaming that Bella was biting her bottom. We were both relieved when morning finally arrived and we could leave.

Sunday 12 March was a beautiful sunny day, very still, and we walked up the valley into dry, red hills where we saw extraordinary underground houses, burrowed out of the earth like rabbit warrens. Often only a chimney sitting on the ground gave them away. The inhabitants lived in almost complete darkness, but it must have been beautifully cool down there. Occasionally they came out, like moles, blinking into the sunlight and exclaiming at the donkey as if she were a long-lost relation. Emu, fascinated by the wrinkled, brown faces of these little old people, christened them 'walnuts'.

It was the hottest day so far and my arms came up in an agonizing heat rash. Both the animals were playing up; George pulled on her lead into the road and Bella kept stopping. Her bottom was swollen and I suspected she was having her period so I tried to be sympathetic, but we ended up bribing her along with the last of the oranges. I was hot, hungry and incredibly tired – we hadn't slept properly for days – and we were almost delirious by the time we arrived in Hondon.

We found a bar beside the church, and I sat in the shade outside with the animals while Emu went in to buy two litres of Coke. I hoped we'd be able to rest here until the worst of the day's heat was over, but a few minutes later the doors of the church opened and the townspeople poured outside. Emu returned with the drinks to find Georgie, Bella and me surrounded by about 200 men, women and children chanting, 'Burro! Burro! Burro!' They were moving closer and trying to touch us. I wanted to curl up in a ball and die.

Emu stood up to her full height, waved her arms around, and shouted, 'Hello everybody, and welcome to the circus! Yes, we're compleeeetely maaaad!'

Unfortunately her performance only drew more spectators, and when they started prodding her too (to see if she was real?), she gave up and sat down on the pavement with me. We drank our Coke, and then I had the idea that if we must suffer this mob, we might as well get some money out of them. I found the MENCAP collecting box and shook it under their noses. About a quarter of them left, apparently disappointed that we were nothing but beggars, but the main body of chanters were made of sterner stuff and wouldn't be put off by appeals to their conscience. Some spat at the tin, and then a few children started kicking it around like a football. We admitted defeat, packed up and left. We were too shocked and tired even to talk to each other as we trudged on, feeling desperately sorry for ourselves, hating Spain, hating the weather, hating this endless road.

Walking along I looked at Emu, her face burnt from the sun and filthy from the dust on the road, her hair standing on end, and her eyes so blue that they looked as if they'd absorbed the sky, and I burst out laughing. No wonder they thought we were strange! Perhaps we really *were* going mad! With our drop-waisted English dresses and heavy boots, our freckled faces and ribboned straw hats, I realized it was silly to hope we could be inconspicuous.

We asked directions to Cannelosa. Luck was on our side for once – there was a direct track leading from behind the bar. We were all happier off the main road, it was now cooler and we had a good walk up to the hills. The Sierra del Argallet towered before us, a craggy mountain range over 3000 feet high. Tomorrow we'd have to cross it and according to my 1941 maps there was a track across the top. It looked frighteningly large.

The sun was behind us, and we discovered that with our hats on the back of our heads, our shadows looked just like the space men from the Smash potato adverts. This cheered us up and our spirits were high as we entered the village of Cannelosa Altat at the foot of the Argallet mountains.

The shop was open, so we bought some food for supper, and an old walnut with black teeth started talking to us. At first I was so fascinated by his mouth that I didn't listen to what he was saying, but when he began poking around in our saddle bags, picking out a saucepan and the washing up bowl, I realized he thought we were gypsies selling our wares! He was offering such a good price for the bowl that I was tempted, but realized we couldn't manage without it. He turned out to be very helpful and led us to a patch of land at the edge of the village, close to a house where they agreed to keep an eye and an ear open for us.

We opened some wine and climbed up on to the hill behind the house to watch the sunset, but three little boys began throwing stones at Bella so we had to come back down and sit with her. I'd never understand how children could be so vindictive towards a harmless donkey. The only way to get rid of these brats was chucking the stones at them harder than they could throw them back. Not very virtuous, maybe, but effective.

The next morning we set off at half past eight, the earliest yet. We walked along the upper road out of the village, passing friendly walnuts and more of the remarkable underground houses. These were the first homes I had seen that seemed loved, with newly painted doors and flowers outside, vegetable patches on the roofs and the delicious smell of burning olive wood coming from the chimneys.

The road became a dust track. I hoped we were going the right way, but when it began to divide I stopped at a house to ask directions. I found a lovely old couple who drew the funniest map for us as they explained that there was once a path over the mountain but it had not been used for so long that it would now be impossible to find and we would be foolish to look for it. We would have to go the long way round.

We wandered happily along tracks for another two hours, joining the main road after lunch. It was scorching hot again, juggernauts roared past, the drivers shouting obscenities at us, and my heat rash was now blistering. Our singing descended to the level of *There'll Be Ten Bottles of Beer Waiting in the Bar* as we struggled on to the tiny village of La Romaneta.

We perked up when we caught sight of the bar, but inside Emu was the first to notice something strange. She turned to me and whispered:

'I think we're about to take part in the *Rocky Horror Show*.'

Everyone looked like relics from the sixties and seventies. The woman in charge was tall and thin, with long black hair pulled back severely from her heavily made-up face. She wore false eyelashes, thick black eyeliner, and was dressed in a tight green cardigan above a mini-kilt, bright red tights and platform-heeled boots. She was arguing noisily with a man whose sideburns were enormous, and who was wearing a purple shirt over flared jeans. In fact everywhere jeans flared as their marinated owners gnawed raw beans, spitting the empty pods on the floor. On the wall was the enormous head of a wild boar, a baby's dummy stuck in its mouth. Above the fireplace were some cattle-branding irons, and spurs from old riding boots. We made a pretty hip exit.

That night we camped outside an isolated farmhouse. We'd almost run out of food and Emu made a strange stew out of everything we had left mixed together. It tasted revolting; even George didn't like it, and I gave mine to the farmer's crazy dog, a beautiful animal with long red hair, just like a fox. He kept us awake half the night, barking at the donkey and hurling her water bowl up in the air, leaping on to the tent and burrowing underneath. I got so angry I shoved three sleeping pills down Foxy's throat, but it didn't seem to make any difference.

In the morning we left the mountains and entered a flat, cultivated plain. The weather was miserable, an endless grey drizzle, and we both felt depressed and hungry. I conjured up images of the lovely warm café we were going to find in the next village, another one called Hondon. I hoped there'd be a shop too, for we needed supplies before we could cross the next mountain range, the Sierra de Salinas.

I still shiver when I think of Hondon the Second. It's the closest I've ever seen to a ghost town: deserted and decaying, broken shutters banging in the wind. There was a large house which had obviously once been very grand, with a great columned entrance and long balconies, straight out of *Gone With the Wind*. The garden was a wilderness and the barns and rows of workers' cottages further along the road were similarly dilapidated. Just beyond them we found a surprisingly well-kept playground area. Next to it was a modern building which I realized was a school, apparently built in 1963 as part of General Franco's rural education programme. We looked inside for clues, but it was in a disgusting state, the floor covered in broken bottles and cigarette butts.

We were starving, so we decided to boil up some soup, while Bella grazed in a surprisingly green field by the playground. It was not our lucky day; the Calor gas ran out when the water was only lukewarm, and there was no wood around to make a fire. My stomach groaned in agony; in desperation I tried eating dry powdered milk from a spoon and nearly choked. I now hadn't eaten for twenty-four hours and I felt terrible.

I was frightened many times on my journey, but I was never so wretchedly miserable and depressed as that moment in Hondon, when I sat shivering under drizzling grey skies wondering what the hell I was doing wandering about in the middle of Spain with a donkey.

Chapter 5
An Addition to the Family

My self-pity didn't last long. A man suddenly came charging up with a gun threatening to shoot us all if we didn't get that bloody donkey off his crops. Oops! We decided to make a detour eastwards to Monovar, a town large enough to replenish our supplies.

We reached the outskirts at five o'clock, by which time we were absolutely famished – I hadn't eaten since yesterday lunchtime. We walked past smart modern houses and carefully tended almond orchards, until finally we saw it: a great white building with RESTAURANTE written in large, beautiful, delicious letters across the front. I staggered up the drive, visions of steak and chips, huge paellas, oozing pasta and chocolate gâteaux dancing before my eyes. I was going to treat my stomach to the greatest pigout it had ever known. A woman came out to greet us.

'*Una tavola para dos*,' I gasped.

She said she was very sorry, but they were closed on Tuesdays; then watched in amazement while I rolled on the ground with my legs in the air screaming and shouting hysterically.

Emu convinced me that we should find a place to camp before continuing our food-finding mission, so we stopped at a house with a large field of scrub in front of it. We knocked on the door and a beautiful blue-eyed walnut appeared. We had made a good choice – this man owned not only the field, but the restaurant and most of the surrounding land. His name was Cesar and of course we could stay in his field.

We tethered Bella, unloaded the packs and walked back into town. Stopping at the first café we came to, I at last ate; though only a sandwich as Emu had gone crazy in a supermarket and wanted to cook a gourmet meal later.

As we walked back to camp I caught sight of my reflection in a shop window and hardly recognized myself. My hair was defying gravity, curling upwards and outwards, the texture of a greasy Brillo pad and a strange dusty brown colour. I realized I hadn't washed it for a week. Emu's hair had been standing on end for days, but since she spends hours at home with the gel and mousse

37

trying to achieve the same effect, it hadn't struck me as odd. We decided to treat ourselves to a visit to the hairdresser's and spent the next hour in heaven, being pampered among the pink cushions and synthetic smells of another world, reading women's magazines and drinking cups of coffee. I felt very sorry for the poor girl who was set to work on my hair – it was only after the third shampoo that she managed to make a lather and it took her fifteen minutes to comb the knots out. It was fascinating watching my appearance slowly return to normal in the mirror. Underneath the muck, my hair had become surprisingly blonde and my face was now tanned and freckled: I almost looked attractive again.

It was dark when we finally emerged and groped our way back to the field. Bella came running up to us eeyoring madly, furious that we had left her alone for so long. Cesar brought us some wood and Emu built a superb fire while I struggled with the tent, cursing myself for not having put it up while it was light. As promised, Emu's meal was delicious, a concoction of pasta, cream cheese, peppers and sausages. We ended the evening by boiling up a huge bowl of water and having a proper wash, scrubbing our bodies into the same condition as our hair.

In the morning I realized that Bella's *guia* needed renewing already. I looked at the restaurant standing on the hill above us, thought of eating a proper sit-down meal and declared a day off.

Monovar would make Prince Charles weep. The old houses were absolutely beautiful – elegant, three-storey buildings with carved wooden balconies and doors, tiled façades and ornate, stencilled decorations in lovely eggy colours – yet most of them stood empty and decaying. Some were being demolished and huge concrete monstrosities built in their place. Behind the main shopping street we found an old *plaza* of ornamental gardens which must have been exquisite once, but now it was overgrown and littered, the fountain empty and covered in graffiti. It was horribly depressing.

I left Emu drawing the Moorish castle on the hill while George and I went off in search of a vet. When I eventually tracked him down he said he had no authority to renew my *guia*, and told me to go to the *Oficina de Extensión Agraria* in Novelda, about eight miles away. There was no bus until the evening so I decided to hitch, hoping Georgie's presence would put off any murderers and rapists. A lorry driver stopped for me, but five minutes into the journey he unbuttoned his flies and started wanking furiously, leering at me with his tongue out. I was less frightened of being raped than that he'd crash into something, and I jumped out at some traffic lights and tried again. Eventually I was picked up by a friendly girl who took me all the way to Novelda.

The man in the OEA was bemused by my request. He told me that the only vet who had the authority to renew my *guia* was in Pinosa, thirty kilometres away, and he would not be back until tomorrow. At this I burst into tears. The poor man was very embarrassed; taking pity, he told me conspiratorially that if he were me he wouldn't bother with a *guia*. The only officials who could demand to see it were the *Guardia Civil* and, he assured me, none of them would have heard of it anyway. The only area where I might have some trouble, he said, was up in Catalonia, where they were still free of African Horse Sickness and were passing strict measures to prevent infected animals getting in.

Thus I decided to forget the wretched *guia,* hoping that feigned ignorance would save me from a fine if ever I were caught. It was market day at Novelda so I bought a huge bag of shrimps to cheer myself up and hitched back to Monovar. I found Emu and we returned to camp, cooked my prawns in an enormous quantity of garlic and siesta'd under some olive trees. My optimism returned and we persuaded each other to do something useful with our day off. I sewed extra straps on to the saddle bags and Emu washed some clothes.

It was a beautiful and peaceful afternoon, until Bella decided to have some fun. She pulled her tethering post out of the ground and shot off down the road to Monovar at the most astonishing speed, with Emu and me in hot pursuit. I was terrified that she would crash headlong into a car, but couldn't help laughing at the sight of my placid little donkey running so determinedly to God knows where. Taking a sharp left up someone's drive, she swerved round the house and came to an abrupt halt at the edge of a swimming pool. By the time we arrived she was affectionately nudging the astonished owners and looking immensely pleased with herself. I hadn't realized the spirit and sense of humour hidden behind those dopey eyes. She returned to the field quite happily and I tied her rope securely to a tree.

In the evening we put on our cleanest clothes and went to the restaurant for dinner: huge steaks, with mountains of potato and salad, followed by a delicious caramel custard. Cesar's daughter, Isabella, came out to talk to us. The same age as me, pretty and vivacious, she was under enormous pressure from her father to marry and have children. She asked all about England. All she wanted to do was travel and see the world, but not like us; she thought we were crazy to seek out old people and isolated places when we could have so much more fun in the cities and coastal resorts.

Cesar came with us the next morning to show us the way to Elda. He took us cross-country over the hills, not saying goodbye until

Elda was in sight. I wished that I had something to give him to thank him; my words seemed inadequate. But it was he who gave us a present, a huge bag of wild asparagus. If we looked carefully while we were walking, he said, we'd be able to find more of it.

Cesar's simple generosity and friendliness touched me deeply. He had not embarrassed us or impinged on our privacy by insisting we come into his house or eat his food, but had provided us with water, firewood and grass for Bella, and he'd given us his protection. It made me wonder how people at home would treat a couple of foreign girls who turned up on their doorstep, and we amused ourselves over the next few hours deciding how all our parents' friends would react. Mrs B. would undoubtedly inform the police; Mr and Mrs C. would see it as an excuse for a party, open a bottle of wine and invite us inside; and Mrs T. would probably set the dogs on us.

Thursday 16 March. Elda is a town that shocks the senses. Set among beautiful rugged mountains, it is a hideous place made up of shoddy apartment blocks and huge factories. Trying to avoid the modern area, we walked through the slums, and we saw something of the real poverty of southern Spain. The people here were Arabic; descendants of the Moors, I was later told. They live in an amazing amalgam of old, rotting houses, homemade wooden huts and corrugated iron lean-tos; shelters made out of anything from plastic crates to pieces of carpet. But for the children, shouting and playing, crying and laughing and displaying the riches of human character, the place would have been hell on earth.

We eventually reached the road to Castalla and climbed up to the hills above the town. The Sierra del Maigmo rose before us, climbing to an amazing Arizona-style tabletop mountain in the distance.

We stopped at a bar for lunch, where we spent far too long drinking the local liqueur. It gave Bella a chance to have a little feast of her own. She had managed to tear open the saddle bag containing our replenished food supplies and had eaten virtually everything: peppers, courgettes, mushrooms, *the wild asparagus*, crisps, rice, pasta, bread, cheese, frankfurters, teabags, two packets of chocolate biscuits, tomato sauce . . . What she hadn't consumed she had smashed: olive oil, eggs, milk and wine now saturated our clothes, which she had tossed over the ground. Luckily for Bella, we were so drunk we could do nothing but collapse into helpless laughter. The staff at the restaurant thought we'd completely cracked.

We tidied up as well as we could and set off again, following a stream through beautiful hills towards our tabletop mountain. I realized that the countryside was becoming much greener and there were many more trees than I had seen before – pine

40

plantations, old almonds and olives, and even some cherry trees.

We camped below a hotel that was being renovated and the caretaker and his wife kindly gave us some milk (Bella had left us with nothing but coffee, tinned tomatoes and dog food). It was a beautiful evening and as we looked out over the red sky and the deserted hills that seemed to stretch on to eternity, the slums of Elda seemed a world away.

We were so tired and hungover that we fell asleep immediately. In the morning the weather had changed; a wind had blown up and there were thick white clouds in the sky. We climbed up to the tip of the scar and stared down at the huge plain below us. I saw how Castalla had got its name, for it stood on a small round hill surrounded by perfectly flat land and looked like a battleship on the ocean. I took out my camera for a picture and discovered that the lens had been smashed. I was furious; I'd been so careful with it and Lord knew when I'd next pass a camera shop.

The road to the plain plunged straight downhill, making no allowances for the gradient. Bella was marvellous; when she started to slip, she devised a way of zigzagging down the mountain without any guidance. The saddle bags lurched from side to side, but never actually fell off.

In Castalla – another once pretty town intent on disfiguring itself – we stopped at a café to ask directions. It was full of old walnuts and I asked them where I could find the track to Fontanella. They looked at me blankly, so I spread out my map on the table, pointed to Fontanella, and asked,

'How do I get there?'

At least half a dozen men crowded round the map, spreading it out to its full size and poring over it. Five minutes later the oldest walnut gave me a triumphant grin.

'You are here!' he said, pointing to Castalla on the map. 'You are not in Fontanella, you are in Castalla!'

Oh dear. I looked at the circle of proud smiles, and realized that most of these men had probably never seen a map before. I folded it away and tried again.

'I want to go to Fontanella. Where is the track to Fontanella?'

'Why do you want to go to Fontanella?'

'Because I'm heading north.'

'Where are you going after that?'

'Towards Ontinyent.'

'Ah well, if you're going to Ontinyent you don't want to go to Fontanella, because there's a fantastic new road that goes straight to Ontinyent, it cuts the distance by almost half.'

'But I'm walking with a donkey,' I pleaded, 'I want to go by track.'

'Don't worry,' they tried to reassure me, 'I'm sure donkeys are allowed on the new road.'

I gave up.

We never did find the track to Fontanella. Instead we walked towards the small town of Onil, nestled at the foot of the hills. As we passed through it started drizzling. We considered waiting in a café until the rain stopped, but it was already after four so we covered Bella's pack in a plastic sheet and pressed on towards the hills. Five minutes later the storm broke; thunder and lightning tore the heavens apart and water poured down in sheets. We gave up looking for waterproofs and ran back to Onil to find shelter.

Some carpenters in a workshop let Bella stand in with them while Emu and I took refuge in a café across the road. I hoped that it would just be a passing squall, but half an hour later it started hailing, fierce hard bullets hurtling against the windows. Realizing that it would be stupid to try camping outside I began asking about places to stay and discovered with delight that there was a hotel in the town. The thought of it overwhelmed me. To relax, to turn a key in a door and know that we were safe. To enjoy comforts without having to rely on other people's generosity, without having to smile in constant gratitude. To sleep!

A friend of the carpenters was happy to let Bella spend the night in his garage, and I bought her some barley and stale bread. She seemed happy, so we locked her up and hauled our stuff over to the '*Hotel Onyx*'.

The storm lasted all weekend and we were forced to stay in the hotel for three nights. It was not the peaceful resting place I had imagined. Rain leaked through the ceiling on to our beds, there was no hot water and the place was filthy, but whenever we complained we received a torrent of abuse. The owner's wife attacked Emu with a broom when she discovered George in our room, even though her husband had previously said it would be OK, and the cook spat at me and called me a *gitana obscena* (filthy gypsy) when I dared to mention that the food was cold.

On Monday morning I was presented with a bill for over £100 and when I protested they threatened to bring in the *Guardia Civil*. Terrified that they would discover my lack of *guia*, I swallowed my pride and paid up, wishing that we'd all camped with Bella in her garage.

On Saturday I'd been to the police station for advice on where to find hay, and met Marco, who must be the dishiest policeman in Spain. He drove me to a tiny farmstead where the oldest walnut I'd ever seen came out to greet us. He laughed when I said I wanted hay, telling me they didn't feed their horses hay round here – they give them a mixture of chopped straw and barley. He gave me a whole bale of straw and a bucketful of barley, and wouldn't accept a peseta for them, but said he wanted to come and see my *burrica*. We put the feed in Marco's car and drove to the garage, where Bella received admiring praise from the old walnut; my saddle arrangements, however, did not.

'*No es bueno*,' he kept saying, then a twinkle came into his eye. He asked Marco to help him fetch something and they drove off in the car, returning twenty minutes later with a huge contraption covered in hessian cloth. As they carried it towards Bella, I realized that it was a real old-fashioned pack saddle, straight out of the Bible.

It was a huge, heavy thing made of wood, leather, cloth and twine. Bella tried it on for size and seemed dwarfed by it. The old man declared it a perfect fit. A great pannier went over the top to form two baskets and the girth and backstraps were fastened with dried cobs of corn. It was beautiful, but I wasn't too sure about its suitability for my journey. I'd worked out a good arrangement by now with my own assortment of homemade padding and canvas bags, and the expression on Bella's face trussed up under this museum piece was a definite negative. I tried to tell the old man that I couldn't possibly accept it, but he insisted, so I bought him a glass of cognac at the bar over the road to thank him and he left us with a great smile on his face.

Marco asked if there was anything else he could do for me. I could think of many things but I controlled myself and asked instead if he knew where I might find a guard dog. I wondered if there was maybe an animal rescue home nearby?

'We shoot strays round here,' Marco said, but he kindly took me to see a friend of his, Tomas, in Castalla. He was nuts about dogs, talked about little else and prided himself on knowing every canine in the area.

He explained that trained guard dogs are big business in Spain, fetching anything from £400 to over £1000. We drove out to two 'training centres' and tried to persuade them to cut their prices for charity, but had no luck. I couldn't afford to pay more than £100 so Tomas suggested we look for a dog with something wrong with it. He took me to see an Alsatian, on sale because he was too friendly, and then to a farm to see a Dobermann who was going to be destroyed because he was too vicious. The previous week he had bitten his owner's sister's fingers off.

At last Tomas remembered a very badly treated dog in the area, whose owner might be persuaded to let me have her for nothing.

43

We drove to an isolated warehouse, and through the driving rain I saw a black dog chained up at the entrance.

I had never seen an animal so thin in my life. She was a Dobermann, black and tan with a docked tail and shortened ears that were scabbed and bleeding. She was covered in sores and tethered with a heavy chain. She had no shelter, not even a bowl of water. As I approached she growled and backed away in confusion. Her eyes were running, her nose was blocked with catarrh, she was covered in ticks and, no doubt, had fleas as well. I felt desperately sorry for her.

I can't take on a dog like this, I thought; she would probably die on me in a week. Her feet looked so sore that she would never be able to cope with the walking. I had to say no. As I turned away my eyes filled with tears. I was leaving her to almost certain death. If I didn't help her, no one would. There did seem a crazy logic in my being so in need of a guard dog, and this poor animal being so in need of a good home. I couldn't just walk away. I looked at her and she looked at me and I knew that the sorrow in those deep brown eyes would haunt me forever if I didn't give her a chance. Taking a deep breath, I turned to Tomas and said yes, I wanted her – he could go to the owner and do his best.

By the time Tomas found him the next day, the owner had heard that I was willing to pay £100 for a dog and wouldn't let Collie go for anything less. By then I'd set my heart on her, so I paid the money anyway. The first thing I did was change her name. She didn't respond to it, and I felt silly calling a Dobermann 'Collie'. 'Bogus' was the name of Hannibal's soothsayer who warded off hobgoblins and evil spirits, thus enabling Hannibal and his army to reach Italy – it seemed appropriate.

I was determined not to get too fond of her, to treat her as a guard dog, not a lap dog, so that when I reached Rome I would be able to leave her behind without too much heartache. Or so I thought.

Chapter 6
Easter Pilgrims and 'Crezzy Lezbins'

We did not leave Onil quietly. Marco, Tomas and the old walnut all came to see us off. Emu and I transferred our gear from the canvas saddle bags into the wicker panniers, trying to balance the weights evenly, while Bella stood patiently underneath. At last we were ready. Bella stepped down off the pavement, the panniers lurched to the left and suddenly the entire pack saddle swung under her belly. Our stuff scattered all over the road, eggs smashed and milk cartons burst.

Why, when something like this happens, does the wrong person always find the most embarrassing articles? Why did Marco have to pick up the dirty underwear bag? Why did six months' supply of contraceptive pills have to fly from the sponge bag into the middle of the street? I wanted to curl up and die of embarrassment.

Second time round, the old man organized the packing: heavy things at the bottom of the baskets, clothes on top. Finally we left Onil, with Bogus walking calmly beside me on a lead. We climbed up into the wooded hills to the north and celebrated the arrival of our guard dog by making our first truly wild camp. I had bought a thirty-foot chain, attaching Bogus at one end and a tree at the other, and I made a bed for her out of hessian sacks. George was thrilled to have a companion, and kept running round Bogus wanting to play. The Dobermann, however, just sat and watched her sadly, as if she didn't know how. She was completely unresponsive, and I wondered whether she might be deaf. A deaf guard dog! Good one, Sophie! She wolfed down two kilograms of the Pedigree Chum we had miraculously found in the supermarket at Onil and I gave her half a dozen eggs as well. I was determined to get her into good condition; it was to be a struggle that lasted the entire journey.

It was a shock to see the state Bogus was in the next morning. The hessian sacks she had lain on were saturated with blood: she had licked her sores in the night, and I saw that the ones on her back legs were raw to the bone. Flies swarmed round her and I reckoned she probably had septicaemia already. I found the first-aid kit, rubbed Germolene on the sores and bandaged her back legs. She just stood and let me do anything to her, as if she had no will to contest anything. We had to move on, but I felt cruel doing so; she needed a warm bed and a long rest, neither of which I could give her. I wished I hadn't taken her on.

My map showed a track going north across the Sierra de Mariola to the village of Alfafara, and I was pleased and rather amazed to find that it existed, cutting through a newly planted pine forest. We made camp at the edge of the forest; to the north lay barren, desert-like country, with a sharp escarpment to the east and harsh grey mountains to the west. It was an intimidating sight, but according to the map, Alfafara was just eight kilometres away. We made an early start in the morning as we hadn't much water left and I wanted to reach the village before the shops shut.

The track led out of the forest into a dry, rolling wilderness. The scrub was black and scorched as if a fire had recently swept across it; the recent rains had left no mark here, and it was almost impossible to recall the cold of the weekend as the fierce sun began burning our arms and faces.

After about two hours the track petered out among some pine stumps; we had been diligently following nothing but a forester's dead-end track. Damn. It was now eleven o'clock and we were hot and tired. Alfafara couldn't be more than two miles away, I reckoned, so I decided it was worth trying to walk cross-country using the compass.

With her cumbersome pack saddle Bella had lost her customary agility and she continually stumbled on the undergrowth as the panniers lurched perilously from side to side. The area was gutted with deep, dry channels carved out by sudden rain, and while it was all too easy to get into them, it was almost impossible to climb out. We soon got stuck.

It was now painfully hot and we had finished all the water. We decided to head back to the forest, but by the time we found a way out of the gully we were a long way from the original track. We stumbled through the scorched undergrowth, but all we could find were more gullies cutting across our path. I began to panic. We were desperately thirsty, it was becoming difficult to talk and Emu was complaining of a headache.

For the umpteenth time Bella's load swung under her belly. I thanked God I had kept the old saddle arrangements and I sat down with a needle and thread to sew them back together (I had cut off the straps and used them to hold the wicker panniers steady). Unceremoniously we ditched the old walnut's pack saddle.

It was now midday and the heat was like a burning furnace, the air dry and choking. I'd never felt thirst like this before; breathing was difficult and concentrating was an enormous effort. The poor dogs looked miserable, but followed us unquestioningly and I felt horribly guilty for my incompetence. Emu was moaning and kept asking what I was going to do now, and I wished I was alone. I'd got us into this mess, and I wished that I was the only one who had to suffer for it. Emu felt like a heavy burden round my neck.

We could see the pine forest in the distance, but trying to find a way to it was impossible. One of us stayed with the animals while the other went on a recce, calling when we had found a way across the next gully with the whistles we had bought in Onil. On one of Emu's searches, she started whistling frantically. I ran in the direction of the noise, thinking she had hurt herself, but when I reached her I laughed out loud. Her beautiful bottom was sticking up in the air as she crouched on all fours and buried her head in the sand. She had found a tiny spring! A trickle of water ran across the earth for about five feet before disappearing again. The dogs fell on it, lapping desperately, and I crouched down too and sucked, sieving the sand out with my lips. It was delicious and instantly cured my headache. Then Bella came and slurped up the whole lot, leaving us with nothing but damp sand. We set off again and this time, with clearer heads, we managed to find our original track. By one o'clock we'd reached the heavenly shade of the forest, and passed the camp we had left five hours earlier. I longed to stop, but we needed to find a proper water supply.

Just before we reached the road we passed a muddy pool by the side of the track. Without a word Emu and I jumped into it. It was too filthy to drink, but we sat there absorbing its coolness, and then we started throwing it over each other, laughing hysterically and getting rid of all the tension and anger we had pent up against each other. I wish that I had a photo of us then, covered in mud and gloriously happy to be alive. The dogs waded in to cool their paws and bellies, and Bella looked on scornfully, wondering what morons she had somehow acquired for owners.

There was a painful irony in the name of the town we reached after nearly dying of thirst. *Bañeres* means 'baths'; it is a lovely old spa town built on the Rio Vinalopo, the biggest river I'd ever seen in Spain; there was even a waterfall. Textile mills were built among the greenest, lushest grass I had seen since leaving England. A mile before the town there was a huge trough at the side of the road, an old watering hole for passing horses. We rushed up to it and stuck our faces in – we had learnt from Bella that the easiest way to drink water from a large container is to suck rather than scoop with the hands. I gulped and gulped, then Emu picked up my legs and dropped me right in, head first. It was so cold I couldn't even scream, but the agony was exquisite and I ended up staying in for five minutes. We gave the dogs a soaking and they drank their fill, but Bella steadfastly refused to touch a drop.

I wanted to camp near the river, so we pitched the tent on a hidden, grassy terrace between the road and the river which was screened by almond trees. We left the animals eating there and walked into the town to find food for ourselves.

The *Policia Municipal* were fast becoming my favourite people. We found one of them at the edge of the town and asked him where we could go for a good cheap meal. He led us to a tiny place that looked no more than a scruffy old bar from the outside. Wooden chairs were piled up at one side of the room, and an old lady was cleaning the floor. 'They need a lot of something hot,' the policeman said to her, and bade us farewell.

The old lady was lovely. She set up a table and two chairs in the middle of the room, put on a clean white cloth, and brought two glasses and a bottle of wine.

'Sit down and drink up,' she said, 'then you'll be able to talk.'

She told us we looked terrible, and asked what had happened. When we explained she turned her eyes to heaven and said she had heard the English were completely *loco,* but up till now she had never believed it. She brought us a huge pan of paella – solid rice, with just a few rabbit bones. The wine went straight to my head and the world soon seemed a wonderful place again, the morning's antics suddenly terribly funny. We were soon talking and laughing with the walnuts who had come in to see 'the crazy blonde girls who'd bathed in the horse trough'.

On Thursday 23 March we walked along the main road to Bocairent; I'd had enough of tracks for a while, and enjoyed the mindless certainty of walking on tarmac. Just beyond the town I noticed a riding school and stopped to make blacksmith enquiries. A friendly gypsy man trimmed Bella's hooves for me, saying that if I found a blacksmith, all well and good, but her feet were wonderfully hard and she seemed happy to be barefoot.

In the afternoon the road became much narrower and took us through a rocky mountain canyon, along precipitous ledges with 200-foot drops to the river below. It wiggled and convoluted through the steep-sided gorge, with blind hairpin bends and sudden dips. The Spanish drivers tore along at breakneck speed, honking their horns before each blind spot as if that alone would miraculously clear any obstacles. I was sure we were going to be run down, or else be the cause of a dreadful accident, or Bella would be spooked and pull us all off the edge. We sang *Onward*

Christian Soldiers and *Jerusalem* to keep our courage up, punctuated by screams of '*juggernaut coming!*'

I was stunned by the beauty of the gorge, with caves hidden among sheer rocks, trees clinging on to tiny ledges, and way down below clear water sparkling through lush vegetation. Spain was proving to be such a land of extremes. Only yesterday we were crawling about in the sand searching for water like desperate gold-diggers in the Australian outback. Now we had been transported to the American Rockies and were contending with maniacal lorry drivers determined to run us over. *Serves me right for wanting more excitement in my life*, I thought, as I stuck up a finger to a greasy-haired bastard in an Alfa Romeo who'd come within inches of us.

Snake Pass continued for eight kilometres and by the end of it we were shattered. As the gradient lessened we saw some ruined mills by the river, Dickensian structures which reminded me of Lancashire and England's 'dark satanic' places that we had just been singing about. We were on the outskirts of Ontinyent before we found anywhere flat enough to camp.

That night was the first of cooking up butcher's handouts for the dogs. They'd finished the Chum and I hadn't been able to find any more tinned food in Bañeres, so I'd asked at a butcher's for anything cheap that we could give to them. He'd given me a disgusting mixture of offal – tongues and trotters, hearts and kidneys, chicken heads and pork fat. My fussy dogs, even the half-starved Bogus, refused to eat it raw, so we had to chop it up and boil it. I'm ashamed to say that my stoicism failed me completely and Emu had to do it. Once it was cooked the dogs loved the stuff, and I realized that if I could bear it, offal was the best food to give them, much cheaper than tinned and better for them.

The next morning we tried to buy bread in Ontinyent, but the bakeries were selling nothing but extraordinary giant *ensamadas*, rings of sweet dough topped with meringue and whole white hard-boiled eggs stuck in the middle. Some were enormous, over two feet wide, and extravagantly decorated. *What a peculiar town*, I thought; and then I realized that it was Good Friday, and these must be the Spanish equivalent of hot cross buns. I bought one of the biggest and we all ate it on the pavement. Bella loved it, but got meringue stuck on her nose and she had great difficulty in licking it off. The dogs ate the eggs, shells and all.

As we zigzagged our way up the small road to Vallada, through heather-covered hills towards the dramatic mountains of the Sierra Grossa, the weather was perfect. We had bought new straw hats and we covered them with the pink heather; in our flowery cotton dresses, we looked like we'd jumped out of a Laura Ashley catalogue. Bogey joined George sniffing for birds and rabbits, and for the first time seemed happy to be alive. I realized that Dobermanns are designed to run; when she walked she was awkward but when she ran Bogey was magnificent. Her bandages spoilt the image a little, for her sores still bled a lot and we were having to change the dressings twice a day; I'd found that sanitary towels made the best padding. I wonder what the makers of Simplicity would think if they knew!

We spent a glorious afternoon climbing slowly upwards, singing all the Easter songs we could remember. The view from the top of our mountain pass was breathtaking. To the west were the ruins of a monastery stuck on the flat top of a huge rock. The blue-tiled dome of a church shone up at us from about a mile below, and as we headed for it, we ran straight into an Easter procession. The people seemed to take us for pilgrims; we were warmly greeted and invited to spend the night on the terraces near their church.

Here we met a group of pot-holers, who turned out to be the Spanish equivalent of yuppies: they listened to Elton John on their CD player, they wore Levi 501s, Reeboks and Tom Cruise sunglasses, and they were wonderfully harmless. That evening, as I sat down to write the diary and watched the sun disappear over the mountains, I felt calm and contented; we'd camped early enough to enjoy the end of the day at leisure. Darkness had become our enemy, holding total sway over our routine. The time as told by a clock had become meaningless. We rose when it was light and slept when it was dark; time had become that simple and that important.

But our peace was suddenly shattered by five eighteen-year-old morons on mopeds. They sat revving their engines for almost ten minutes, and then tried to talk to us, using such easy conversation starters as, 'You have very big boobies' and 'Do you want to fuck?'

We pretended we couldn't speak Spanish, but that didn't work. They developed a rather peculiar argument which began as 'foreigners should not come to Spain unless they speak Spanish', progressed to 'you should not come near our town unless you are here to please us', and ended up as 'English girls should only come to Spain if they are happy and willing to be fucked by any Spaniard who wants them'. When we still ignored them they started getting aggressive. I'd had enough. I grabbed my axe in one hand, Bogey by the collar in the other, and marched towards them. The wimps zoomed off, terrified, threatening violent retribution for the 'crezzy lezbins'.

They returned later that evening and zoomed up and down past our tent, throwing matches and screaming obscenities. Bogey barked in terror and confusion, and with each approaching roar I was convinced they were going to plough right through us.

Pot-holers to the rescue! They were big hefty fellows, and grabbed their picks as they came running over to defend us. The bikers fled down the hill, and we peered out of the tent to thank the heroic three. They really were yuppies, they were wearing Paisley boxer shorts! We opened a bottle of wine and talked to them while our nerves calmed down. They were lovely blokes, and it was fun talking to people of our own generation for a change.

The next day I wanted to reach Enguera, but the heat was suffocating. We had a bleak, barren mountain to cross and had been warned that the track hadn't been used for years and would be difficult to find. There was a much better track from Montesa, six kilometres along the main Valencia road; and at Montesa there was a railway station. Emu was due to start work in Majorca at the beginning of April and it was already 25 March. A roadless wilderness stretched beyond Enguera, so she decided it would be best to leave me now.

The station master at Montesa turned out to be a Hannibal nut! He thought we were marvellous and was the first person to recognize the origins of Hasdrubella's and Bogey's names. He let us stay at the station overnight, since there wasn't a train to Valencia till the next morning.

I went through my gear, sifting out all that had proved useless for Emu to take with her and tying it up in Bella's hay net. Emu boarded the 8.31 a.m. to Valencia, looking rather tramp-like compared with the civilized people on the train. (She later told me her carriage emptied after she sat down.)

When she had gone I locked myself in the loo and burst into tears. I felt frightened and very alone in this strange, sometimes hostile country. I hardly recognized my haunted face in the mirror: my skin was browner than ever in my life, my hair a huge golden mess, my lashes and brows bleached almost white by the sun, and my eyes looked like little blue marbles. I set to with the make-up Emu had left me; when I'm upset I find that putting on make-up calms me, and as my face returned to a semblance of normality my confidence grew. I was quite impressed by what I could do with nothing but a brown kohl pencil and a stick of mascara.

I set off towards the beautiful castle of Montesa and from there found the track to Enguera. The animals seemed confused by Emu's departure. Bella kept stopping and looking back, as if trying to tell me we'd left Emu behind. Watching her, I found it difficult not to cry.

I stopped to get some water from the saddle bags and my doldrums suddenly left me when I realized I had left a pair of pink spotted knickers sitting on the waiting-room bench at Montesa station! I had washed them that morning and forgotten to pack them. At least they're clean, I remember thinking, and I couldn't stop laughing. I looked around at the beautiful mountains, up at the clear blue sky and suddenly life seemed good again.

Chapter 7
Alone on the Moors

Sunday 26 March. I couldn't stop walking, the day Emu left. At Enguera I went into the church and lit a candle for my little sister, and then one for myself too. I knelt down and said one of my rare prayers – *if there's anyone up there, I could do with a bit of help right now*. This was the beginning of the journey as I had originally conceived of it, the start of my solo wanderings. Up till now it had only been a dress rehearsal. Now I was alone, and I was scared. Sophie vs. Spain, Round One.

On the road to Benali we passed a donkey, the first I had seen other than Bella. We all stopped and stared in admiration at the beautiful creature coming towards us at a brisk trot. He was huge, much bigger than Bella – I would have said he was a mule but for the size of his ears. His balls were so big he must have been an untouched stallion. He was pulling a cart of logs, with a young man sitting at the front holding the reins, and neither man nor jack gave me or my jenny a second glance as they passed. Arrogant bastards! Bella bellowed at him – the loudest eeyore I'd ever heard from her – and stamped her foot in indignation.

I made camp about six kilometres into a pine forest beyond Enguera, well away from the road but I was paranoid, terrified of every sound. I was furious with Bella for continually advertising our whereabouts. She was in love, and eeyored incessantly back towards Enguera; for the first time I sympathized with the army practice of removing the voice boxes from donkeys in wartime. I couldn't face cooking just for myself, but finished a whole bottle of wine while I brought the diary up to date. The tent seemed big and empty, so I let Bogey come in too.

I'd rid her of fleas and ticks, and what I hoped were most of the worms, but physically she hadn't improved much in a week. I'd expected her health to return the instant she was fed and treated well, but she was no fatter and her sores were still in a terrible state. I changed the dressings twice a day and each night I boiled up her bandages in disinfectant to remove the blood. Her strengthening was going to be a slow process. Her trust in me was growing, though, and I found her mental awakening very moving. She now understood what stroking meant, no longer growling and cowering in confusion when I tried to touch her; and she responded to her name, her little stump wagging in delight when I called her.

There was low cotton-wool cloud that evening, pretty but foreboding, and the next morning the weather had changed. It was damp and grey, a still mist clinging to the trees and giving a ghostly look to the forest and I felt spooked. The village of Benali turned out to be nothing but a farm so I couldn't stock up on food, but the farmer gave me a few scraps for the dogs and directions to Bicorp thirty kilometres to the north.

The track took me into wild open country which reminded me of the Yorkshire moors, with thick gorse and gnarled old trees, the sparse grass nibbled to the core by sheep. I stopped for lunch by a deserted farmhouse and boiled up a huge bowl of chicken stock for myself and the dogs. I considered staying the night, but decided to press on due to our lack of food. Soon afterwards the track was met by another from the right, but it was unmarked so I decided to ignore it.

The fog had thickened and I couldn't see more than ten yards ahead; it was swirling around us, suddenly revealing huge boulders or large trees and I felt frightened. I thought I could hear a car, but nothing came, and my own voice echoed back to me when I called. I panicked at the thought that maybe I was reading my compass wrong – perhaps the white end pointed north, not the red? – and I nearly went mad trying to work out where my shadow was falling. I turned back and tried the other track, but I was soon convinced I had made the wrong decision. This track had not been used for months. It was covered in sheep droppings, and ant mounds sat undisturbed in the smooth unmarked earth. I heard the bells of goats and sheep on the hillside somewhere to my right and I yelled over, hoping there would be a friendly farmer with them. No one answered. I carried on rather hopelessly, having no idea of the time as Emu had taken the clock with her. Bella seemed to share my fears and was walking much faster than her usual 2 mph. I shared my last piece of chocolate with her to try to cheer us up.

Suddenly I reached a fork in the track and – I couldn't believe it – *signposts*. *Both* tracks were signed to Bicorp! Each was via a different place, neither of which was shown on my map, so I took the more northerly one, sang *If You're Happy and You Know It*, and smoked my last cigarette in celebration. The weather improved along with my mood and the mist cleared to reveal dramatic scenery, much more mountainous than before, with wooded slopes and sudden gorges, the earth a beautiful reddy colour. The track climbed, fell and twisted, and I was amazed by Bella's energy. We must have walked well over twenty kilometres already, but she seemed happy to go on.

As the sun sank there was still no sign of a village; nor was there anywhere suitable for camping. It was dark by the time I found somewhere to stop, and looking back it seems a crazy place to have camped. We had entered a pink, steep-sided canyon and just below the track was a long, flat terrace about fifteen feet wide. I found a path down to it, tied Bella's rope and Bogey's chain around the trees to make an enclosure and we spent the night there on the ledge above a fifty-foot drop. As I drifted off to sleep I thought of the lethal consequences of sleepwalking in such a place, but I was too exhausted to worry for long.

I reached Bicorp at ten the next morning. It was a pretty little place. After several *cafés con leche*, which were two parts sweetened condensed milk to one part coffee (more like a pudding than a drink but absolutely delicious), I rang Mum and discovered that Rachel and Polly, my two pet sheep, had both given birth to triplets the day before. This made me homesick, for I love springtime at home. I wished I was back amongst it all as I peeled off my stinking socks for the first time in two days and counted my blisters.

I did a big shop, treating myself as well as the dogs to some meat, and at one o'clock I set off for Millares, a village twenty kilometres to the north. I passed a man with a horse and cart, who told me a storm was coming. The sky seemed brighter to me, so I dismissed such pessimism and carried on. We were back in wild, open Brontë country; it was barren and neglected, without a living creature in sight.

The rain came suddenly, with the full force of the wind stinging our faces, and Bella tried to hide her head behind my back. I put on my waterproofs, hitching my full skirt up round my bum so it felt as if I was wearing a nappy. We were drenched and miserable by the time I spotted a sturdy-looking croft to the left of the road. The wooden door swung open when I touched it; it was too dark to see much inside, but I was too desperate to be dry to feel frightened. Bella came in too and I unloaded her. It was already late afternoon – this would have to do for the night. I peered out at the black clouds and shivered; we were in for a heavy storm. I thought of Onil and prayed that this one wouldn't last for three days.

My eyes were becoming accustomed to the light, so I began exploring my refuge. It was a stone building, about twelve feet by fifteen, with the back wall higher than the front and a sloping roof. The only light came from a hole above the fireplace in the far corner. There was a small well by the door, with an ancient rusty bucket and chain. By the fireplace were two pans, a spoon and a knife, and a few old jars and bottles with wrinkled green nuggets inside. There was a pair of old leather boots, so dusty that they looked like plaster casts. No one could have set foot in the place for years, yet whoever had lived here seemed to have left a strong presence.

The dogs were hungry, so I lit a fire to cook their food and hoped it would brighten the place up and maybe scare the ghosts away. The grocer in Bicorp had given me some rotten vegetables for Bella and she happily tucked into these while I sat down by the doorway and began reading the book I had brought from England with me but so far had not even opened. It was Christabel Beilenberg's *The Past Is Myself*, an account of her life as an English-woman in Nazi Germany, and I was soon completely absorbed. As the light faded I went on a foray for more wood and then moved inside to the fire. I tied Bella so that she could graze in the lee of the croft, but she preferred to be inside and lay down with the dogs on the dusty floor, unperturbed by the fire and noisily eating the oranges I had bought in Bicorp.

As the storm raged outside I sat in that smoky room peeling oranges for my donkey and reading about the bravery of an English girl faced with an all too real enemy. I forgot my strange surroundings, and threw the last of my wood on to the fire to keep up enough flames to read by.

When Christabel's husband was called up for military service I stopped to cook my supper. I discovered that the meat I had bought for myself was lamb, so the dogs did well that night – I haven't eaten lamb for years, I love my sheep too much – and I made an omelette instead.

As I was brewing some coffee, I noticed in the firelight some engravings on the wall, and I moved closer to read them. The name 'Bernadetta' had been carved over and over again, and there was some other writing too, a vulgar but rather endearing love poem. I noticed some more and, fascinated, I got out my torch and dictionary as I brushed the cobwebs away. I gasped in surprise – there was nothing romantic about *these* engravings. There were some crude pictures of a woman, hands tied and legs splayed, and more writing. 'Bernadetta', it seems, was a beautiful girl whom my crofter had courted. But she had spurned his love and married another, and his love had turned to obsessive, vindictive hate. He'd planned dozens of ways to punish her; he wanted to torture her, to whip her, to disfigure and humiliate her. The wall was covered with his cravings; I was shocked but couldn't stop reading. When I'd read them all, I sat down and I realized I was trembling. What monster had lived in this house? Had he actually done any of these things to Bernadetta? What if he came back? What if he mistook me for

Bernadetta? What if he did those things to *me*?

I worked myself into a state of complete terror as I became convinced that the crofter would return. I tried to bolt the door, tying Bogey's chain across. Sitting by the fire, knife in hand and axe by my side, I smoked cigarette after cigarette and tried to get back into my book. I burnt the stool, the cupboard and a bedhead in an attempt to keep the fire going, and then I ran out the batteries for my torch; for the first time in my life I was terrified of the dark. That night I had horrible dreams. Stormtroopers burst through the door and kicked me with studded black boots before riddling my body with bullets; rats gnawed at my face; and I was chased by a black-eyed priest screaming, '*Bernadetta, whore, Bernadetta, whore, Bernadetta . . .*'

I woke at dawn bathed in sweat. It was still raining, but I left anyway. The weather's punishment could not have been worse than my own imagination.

The bare moorland came to a sudden end at a sheer escarpment to reveal the most dramatic scenery I'd ever seen. The deep valley of the Rio Jucar cut across my path and steep, abrupt mountains rose to the east. Below me I could see the roof tops of Millares nestled into the hillside. A van passed me, the first sign of traffic I had seen all day, and the driver stopped.

'Where've you been?' he called.

'What?'

'We've been worried about you in the storm. Someone rang from Bicorp yesterday saying you were coming, and when you didn't turn up last night some of us drove out to try to find you, but you'd disappeared.'

Bush telegraph, it seems, is alive and well in Valencia! When I entered the bar at Millares an hour later I was greeted like the prodigal daughter and I collapsed gratefully over a tortilla sandwich and a glass of wine. The only other female there was the lady behind the bar, a great fat woman whom everyone referred to as '*la jefe*', the chief. Later I was shown to a patch of grassy land by an orange grove near the river. I put up the tent and left the animals there while I explored the village.

Millares is built on a series of terraces. It was rather like Toytown; everything was in miniature and colourful Easter flowers had been painted all over the paving stones in the streets. None of the shops were marked on the outside; I kept having to ask directions, and twice I burst into people's living rooms before I managed to find the grocer's.

I was sad to leave Millares the next morning. The sun appeared through the watery skies, and I shut my eyes and dreamed of being clean. At least my hair was now OK, but I hadn't had a bath for ten days, and I hadn't been able to wash my clothes because of the wet weather – nothing would dry. I was beginning to smell as well as feel like a seasoned gypsy. Dubious skies returned before my saturated saddle bags had had time to dry out.

I stopped for a rest in the middle of the afternoon and took off my boots to rub my aching feet. I couldn't believe the state they were in. The arches were a purply-blue colour, the muscles bruised and tender, and the joints of my toes were swollen, looking puffy and rheumatoid. Both my little toenails had been completely worn away, which for some reason I found terribly sad. I'd always liked my feet before; now they were grotesque and ugly. They suddenly hurt ten times more now I knew how they looked and I felt faint and weepy. I packed up Bella and set off again in the drizzle, feeling pathetically sorry for myself. If only we could find a warm, dry and safe place to stay until the weather improved.

The sign said 'Bar-Restaurante Llanorel, open all year, 1700 metres'. I hobbled desperately towards it – never had a mile seemed so long. A ladies' tea party was going on inside and I was plied with hot coffee and doughnuts before I'd even introduced myself. I finally gathered enough energy to explain what I was doing and what I wanted, and a plump, smiling couple called Juan and Juana said that of course I could stay.

I settled the animals, then went to the swimming pool and sank my swollen feet into the cool, soft water. It was heaven. I was soon brought sharply back to earth.

'*No!*' bellowed Juan. '*Viene aqui!*'

I followed him into the house, apologizing profusely for my breach of etiquette. There Juana took hold of my arm and led me to the bathroom. She'd run a hot bath, smelling deliciously of bath salts, and had laid out clean clothes for me on a chair. I tried but couldn't think of adequate words to thank her. She told me to take as long as I liked and left me to soak in that glorious tub of hot soapy water. What fantastic people! What a wonderful world!

I scrubbed and scrubbed at myself and the water was a muddy brown colour when I'd finished. Then I rubbed Juana's handcream into my poor old feet and covered myself in her honeysuckle-scented powder. I couldn't help smiling when I saw the clothes she'd put out for me: there were huge lacy knickers that came up to my chest, and one of those reinforced vests that acts as a bra as well; on top went bright blue nylon trousers, about six inches too short and huge round the waist, then a shirt that was too small so I had to leave it unbuttoned under a huge red Superman sweatshirt. Pop socks and Dr Scholl sandals completed the outfit. I laughed out loud when I saw my reflection, but it felt so wonderful to be clean that I didn't care how bizarre I looked. I smelled delicious and I looked respectable.

'You are to sleep inside,' said Juana, and showed me to a bedroom. It was her son's, but Juana insisted he would be happy to sleep on the sofa. She sat me down in the sitting room by the fire and both she and Juan told me how I must think of them as family and of their house as my home, that I could stay as long as I liked and that I must ask for anything I wanted. Their kindness was overwhelming, almost embarrassing. I helped Juana set the table for supper.

'Are you hungry?' she asked.

'Yes, I'm starving,' I replied truthfully.

But my hunger vanished as she brought in the food – fried eggs and *sobresadas!* Oh, no! The whites of the eggs were still transparent and runny, and the huge pile of red sausages was swimming in grease. There wasn't even any bread to help it down. How on earth was I going to get through this nightmare? I tried a bit of sausage and hated myself for being such a fussy eater.

'Delicious!' I smiled at Juana's anxious, enquiring face and prayed for deliverance. My chance came when the phone rang. Juan went to answer it in the next room and called to Juana to join him: it was one of their sons. Grabbing the roll of loo paper I always kept in my shoulder bag, I quickly wrapped up half the sausages and one of the eggs, shoving them into my bag just as Juan and Juana put the phone down. They returned and sat down again, and both looked towards my plate in astonishment. Looking down, I saw my bright pink loo roll sitting on the edge of my place mat!

I tore off a couple of sheets, noisily blew my nose and placed the incriminating object back in my bag as if it were the most normal thing in the world. They looked at each other in amazement, but seemed to accept my strange behaviour as something to expect from a foreigner and continued their meal.

The next morning it was raining hard, and Juan insisted that I stay until the weather improved, so I spent the day helping Juana with the restaurant. It was a friendly, informal affair; they knew everyone who came in, and sat down to talk with them while they ate. At about eleven o'clock a great party of men appeared; they had been working in the fields since dawn and were only now stopping for breakfast. They found my story hilarious, and went out to have a look at my donkey. They prodded and poked poor old Bella, giving opinions as to her age and price. I was amused and pleased to see that none of them would go anywhere near Bogey.

I gossiped with Juana, who like most of the older Spanish ladies I'd met was dying to know if I had a *novio* – an 'intended one', half way between a boyfriend and a fiancé. Not wanting to disappoint her, I made one up, and had such fun inventing the man of my dreams that over the next few months I created many different versions of him, combining the best features of all the men I've ever loved, liked or lusted after. This one was a lawyer called Richard, a great blond hunk who was dying to marry me, but respected my decision to see the world and build my career first. 'Sounds like a wimp to me,' Juan said.

Bella's feet had worn down too quickly over the past week, and I had reluctantly decided that I must get her shod. The local policeman gave me the address of Fernando, the blacksmith in Buñol, about twelve kilometres away. But I must get there tomorrow; Sunday, Monday and Tuesday were fiesta days and no one in Valencia would be working.

I took out what food I could to George and Bogey, but Juan and Juana seemed to resent my asking for scraps for the dogs. Apparently I pampered my animals too much. In their book dogs are not meant to be fussed over, and they thought I was ruining Bogey as a guard dog by showing her affection. As for being fond of a *burro*, they were incredulous and rather appalled.

My own food problems continued. On Friday Juana asked me if I liked squid. I *thought* I did – I mean I always had before – but when a huge purple animal arrived, eyes, arms and body still intact, I felt weak. It had just been grilled, whole, with salt. When I sneaked it to the dogs later they looked at me as if I was mad. *Eat that?* They rolled in it instead, and stank for days.

The bar gradually filled up with people arriving from Valencia for the bank holiday. A doctor had a look at Bogey's sores for me. He gave me more supplies of bandages, gauze and antiseptic, and a prescription for some powder to keep the flies off.

In the evening I sat on the steps outside the bar and talked to the children. We taught each other swear words from our respective languages, and they asked me the English for '*burro*'; they then went round yelling 'You're a donkey! You're a donkey!' and screaming with laughter. For the first time I was able to laugh at my misfortune in owning an animal whose name was the most common swear word in Spain.

I woke on Saturday morning to clear blue skies, and happily said my thankyous and goodbyes. Juan and Juana were lovely people, but their kindness was almost suffocating. Bella had polished off most of their lawn and I feared we were beginning to outstay our welcome. I ate three of Juana's delicious homemade doughnuts for breakfast and was given a Valencian flag by the children, which I stuck out of the back saddle bags. Then I set off once more, waving until they were out of sight.

Chapter 8
Men

Saturday 1 April. I walked along the quiet road to Bunol singing at the top of my voice. I was trying to see how many Abba songs I could remember and had reached number fourteen when a green jeep with *Guardia Civil* emblazoned on the side drove past. It parked fifty yards ahead of me and *Super Trooper* came to an abrupt halt. Four enormous uniformed men got out and started walking towards me clutching their guns.

'Hello!' I said as innocently as I knew how, deciding to pretend not to speak any Spanish.

'*Documentos! Papelles!*' screamed Front Right.

Here we go, I thought; criminal record, here we come. I wondered vaguely if Bar school would still accept me. I scrabbled about in my bag for my passport and handed it over, trying not to look as guilty as I felt, waiting for the demand for the donkey papers. Front Right and Left walked back to the jeep with my passport and began making phone calls while frantically leafing through it.

The back two stayed with me (so we couldn't make a quick getaway?) They stared at me, looking me up and down without a hint of humour. I did up the top buttons on my dress and hated the pathetic little would-be Rambos. God, you're ugly, I thought, as I smiled sweetly and offered them a Polo. (They refused.)

The other two came back and yelled at me,

'*No es correcto! Nos faltan mas papelles!*'

Inwardly I panicked, cursing the man who had said the *Guardia Civil* would never know about the *guia* law. But as they continued screaming at me I realized what they were worried about was the absence of an address in my passport. Producing my driving licence seemed to satisfy officialdom and my passport was returned. Then Front Left revealed his utter imbecility by trying to speak to me in German! He'd just spent ten minutes studying my very British passport and he thought I was German! Behind those big guns and smart uniforms I realized there wasn't much brain – the vets had been right. Then they told me that I was crazy to be wandering around on my own, that I would get raped and/or killed, that

Spanish men would think I was wanting it. I was tempted to set Bogey on the bastards as they swanked back to their jeep. Wanting it! If I wanted sex, what a weird way of going about it, wandering along country lanes with a donkey and two guard dogs!

When I finally found the right address in Bunol I was told that Fernando the blacksmith was in Chiva and would not be back till Wednesday. I set off despondently through the sprawling industrial town and spent an uncomfortable night on some waste ground behind a factory.

I packed up as soon as it was light and walked along the main road to Chiva. Luckily there was a hard shoulder so the traffic didn't seem so bad, and I sang as loudly as I could to drown the roar of the lorries. About a mile outside the town a car stopped in front of me and I was forced to walk out into the road to pass it. As I did so the driver knelt on his seat by the open window and waggled his very pink penis at me.

'This is for you, gypsy girl,' he said. 'Put your mouth over it, I know it's what you want, I've been watching you, I can see it in your eyes that you're desperate for it.'

I wished that Bogey would bite it off, and walked on as quickly as I could. I hated myself for feeling upset. Damn the bastard, for ruining my good mood! I wished I was one of those women who can just laugh it off. Why did I have to take it as an affront to my femininity, my sexuality, my dignity? I felt furious, I hated men, and would gladly have castrated the whole lot of them there and then.

Chiva was a lovely old town, with a fantastic bakery where I stopped for bread and treated myself to a creamy strawberry meringue creation. I was about to bite into it when I realized it bore a remarkable resemblance to what had just been thrust at me through a car window. I took my knife from my pocket and very slowly sliced the top off. Would this count as voodoo? I earnestly hoped so as I hacked the rest of it into a mushy pink mess and fed it to the dogs, laughing in as witch-like a manner as I could muster. The baker looked on in astonishment.

'Private joke,' I smiled to him, and with relief I realized that my anger had left me. There was no point in getting wound up about perverts – it would be like admitting defeat. I wasn't going to let them spoil my journey.

I set off along the road to Gastalgar and passed a mule, a horse and a donkey all within the space of half an hour – Bella was beside herself with excitement. All were pulling carts into Chiva; the donkey was unshod and the mule was wearing terrible front shoes which were much too big for him, so I wasn't given much hope about farriers. It became very hot at midday, so when I saw a sign to some fountains we followed it and found a river, with some beautiful green grass for Bella. The water was freezing and I was too chicken to swim, but I set about washing as many of my clothes as I decently could. It was strangely satisfying to see the filth ooze out of them. A friendly young chap called Iago came to wash his battered old car in the river, and then he sat down on the bank with me and tried to talk to me for a while. He was nice enough, but I couldn't relax and wouldn't let Bogey leave my side. I knew it was crazy, that he was probably just a simple chap without a malicious thought in his head, but when he started trying to chat me up I panicked and screamed at him to go away or I'd set my dog on him. The poor guy looked completely bewildered, but did as I asked.

I left at six. Black clouds spoiled what I had hoped would be a perfect sunset and I grew worried about the lack of sheltered places to sleep. We entered another holiday home area where a family in one of the less smart houses let me camp in their field. I'd just put up the tent when it began raining; they insisted I come inside and I sat in their sitting room drinking hot coffee and watching boxing on the telly until it stopped. I breakfasted with them the next morning and they gave me a big sackful of dried broad beans for Bella.

I set off again through the endless orange groves; the smell was intoxicating, fresh and strong after the previous day's rain. The skies were dubious, but I didn't expect the ferocious storm that hit us just three kilometres from Pedralba. We ran for cover under an orange tree, but the rain went on and on and we got soaked anyhow. Bella put her bum to the wind and chomped her way through twenty kilos of broad beans, while I hit the bottle, George hid up my jacket and Bogey balanced on my lap.

By the time the rain stopped a good two hours later, I was frozen, sodden, stiff and rather drunk. We plodded along towards Pedralba and came to a large roadside café full of people, great parties at long tables enjoying the end of what appeared to have been a quite sumptuous meal, and I remembered that it was a fiesta day. I staggered to the bar and asked for food, but was told I was too late. I groaned, and I think I nearly fainted because I was suddenly being seated in an armchair and given some brandy. They said they had some broth I could have, and I also persuaded them to give two buckets of leftovers to the dogs. Normally I would have found the soup revolting – greasy yellow water with lumps of skin floating in it – but it was hot and tasted delicious to my desperate tongue.

As I warmed up I felt incredibly tired and I tried to snooze for a while, but I was driven mad by people coming up to talk to me.

An argument broke out about Bella's age, and one man sat down beside me insisting that she was five, grasping my cheek and shaking it to prove his point. Another arrived saying he knew all about donkeys and mine was definitely twenty-two, and he kept slapping my knee for emphasis. A fat woman with dyed red hair and a huge floral dress started talking to me in a strange accent I couldn't understand; she yelled at me louder and louder, and then began poking at me with her finger to make me listen to her.

Stop touching me! I wanted to scream, and I tried to pull my chair away. Finally I could stand no more and left.

I scoured the village for food supplies but found nothing open save a bar selling Twix and Mars bars, so my supper was very unhealthy that evening. I made camp in one of the orange groves just outside the village, realizing that they were excellent places to hide, for my tent was the same colour as the leaves. Never again, though – Bella collected windfall oranges, deposited them outside the tent and eeyored at me until I came out to peel them for her. What had at first been a quaint little habit no longer seemed so amusing!

I was in a surprisingly good mood the next morning as I crossed the plain to Casinos. Walnuts were picking artichokes in the fields and I was given so many that I couldn't carry them all.

'*Donde vae con la burrica?*' they would ask, and when I replied, '*A Roma!*' they would laugh and shake their heads. Many asked me to mention them to '*el Papa*', assuming I was on some kind of pilgrimage. I was smiling and waving to everyone when a car passed me, so I smiled and waved to it too. It stopped and the driver wound down his window as I approached. He was smartly dressed and had a thick gold ring on his wedding finger.

'You want to make love?' he said.

'Of course not!'

'But you waved . . . I thought . . . You shouldn't act like that if you don't want a man to think you desire him.'

I was too flabbergasted to say anything more than 'Fuck off!' I grabbed Bogey and held her beside me like a shield as I walked on, but he didn't give up, stopping if I stopped and speeding up if I made Bella trot.

'You have very beautiful eyes,' he said.

Boy, you're original, I thought, and tried to ignore him. But he went on and on with his banal attempts at flattery and in the end I screamed at him to go away and leave me in peace, whereupon he called me a bitch and a tease, and I'd be in trouble soon if I continued treating Spanish men so badly. What I needed, apparently, was a good fuck – from him, of course. At this I kicked his car and made a beautiful dent in the side door; he was so angry that if I hadn't had Bogey I'm sure he would have come out and hit me – men and their precious cars! It made him go, though.

I was seething. What I hated was the implication that I was asking for it, that somehow I was to blame for men acting like that. I contemplated shaving my head, blackening my teeth and walking with a limp the next time it happened.

I reached Casinos by midday on 4 April and was relieved to find the bank and shops open. I went on a mad shopping spree and bought enough food to last a week, treating myself to a steak at the butcher's, and then I found a tiny shop selling nothing but cured hams, and I tried so many that I felt I couldn't walk out without buying any. Casinos is famous for its sugared almonds and its marzipan; needless to say, I felt rather sick by the time I left.

My map showed a track to Segorbe and I stopped at a bar to ask for directions, causing the usual response as walnuts crowded round my map and argued fiercely amongst themselves. I went to the loo and had a wash while they were at it and I don't think anyone noticed that I'd gone. I was given such conflicting advice that in the end I set off and tried to find my own way.

I walked along a straight road heading east, and was busily trying to remember the words to the Carpenters' *On the Bayou* when a little man pedalled up to me on a bicycle. He was fortyish, dressed in filthy blue overalls and heavy boots, with rotting teeth and a vile grin on his face.

'How much?' he kept asking. I tried to ignore him, but he thought I just didn't understand so moved on to sign language, pointing at his crotch, grunting strangely and then indicating a little shed about fifty yards away, rubbing his fingers and thumb together as a money sign. I felt my anger rising, but as I watched him leering and grunting at me I started thinking, Damn you, you little wanker, I'm not going to let you frighten me. *I'm* going to have the last laugh this time.

I put on my smartest Castilian accent, smiled sweetly and gave him a list of prices.

'If you just want me, it's 30,000 pesetas. It's 20,000 more for each of the dogs, but if you want the donkey too it's 100,000.' I twinkled my eyes at him. 'We're all girls, you see.'

I thought his eyes would pop out of his head. The grunting suddenly stopped and without a word he scrambled on to his bicycle and pedalled frantically towards Casinos – whether to escape, to spread the news or go to the bank I'm still not sure.

Lord knows what I would have done if he'd taken his wallet out and said, 'It's a deal,' but it made me laugh for a good half hour as

I ambled along the side of the Canal del Generalissimo and then up what I hoped was the right track to Segorbe.

My diary entry for that evening reads: 'I am sitting on a beautiful wooded mountainside beside my tent and camp fire; all is just as it should be, except that I am completely and utterly lost.'

My track-finding endeavours had proven disastrous. I'd wandered about on that mountain for hours, finally giving up and making camp in a clearing. My mood, however, was surprisingly bright; the sun had appeared briefly before it went down, and the air was thick with the smell of wild rosemary. I had a delicious meal – artichokes followed by steak, which I'd grilled over some pine branches. I sat sucking sugared almonds with a contented dog on each side of me while I pored over the map deciding where to go the next day.

In the morning I headed east because the sun was shining brightly for the first time in what felt like ages and I wanted to feel it on my face. We walked along the sandy path by the canal and I sang the songs from *Evita;* I remembered every line of *Another Suitcase, Another Hall*, but nearly went barmy trying to remember the words to *Don't Cry For Me Argentina*.

I found the track to Marines Viejo, heading up a valley through strange, barren land with high, barbed-wire fencing. I was not far along it when I heard banging. As I continued, the noise became unmistakably that of gunfire, and when a little man in green ran up to me yelling and waving his arms about, I called it a day and turned back. Typical! The one track I manage to get right and it goes through a war zone!

I retraced my steps and continued southeast along the canal to Marines, where I stopped at a bar for some coffee. I came to a sudden halt when I walked through the door, for blasting from the radio was *Don't Cry For Me Argentina*. How weird. The man behind the bar laughed when I told him where I'd been; apparently I'd walked into an army training ground and was lucky not to have been shot.

As I drank my second cup of coffee I found myself staring at a beautiful young man a few yards from me. He was incredibly attractive, Spanish in the best possible way, with black wavy hair, unbelievably long lashes framing warm brown eyes, wide cheekbones and a perfect mouth; not too big, just right for his smile. Beneath the open shirt I caught glimpses of an amazing body, deeply tanned, strong and lean, not an ounce of fat. I couldn't keep my eyes off him, and began to remember why I wasn't a lesbian. I longed to be able to sit next to him and chat, to flirt, to feel attractive in the company of an attractive man. I shut my eyes and dreamed of wearing high heels and a mini-skirt, of bopping and laughing at a nightclub, of being charming and witty and sexy. I wanted to feel desired without feeling threatened – I'd almost forgotten what that was like. How different this trip would be if I were a man, I thought; I could walk around in nothing but a pair of shorts, and I could Don Juan my way across Europe without ever experiencing that underlying fear of the opposite sex.

Life's not fair, I thought, then I caught a glimpse of myself in a mirror and had to laugh. I looked *dreadful*. I was filthy; my greasy hair was pulled back severely, my face was flushed and red from the sudden warmth of the bar and I looked about as sexy as Worzel Gummidge. No man worth having would give me a second glance.

Chapter 9
Woozling

I walked uphill for the next three hours, through the friendly village of Olocan and up into the beautiful craggy mountains of the Cruz de la Hoya. We were all tired when we reached Marines Viejo, a tiny village without a single modern building, stuck on a steep hillside. On the far side of the village I saw some perfect grassy terraces. Sheep were grazing, tended by an ancient lady walnut who told me I could happily camp there. She accepted a glass of cider and we talked for about an hour, as we watched the sun disappear over the ridge of mountains on the far side of the valley. She chuckled at my photos of the sheep back home, amazed by the bright green of the fields and the size of the Suffolks.

Eva was a widow and lived farther up the valley. She had about fifty sheep whom she roamed about with all day, locking them up in a barn at night. It was fascinating watching her with them; they followed her when she called, and she made an extraordinary variety of clicking and hissing noises with her tongue to stop them straying. She also owned a fair number of almond and olive trees, though she didn't seem to mind when Bella started demolishing one of them. Eva thoroughly approved of the disgusting offal mixture I cooked up for the dogs, but looked suspiciously at the cheesy pasta I was making for myself.

'A big girl like you needs meat,' she said.

Thanks, I thought, and realized I was almost double her size.

Eva looked inside my tent, fascinated, and she thought my sleeping bag was fantastic, but was flummoxed by what I was doing. If my parents lived in such a big house, she said, pointing to my photograph of home, what was I doing living like a gypsy? Had I done something wrong? Had they kicked me out? I tried to explain, saying I was on a sort of holiday, that afterwards I'd be going home and leading a normal life again. She nodded, not understanding at all.

'But what about your boyfriend? Doesn't he mind your wandering about on your own?'

I told her it was OK, he was an understanding sort of guy.

It was very cold the morning I walked through the beautiful, craggy mountains of Cruz de la Hoya. At Gatova I stopped at the bakery, tying Bella and the dogs outside. I joined the queue of ladies and stood salivating at the baskets of fresh pastries and delicious smells coming from the ovens. I'd been impressed by Spanish bread; it rivalled the French in quality and was much cheaper, and the bakeries usually sold delicious cakes and biscuits as well.

I had just reached the front of the queue and was considering treating myself to some almond meringues when someone at the door of the shop screamed. I heard a clattering of hooves and looked round to see Bella charging towards us, saddle bags round her belly and lead trailing on the ground. She barged through the door and plunged her head into a tray of *ensamadas* before I had time to reach her. Ladies screamed and fled, and I thought the baker was going to have a coronary. It was hell getting her out, as the room was too small to turn her round and donkeys are notorious for refusing to walk backwards.

I eventually managed it, and then grovelled apologies to the baker, offering to pay for all the damaged *ensamadas*. Luckily he saw the funny side of the situation and was incredibly good humoured, even giving Bella a basket of stale bread. A large crowd had gathered, and the baker's kindness sparked off a strange bout of generosity. The old ladies decided that I was a pilgrim and that my animals and I were desperately in need of food. They started bringing us things – broad beans and corn for the donkey, bones and scraps for the dogs, and for me some magdalenas, a bag of chocolate and a dozen eggs. Someone brought me a cup of sweet coffee laced with Cognac, and an old man gave me one of his black cigarettes, which was a bit hard to take so early in the morning but I didn't want to spoil the atmosphere of this spontaneous gathering, so I accepted gratefully and tried not to cough. They seemed to think that I was French, and we spoke in a strange mixture of languages. They told me to remember them to Papa when I reached Rome (it was lovely, as if they were talking of an old friend). I bade them farewell and felt wonderfully happy as I set off again.

The scenery was breathtaking but the walking was tough that day and I was exhausted by the time we reached the Palancia valley. As we approached Altura I noticed a camp site. Yippee! I couldn't believe my luck and hoped there might be some English people here. I was now reading *The Past Is Myself* for the third time; perhaps I would be able to do a book swap.

The owner was polite but firm: the site was not yet open for the season. I begged and pleaded and showed him the newspaper articles about me and eventually he relented, letting me stay for one night as long as I promised to clear up all Bella's mess.

I made the most of the hot water and washed all my dirty clothes. As I was searching through my saddle bags to find a missing sock, I found a strange plastic bag I didn't recognize. I looked inside, and gagged; it contained a stinking, maggot-ridden chicken. Yuck! It had been there since Millares over a week ago and I had forgotten completely about it. I felt very ashamed of myself – my standards were really dropping. But at least I now knew that the awful smell wasn't me!

The next day I camped by a river near the town of Segorbe, where I'd been told I could find a blacksmith. I spent the afternoon lazily exploring the town and pretending I was an ordinary tourist, eating ice cream and buying postcards. I replenished my supplies of Calor gas and batteries and bought Bogey's prescription, a strange silver powder that turned out to be a miracle medicine, curer of all external ailments. I gazed through the windows of the smart dress shops, remembering what sophistication looked like, and for a laugh tried on a few outfits. I met some English people and descended on them as if they were old friends. It felt fantastic to speak my own language again and I gabbled away at them desperately. They seemed to think I was a bit of a nutter and walked away as soon as they politely could.

When I got back to camp I found that the inside of Bella's ears had been savagely attacked by mosquitoes and midges – they were in a terrible state, bleeding and inflamed. I smothered them with every disinfectant and repellent I could find, which seemed to keep the insects away but which resulted in the one and only time that Bella bit me – she hated anyone touching her ears. The midges attacked me too in the night, and in the morning my tent was dripping wet inside and out. I swore never again to camp beside a river – it wasn't as idyllic as it sounded.

I got up early on Saturday and arrived at the address I had been given by half past seven. I had tried not to be over-optimistic, and had almost convinced myself that it would be another false lead, so when I actually saw a real farrier banging nails into the hoof of a great chestnut horse I could hardly believe my eyes. Yes, he said, he would shoe my donkey. I was so delighted I wanted to hug him.

Bella was in such ecstasy at seeing another equine she didn't notice the strange noises and smells, and stayed calm even when the smith set to work. He was surprisingly small, but the strength contained within that wiry body was phenomenal. It was fascinating watching him, as he took a six inch strip of iron, heated it in the furnace till it was white hot, bashed it into a curve, cut and trimmed it, then heated it again, and on and on until he'd produced a tiny little shoe, no bigger in width than the rim of a tea cup.

It was years since he had shod a donkey, he said; for although some still work in the fields, few donkeys walk on the roads. He shod only her front feet, saying he only did the back ones if the animal was used for pulling. He didn't have any small nails, just great big thick ones which I thought were going to rip Bella's little hooves apart as he hammered them in. He didn't put her foot between his legs like an English farrier would; instead I had to hold it up for him while he worked from the side, and I was terrified that I was going to lose a finger. The finished products looked like a pair of skates, incredibly clumsy and heavy. I prayed they wouldn't make Bella go lame, paid the smith his 1000 pesetas, and set off through the town.

I soon discovered that they had the effect as well as the appearance of skates; poor old Bella slipped and skidded all over the smooth tarmac roads. Going downhill I had to walk in front with my back against her chest to act as a brake, and she just slid down, snowplough style. Once the road became rougher, she began to get the hang of it, but she kept stopping, picking up her feet and looking at them with a bewildered look on her face, trying to work out what we'd done to her. She was bemused by the noise as well and would look behind her thinking someone was following us.

We were entering what was to be my favourite part of Spain, the beautiful mountains of the Sierra de Espadan, and we passed through the loveliest villages I'd ever seen. They had strange Arabic names, such as Vall de Almonacid, with the ruins of an ancient castle perched on the peak above it, and Algimia de Almonacid, the quaintest of them all, with narrow cobbled streets and tiny round *plazas*. Flowers spilled over the balconies of the tall, thin houses and it was tempting to stop and paint, but I wanted to make the most of the warm weather and walk a reasonable distance.

I reached Matet by late afternoon and stopped at the bar to ask directions to Torralba del Pinar. I would never find the track to Torralba, I was told; much better to take the one going west to Pavias. The landlord gave me detailed instructions, even drawing a little map, and after a couple of beers I set off again. After a few miles I made camp, and as I sat beside the fire cooking my supper, I felt incredibly happy. It had been a day such as I had dreamed of. The countryside was so beautiful, the villages so picturesque, the people so friendly; my donkey was shod and my Dobermann was growing fatter. Everything was going right at last. I was becoming used to my own company and was quite content to be alone with the animals.

The next morning, Sunday 9 April, I went along what I prayed was the right track for Pavias. I reckoned it must be, but there were already hoof marks in the mud, surprisingly similar in size to Bella's, and I kept thinking of Winnie-the-Pooh following his Woozle. It began drizzling and I felt a bit hopeless. I wished I hadn't been so ambitious and had gone by road instead.

But when I saw Pavias down below me, sitting prettily by the side of a river, my spirits lifted. I was very proud of myself for having followed my instructions so successfully. As I approached, however, something seemed wrong. I couldn't work out what it was; though most of the people I passed were waving and smiling at me in a very friendly fashion, others were looking at me quizzically, shaking their heads in apparent surprise. Then I arrived at the *plaza*, which struck me as vaguely familiar, and as I looked round I suddenly realized that this wasn't Pavias at all – I was back in Matet! I had just spent a good five hours walking in a convoluted circle!

The villagers stared and smiled as I collapsed in helpless laughter, and I was still giggling when I entered the bar. The landlord took it as a personal insult that his directions had not led me to where I wanted to go and became the butt of endless jokes around the bar. I decided to change my plans and go east to the village of Villamalur because a small tarmac road led the whole way there. It would be a greater distance, but I couldn't face getting lost again. Before I set off I rang Clare, a friend who in a rash moment had promised to come out and join me for a while. I quite expected her to have changed her mind and was rather astonished when she said she was planning to be with me for my birthday on 20 April. We agreed to speak again in a week's time to organize a meeting place.

The road to Villamalur was lovely, barely more than a track, and only one car passed all afternoon. Halfway there the rain started bucketing down, so hard that even Bella was prompted into a run, and we were drenched by the time we arrived. I burst into the little bar and asked if there was anywhere we could stay for the night. The animals were put up in a woodshed, and for 400 pesetas I spent the night in a damp but clean little bedroom in a house at the far side of the village. I boiled some water up on my stove and filled a basin, and made the most of my privacy by stripping off and having a good scrub down. It was funny seeing my naked body in the mirror; I had the kind of sun tan you get when you're eight years old – my face, arms and lower legs were a deep brown, but the rest of me was as lily white as when I left England. I would have been a horrific sight in a bikini.

Then I looked at my face more closely. Typical! At home I spend a fortune cleansing and pampering it with every concoction devised by the Vichy laboratories, but I still have to coat it in powder before daring to show it in public. Now, the one time in my life when I don't give a damn about my appearance, when I actually *wanted* to look ugly, and my complexion was better than at any time in my life – not a spot, pimple or blackhead in sight.

The weather was brighter the next morning, although a cold north wind was blowing. I left early and snaked my way down from Villa-malur's perch through a wooded valley to Ayodar, a tiny village with an extraordinary blue tiled dome on its church which made it look like a mosque. I stopped at the bakery and asked where I might find the *camino* to Espadilla, but was told there wasn't one – it would by now have fallen away down the steep-sided valley.

This was a serious set-back; I had come this way relying on there being a track through the next mountain range. If not, I'd have to walk an extra thirty kilometres by road.

'Why don't you go on the *pista*?' an old lady enquired.

I'd never heard the word *pista* before and asked what she meant. I felt like screaming when she told me. *Camino*, it seems, refers only to old tracks; a new one is called a *pista*.

It was a steep sandy track leading up a ravine-like valley and then along a ridge at the top. The view over the surrounding mountains was spectacular; I was reminded of the fells at home, but this was on a larger scale and more majestic somehow. I saw what looked like little white maggots down below me, then realized they were sheep. They were on such a steep slope I couldn't believe that they didn't fall off. I crossed the top of the pass and suddenly saw the huge valley of the Rio Mijares far below me, with five little white villages dotted along it, each with a blue domed church shining up at me, and over to the east the river grew into a great, star-shaped lake.

We descended abruptly and suddenly Espadilla was just below us. It was a beautiful village, with flowers growing everywhere, tumbling over balconies and filling every spare piece of ground. Eventually I found the bar; it was like an English pub inside, pan-elled and beamed, and was run by a lovely family who told me I should camp in the children's playground.

'Is it safe?' I asked.

They seemed astonished by my question. 'There aren't any bad people round here,' they said. 'We all know everyone else; we'd know if there was a wicked man on the loose.'

It was strange how the people who were so keen to tell me of the danger I was in, who warned me of the evils of other human beings, were usually the ones who themselves frightened me; whereas sweet people like these tended to think the rest of the world was as kind and harmless as they were. Takes one to know one, kind of thing.

In the morning I breakfasted with the family and the father gave me directions for Lucena del Cid. I set off through the lushest orange groves I've ever seen, then I climbed up out of the valley and over a ridge into the next one; I was beginning to regret travelling north in a country whose rivers ran eastwards. I passed through the pretty village of Argelita, crossed the Rio de Villahermosa and followed the tiny road which wiggled up on to grassy, bare moorland. We were incredibly high – I could see all the way back to Ayodar – but the road seemed determined to take us higher still. Before each bend I would beg it to give our legs a rest, dare it to go downhill just for a while, but it was the middle of the afternoon before it did.

I stopped for a late lunch at a deserted hamlet called Mas de Moro and an old shepherd with an odd mixture of sheep, goats and scruffy grey dogs stopped to say hello. He seemed extraordinarily pleased to discover I was English and was keen to know what I thought of Spain and how the Spanish were treating me. He told me he'd known an Englishman in 1937.

'In the war?' I asked.

He nodded. 'He died helping us.'

For once in my life I was completely at a loss for words. The old man didn't say any more and we sat quietly in private thought. Before he left he insisted on giving me a present. He wanted me to take one of his lambs; I'm not sure what he meant me to do with it, but I was actually quite tempted – I thought it would be fun to have a sheep walking along with us as well. Luckily I stopped myself and refused, so he gave me a knife instead. It was beautiful, with a carved handle and a little leather pouch to keep it in. To bring me luck, he said. Then he walked away into the hills with his animals, waving before he disappeared.

When I'm het up over exams or boyfriends, and depressed by the complexities of my life in London, I can return home to the Lakes and after spending just ten minutes with my little brother, I'm brought back down to earth. As Stevie struggles to put a sentence together, my own problems seem pathetic and irrelevant, and I realize how lucky I am. I felt like that now. Humbled, somehow, and privileged to have met such a man.

Chapter 10
In the Land of the Cid

Wednesday 12 April. Lucena del Cid is a pretty little market town built above a deep gorge; a huge double rainbow framed the church as I approached, making the setting seem even more spectacular. I left the animals in an empty barn while I shopped and explored. At the butcher's I asked as usual for scraps for the dogs and was given a huge dustbin bag full of something. Since it cost only fifty pesetas, I didn't bother enquiring as to its specific contents, but I found out as I was crossing the main street and the bag split. Pounds and pounds of pork fat splurged over the road – huge, thick white slabs of hairy jelly, greasy and slimy and impossible to hold on to. Cars hooted at me to hurry as I desperately tried to pick it all up. Humiliation comes in many forms!

The man at the bank was the first person who actually said, 'But Hannibal didn't come this way . . .', and he found my answer of 'Too many English on the coast' very amusing. He invited me to have lunch with him and his wife, and over a thick vegetable soup they told me something of the history of the area, of how it has borne witness to some of the fiercest fighting in Spain.

The words *el Cid* appear in numerous place names, they told me, because this region was the independent state claimed for him in the eleventh century by Don Rodrigo Diaz de Bivar, the national hero of Spain known as 'the Cid', an Arabic word meaning chieftain. In romantic legend he was a Christian champion who played a crucial part in the reconquest of Spain from the Moors. In reality he was an unprincipled freebooter who fought for whichever side paid him most; he served the Moorish ruler of Saragossa, then fought for the Christian Count of Barcelona in Catalonia, and finally he took this part of Valencia for himself.

I asked them if they knew the track to Chodos; they said no one used it any more, and I would be better going to Adzaneta. I must always take the right turn at every junction I came to, they said. I pictured myself walking round in endless circles, but took their word for it, and tried to remember the various landmarks they described. Just as I was leaving the town there was a heavy downpour of rain. I sat in a café till it stopped, and the men there wouldn't stop laughing when I said I was planning to walk cross-country to Adzaneta. I'd never find it, they said. They tried to persuade me to go by road, but that meant thirty-five kilometres instead of twelve; I said I would at least give the tracks a try.

'When are you wanting to arrive in Rome?' they asked.

'October,' I replied.

'It'll take you that long to reach Adzaneta!' they chortled.

The hardest part of the afternoon's walk was the initial descent from the town down to the River Lucena, for the slope was almost vertical and the path had been tarmacked, so Bella skidded most of the way down, with her front legs turned inwards as if trying to do the snowplough. We both grazed our knees; Bella was pathetic and held hers up to me, as if expecting me to kiss them better.

We then climbed 1000 feet up on to the Sierra de la Cruz. The sun came out as we reached the top and the view was magnificent. I could see the sea! I hadn't realized how close it was. The colour was breathtaking, an incredible turquoise blue; I put on my monocle and saw the waves and the boats, and decided my next journey would be by boat. I'd be able to wash whenever I liked and I wouldn't have to talk to anyone unless I wanted to. My monocle, one cracked lens held together with sticking plaster, was all that remained of the two pairs of glasses which had left England with me. Most of the time, though, I was quite happy without it. The scenery looked better because I never noticed the rubbish or the electricity pylons, and I've always found that human beings are much more beautiful when I'm not wearing my glasses – I don't see the wrinkles or the dandruff.

The clear blue skies suddenly filled with extraordinary cloud formations, bringing hard, driving rain and hail from the west. I guessed my way along the track and didn't really have a clue whether I was right or wrong. But it was a peaceful afternoon and the miles flew by. When I saw the plain below me and what I reckoned must be Adzaneta in the middle of it, I felt very proud of myself, and stuck up two fingers to those men in the bar.

When I reached the village I found an orchard next to the church and struggled with my tent in the dark. I went straight to bed, too tired to cook any supper. As I sank into sleep I heard the church clock strike half past nine, and I smiled. I'm going to be hopeless when I finally return to civilization, I thought, I'll never be able to cope with the night life.

I was woken soon after 2 a.m. by a furious barking outside the tent. There was a loud thud and some groaning, definitely human and male. I peered out and saw a man laid out on his back in the grass; he must have tripped over the guy rope. The animals seemed to have the situation under control – Bogey was leaning over him growling and snarling, while George was running round excitedly, yapping support and pulling at his shoes. The poor man was crossing himself frantically, calling for deliverance from Madonna and '*dios mios*' and anyone else who might help. Then Bella plodded up and leant her head over him to have a look, and as he stared up at her he let out a wail of terror. I tried not to laugh as I pulled the animals away and told him, in as deep a voice as possible, to leave immediately or I'd order my dog to kill him. I could smell the stench of brandy on his breath and from what he was mumbling I realized that he wasn't sure whether this was real or part of a terrible Bacchanalian nightmare. He stumbled away as fast as he drunkenly could.

I made a big fuss of Bogey, my guardian angel, and wondered whether she would actually ever bite anyone. Luckily it seemed that the sight of a Dobermann barking and growling was enough to make most people not want to risk finding out.

The church bells woke me up early in the morning and I felt cold and hungry. I'd just heated up some coffee for breakfast when two *Guardia Civil* men approached me. One was moustached and hairy, the other thin and taut-faced; they were more friendly than the last lot had been, but I didn't much like the look in their eyes. When they asked for my papers I confidently handed over my passport and they flicked through it and gave it back. I was about to heave a sigh of relief when the doors of hell opened.

'And where are the papers for your animals?'

I tried to stay calm as I fumbled about in my bag. I thought an out-of-date *guia* would be better than nothing at all, so handed over the certificate that had last been stamped at Abanilla over a month ago. They saw through it horribly quickly.

'But this isn't valid!'

I tried to look confused and ignorant, but they didn't fall for it at all and began to get angry.

Things got worse: they demanded papers for the dogs. The *dogs*! I hadn't realized I needed anything for *them*!

'You must have proof of their anti-rabies vaccines,' they told me, 'otherwise there is a large fine and we can destroy them.'

I panicked. I had a certificate for George, even one for myself, but nothing for Bogey. I couldn't think of any way of lying myself out of this mess and I burst into genuine tears. Never in my life have I grovelled as I did then, apologizing pathetically, promising to take my animals to a vet immediately, playing the helpless female for all it was worth. Bogey was going to be killed; it was all my fault, and I couldn't think of any way to save her.

'Don't worry, *gitana guapa*,' the hairy one said. 'If you give me a big kiss and promise to go to a vet in the next town you come to, we'll forget all about it.'

I was so overjoyed that I probably would have kissed him anyway. He was horribly smelly, but it seemed a small price to pay for what at the time seemed enormous generosity. He held me hard against him and put his tongue in my mouth, but luckily didn't seem to expect any response and it was all over quickly. They bade me farewell, wished me luck and were gone.

I suppose I should have been shocked, or angry, but all I could feel was relief. Suddenly everything was all right again. I'd been let off, the animals weren't going to die, the journey wasn't going to come to an abrupt end after all. I went to the village store and bought a huge celebratory breakfast for us all – bread and real butter for me, liver for the dogs and two kilos of apples for Bella (she kept letting out great cidery burps all day), and I treated myself to a packet of real Marlboro's. They were more than double the price of Spanish cigarettes, but I savoured every puff.

The road was very straight and boring up the valley of the Boco de la Val, but I was so happy that I didn't mind. The wind was freezing, so at lunchtime I put all my clothes on: thermal underwear, both dresses over my jeans and T-shirts, two jumpers, and my waterproofs on top of all that. I must have looked like the Michelin man, but it was the only way to keep warm, and I hoped it might put the men off as well. In hard, squally rain we climbed up on to the wild, desolate moorland of the Sierra de Espaneguera, entering an area of Spain known as El Maestrazgo, a mountainous region that would take us all the way into Catalonia. We camped in the tiny, isolated village of Villar de Canes, a bleak little place untouched by the modern world, where the wind was so fierce I had to cook my supper on the Calor gas stove inside the tent, hoping we wouldn't go up like a zeppelin. I kept my clothes on inside my sleeping bag and drew the drawstring up over my head, but it was still bitterly cold.

If anything, the wind was stronger in the morning. I drank a litre of hot chocolate before daring to venture from the tent, and the fly sheet nearly flew away as I was folding it up. I decided to walk up the Belluga valley, hoping the rugged mountains on each side might act as a windbreak and give us some protection. No such luck; instead it gusted down the gullies and hit us from all sides. My eyes watered, my nose ran and my fingers were so numb with cold that it was difficult to hold on to Bella's lead, and zipping up my jeans was a major operation. I wished I was a boy and could have a pee without having to expose so much bare flesh to the elements,

Emma and George.
Still smiling – we
hadn't set off yet

Hasdrubella the
beautiful

A road through a Spanish wilderness

Dawn view from the tent near Fortuna

Bogey hated getting up in the morning

Paw George!

Sunshine at last – we couldn't stop smiling

The best time-wasters in the world – Bogey's puppies

Puppy love

Hannibal taking a bath as soon as the packs were off

Let them eat cake!
Bastille Day
celebration in
Puyloubier, France

I'm sure something's not quite the same. In the Rhône Valley, France

Below the ruins of Les Baux, France

and I regretted drinking all that hot chocolate earlier.

The valley itself was breathtakingly beautiful, with rugged peaks above its fertile bottom. I saw some *trees*! Proper big ones, the first I had seen in Spain, and I was so overjoyed that I sat under the biggest and sang *Cottleston Pie* to celebrate. I don't know what kind they were, but they looked very beautiful to me and made me feel incredibly happy. (Was I going potty? Do normal people feel incredibly happy when they see a tree?)

In the village of Cati a friendly lady in the butcher's told me there was a hermitage, La Ermita Santa Ana, a mile to the north, which would be a perfect place to camp, or I could stay at the *campo de futbol* beside it. I bought a chicken to share with the dogs, and walked through the village just as the children were let out of school. I tried to escape unseen, but Bella wasn't very good at quick getaways and we were spotted. I cursed my luck as hordes of little boys clambered round us and started their familiar chant.

The hermitage was spooky, locked up and uncared for, and the side in the lee of the wind was visible to the road. I opted for the football pitch instead; it was walled and sheltered, and had plenty of grass round the edge for Bella. The little boys from the village were fascinated by the tent and they wouldn't leave Bella alone. I asked them to go away, but of course they wouldn't. I was trying to cook a sophisticated meal for a change, stuffing a chicken breast with herbs and garlic and poaching it in wine (Cordon Bleu camping!), but they ruined my enjoyment of it by making revolting puking noises to show me what they thought of my taste in food. I finally got angry, which was my downfall. They turned into absolute little bastards, knocking down my tent, untying Bella's tether, and nicking things out of my saddle bags. I felt like murdering them, and thought for a moment that I had; while hurling stones back I hit one on the head. He fell from the wall and landed flat on his face with a loud thud. His spectacles broke and his nose started bleeding. I'm afraid I didn't feel in the slightest bit sorry for him as he hobbled off towards the village with his friends; my only worry was that his father might organize a posse to come and punish me for hurting his precious *hijo*.

Bella had been walking slowly and seemed tired, so I decided to take the next morning off. I had noticed an old-fashioned washing area in the village – a miniature raised swimming-pool with stone slabs round the side – and thought it would be a good idea to wash my two dresses. (All my clothes were dirty, but I didn't dare wash anything else in case the warm weather didn't last. Smelly dry clothes would be more use than clean wet ones.)

81

About a dozen ladies were already there, scrubbing away at great mounds of family laundry. They looked so professional, rubbing the cloth against the stone slabs with swift, deft strokes and managing to remove every fleck of dirt and grime that I felt utterly incompetent in comparison.

A lot of dirt came out of my dresses, but nothing I could do would make them look clean. There was an area at the side for drying, and as I hung them up I was shamefully aware of the large prominent stains, the ripped hem, and the general muddy tinge I had been unable to wash out. Two dozen critical eyes noticed this too and I felt ridiculously guilty, as if I'd failed some test of womanhood.

Yes, I know! I wanted to yell, I'm no good at washing! I admit it! But I've got a law degree, you see; I spent my childhood learning other things. I can cook! I'm good with children! (or at least I was, before I met yours.) I'm usually good at being a woman, honestly!

I took my dresses and fled from their pitying smiles, aware that I was being over-sensitive but unable to control my feelings. I packed up and set off once more, drying my clothes by my usual method on the back of the donkey. I'd invented a very clever mobile washing line that hung from sticks around Bella's tail. It gave rise to many rude comments, but as long as Bella didn't roll it was most effective.

Chapter 11
Stung for a *Guia*

Saturday 15 April. The weather had improved and it became warm enough to wear just jeans and a jumper over my thermals. I walked northwards through heather-covered hills and stopped for lunch just before I met the Morella road. After my sandwich I settled down for a read, while Bella polished off a good patch of grass. Suddenly Bogey, who'd been scuffling through the undergrowth with George putting up birds and rabbits, gave an enormous yelp and leapt up into the air as if she'd had an electric shock. She hurtled towards me and flung herself into my lap, jerking and snapping in semi-convulsions. It was a few seconds before I saw what had happened and the realization hit me at the same time as the first shot of pain.

Physical agony mixed with terror and blind panic. I jumped up and screamed, flinging Bogey as far away from me as possible. She was covered in hornets, enormous grey and black wasps with huge dangling legs; I'd never in my life seen so many, and hundreds more were zooming towards us. She must have put her nose into their nest, and they were set on revenge, apparently blaming me as well as my dog for the intrusion. I covered my face with my hands and ran, but they followed and swarmed round me. They flew into my hair and on to my clothes, and I screamed and screamed in terror as they began to sting. My jumper was covered with them; I ripped it off and hurled it at them, swiping at the air and stamping on them, but it only made them angrier. The noise was the worst thing, the furious buzzing from the ones stuck in my hair; I thought they were crawling inside my head and I was convinced they were going to kill me. I couldn't stop screaming, wailing in agony as they sank their tails into my skin. I ran along the road, praying that a car would rescue me. As soon as I thought I was rid of them, more would rush at me. It was a nightmare that went on and on, and all I could do was run and scream and swipe hopelessly at the air.

I finally ran far enough. They gave up at last. I stopped crying and tried to calm down, calling the dogs and suddenly remembering Bella, whom I hadn't even tied up. Bogey ran towards me, then lay down on the side of the road and didn't move. I had seen her snap at and eat a good few of the hornets; her throat and stomach must have been stung and I dreaded to think what effect that would have. I had some anti-histamine pills in my first-aid kit, but there was no way I could reach my bags – a swarming black cloud still surrounded them. I needn't have worried about Bella. She was still happily eating in the midst of it all, apparently oblivious to the entire drama; hornets, it seems, do not attack donkeys.

I didn't know what to do except wait, so I sat down at the side of the road and tried to comfort the dogs. Georgie had been stung in her ear and was making a terrible fuss; Bogey lay still beside me. I counted five stings on my scalp, one on my ear, two on my neck and an indeterminate rash of them on my hands and arms. I was in shock rather than agony; I couldn't stop shaking and my heart was still beating incredibly fast. A lorry driver stopped beside me and asked how much I charged; I screamed at him to fuck off and burst into tears again. He seemed to accept this as perfectly normal behaviour from a prostitute; he laughed and threw me a cigarette, said 'Maybe next time,' and drove away.

I was still sitting there half an hour later when a young couple pulled up thinking Bogey had been hit by a car and offering help. I tried to explain what had happened (it was difficult as I didn't know the words), but they lent me a jacket, scarves and gloves and I made my way back towards my stuff; the hornets flew at me, but the little bastards couldn't get through all my layers and I returned unharmed to the road with my donkey and my bags. The poor woman was stung as she tried to shake the hornets from her scarf and I felt awful, but at least I could now give Bogey some anti-histamine and get going again.

I set off along the main road towards Morella. The sky had darkened and was threatening rain. I wanted to make camp as soon as I could, and luckily after just two kilometres we arrived at the tiny hamlet of Vallivana. It was an idyllic place, with a beautiful church and a lovely old *santuario*. A huge building with stables and out-buildings beside it, obviously once a nobleman's house, turned out to be a restaurant. I tied up the animals and entered a large, scruffy room filled with long wooden tables and a bar against the far wall.

The landlord and his family were very kind to me; they let me tether Bella next to the graveyard and said I could take her into a stable if it rained. Their little boy helped me put up the tent next to the house; he was horrified by the state of my tent pegs, and brought out a selection of his father's tools to straighten them – even the ones that I had bent double he managed to bash back into shape. His mother gave me scraps for the dogs and let me use their back room to have a wash.

84

I rang home and Mum gave me a message from Clare – she wasn't able to come out to join me until 24 April. I was going to be alone for my birthday. I tried not to feel sorry for myself and had another brandy – they'd left the bottle on the table beside me, and it was much more effective than aspirin or anti-histamine as a pain-killer.

The *parador* slowly filled up with groups of people coming for an evening meal. A table of men invited me to join them and I threw caution to the wind and accepted. I stopped worrying and decided to enjoy myself. We had a fantastic meal of rabbit and asparagus stew followed by a delicious sheep's milk custard, but I got absolutely plastered as they poured glass after glass of wine for me. I finally stumbled out to my tent and was violently sick, but I slept well, oblivious of the cold and for once indifferent to the dangers.

We had a long trek ahead of us: twenty-five kilometres across the Querol mountains to the town of Morella, where they had promised me last night I would find a vet. We would be entering Catalonia in a few days' time and I wanted to make sure I had valid papers for the animals. Bogey, thank God, was fine this morning, apparently none the worse for her stings. George was still making a hell of a fuss about her ear; my wounds were itchy but not too painful, and the swelling had gone down.

I climbed up on to wild high hills of gorse and heather, where nothing broke the force of the wind as it tore down from the north across the Maestrazgo. Despite all my layers of clothes, it seemed to cut through to my bones. I sucked my fingers to keep the blood moving and tried to keep my brain functioning by remembering the words to as many Edward Lear poems as I could. People often ask what I used to think about as I was walking along; on cold days such as this, it was all I could do to think about anything. They say that when sheep and cows are outside in temperatures below freezing their cerebral activity drops by 80 per cent; I think something similar happened to me.

At midday I met some farmers weighing sheep in a small fenced enclosure. They had some bread, salami and brandy which they offered to share with me, and we shivered together behind their Land Rover while they told me how they had never known an April like it.

I was frozen and exhausted by the time we reached the Bergantes valley and we stopped at the foot of the hill on which stands the walled town of Morella. I left Bella grazing beside a petrol station while I sat in a café drinking gallons of hot soup, thawing out and regaining my energy. I stared up at the telly in the corner and slowly realized that it was talking about England; there'd been another football tragedy, a horrific number had died. Everyone in the room was discussing how terrible the British were, how they should never be allowed to European football matches, how they were a bunch of hooligans. I quickly put my book away and spoke the most fluent Spanish of my life as I asked for the bill.

The town's camp site turned out to be nothing but a clump of pine trees and a cold tap facing the full brunt of the wind. I fed the dogs their meat and then I discovered that while I'd been in the café Bella had eaten the rice and vegetables I had been saving for my supper. I had no food, no wine and I was freezing – I decided the circumstances were dire enough to justify spending the night in a hotel. I tethered Bella to a pine tree and put up the tent for the dogs, leaving them curled up on my sleeping bag, while I walked back into the town and found a room.

Despite the soft bed, I slept badly, worrying about the dogs and unused to the heavy sheets and blankets. In the morning I found that my prayers had been ignored – it was *snowing*! Great white flakes swirled down the streets and filled the skies, obliterating the view and turning the ground into sheer ice. The tent was barely standing when I went to rescue my animals. Bella stood with her bottom to the wind and looked at me miserably, her eyes framed with white, frosted lashes. Her water bucket was frozen solid. I heated up some milk and eggs for the dogs and tried not to despair. I decided we should move on to a village, somewhere smaller that would be friendlier than the inhabitants of this large, touristy town.

But first I had to find a vet. I found two scruffy-looking ones in the *Oficina de Extensión Agraria* and felt pleased to have found them so easily, but their grave expressions when I asked for a *guia* for my donkey wiped the smile from my face. They told me that as of 17 March any equine entering Catalonia must have a blood test, and this blood test took a week. *A week!* I can't wait a week, I wailed, but they told me that I had no choice, for if discovered without a certificate giving evidence of the test, the animal would be destroyed, irrespective of whether it had equine flu or not. They also told me that I could be in deep trouble with the law, for if the test showed that Bella *did* have equine flu and the authorities realized that I had travelled through Spain with an infected animal without a *guia*, I would face criminal charges.

This was all I needed. I agreed to return with Bella in the afternoon, then sat and shivered in a café with the dogs and wondered what God had against me. I looked out of the window at the falling snow and decided that we would all freeze if we had to stay here a week. Over lunch I had my inspiration. If I found somewhere for Bella to stay, the dogs and I could go to Majorca to see Emu! We

86

could catch the ferry from Valencia – I knew dogs were allowed on it, I'd seen them – and I could be there for my birthday. Suddenly I felt happy again and I headed for the town hall to seek out accommodation for my donkey.

The very enthusiastic mayor of Morella found my request hilarious and suggested that Bella stay in the stables of the bullring. Apparently, a man called José, who looked after the place, probably wouldn't mind feeding my donkey if I paid him for it. A policeman was summoned and told to take me there.

José was a sweet, little old man with a huge nose and a dreadful cough; I'm not sure what the policeman said to him but he seemed to think that I was very important, and said it would be a great honour to look after my donkey. The stables were large and clean, opening on to a small, sheltered yard. José said he would fetch hay and corn for Bella, and a bucket for water since she couldn't reach the horse troughs. I was very pleased, and left him fussing over her while I packed up my gear.

The rest of the afternoon didn't go so well, for taking the blood sample was one of the most horrific performances I've ever seen and poor Bella was absolutely terrified. The vets tied her head up so tightly I feared they would break her neck; she was kicking and jumping, whinnying in fear and rolling the whites of her eyes at me, more frantic than I'd ever known her. I tried to protest but they ordered me to keep out of the way while they jabbed frantically at her neck. Blood shot everywhere, except inside the test tubes. They left me to clean her up and calm her down; I was furious, but when I tried to tell them what I thought of them they just laughed, saying they'd heard the English were pathetically soft towards animals. They gave Bogey a rabies vaccine and I arranged to meet them in a week's time for Bella's results.

On returning to the town hall to find out bus and ferry times, I discovered that dogs are not allowed on buses. I hated myself for the decision I then made, but I felt I had no choice. I could hitch-hike to Valencia, but I realized that no one would stop for a Dobermann so I decided to leave Bogey behind and take only George. José agreed to look after Bogey, so I made a warm bed for her in the straw and left all my spare clothes with her to try and make her realize that I'd be coming back. I hoped that a week's rest was just what Bogey needed to build up her strength, but I felt miserable leaving her. She was just beginning to trust me and now I felt I was shattering that trust. I said a very tearful goodbye and set off with George for Majorca.

Chapter 12
Freezing on Top of the World

My week in Majorca passed like a dream; I was in another world and I loved it. Suddenly I was just an ordinary tourist and I felt gloriously free; I could wander through the streets of Cala Ratjada in a mini-skirt without attracting a second glance and I could stay up all night dancing at the discos without worrying about giving the wrong impression. I spent so much time wallowing in the bath I'm surprised I didn't turn into a prune, and I washed my clothes over and over again in the machine. Emu organized a huge party for me on my birthday, 20 April, and it was great to sit and chat with old friends about subjects entirely unrelated to my walk.

After six days, however, I felt strangely pleased to be returning to my gypsy life. I felt unhealthy and tired after all those late nights, and the novelty of being clean had soon worn off. On Sunday evening George and I cheerfully set sail back to the mainland and I waved goodbye to Emu without any of the tears of our previous parting.

Clare was due to arrive at Barcelona airport at three the next afternoon. I'd planned to meet her flight and then we could both travel to Morella together. I felt very nervous as I stood in front of the mirror in the airport loo, brushing and re-brushing my hair, putting on more and more make-up, trying to work miracles with my appearance. I was convinced that Clare would be disgusted by my tramp-like existence.

I didn't recognize my best friend as she approached through customs. Clare had dressed as the perfect hippy student hiker, complete with flared cords and trainers; it was so unlike the picture I'd had in my mind that I collapsed laughing. I suppose I should have known that she was hardly likely to turn up in a Chanel suit and silk stockings. Most people would have looked horrendous in what she was wearing, but Clare is so pretty that she managed to get away with it and still turn heads. My nervousness vanished immediately and it was simply fantastic to see her.

We made our way over to a bar by the road from where we could start hitching to Morella. Clare opened her rucksack to reveal the most wonderful assortment of goodies: ten paperback novels, two kilos of Alpen, a bottle of champagne, a huge packet of smoked salmon and a great parcel of birthday cards and presents from family and friends at home. Our mood was ridiculously merry as we stood in the pouring rain with our thumbs out trying to reach Morella by nightfall. We didn't make it and spent that first night sharing a bed in a grotty *pensione* in a town called Cubelles, where we drank the champagne out of plastic toothmugs and cut up the salmon with my penknife.

We didn't reach Morella till four o'clock the next afternoon, 25 April, and we missed the vets, but we found José up at the bullring with the animals, who were delighted to see us. Bogey had put on a good lot of weight and looked much better; I thanked José for feeding her so well, but he just shrugged his shoulders, commenting that she was a very fussy eater for a dog so thin. He told me that he'd had to spend the whole weekend sitting with Bella, because children had been climbing up on to the bullring walls and throwing stones at her. I walked round the yard and saw that the ground was covered with missiles, some of them large rocks that could have really hurt her. I felt hopelessly angry, and somehow ashamed that Clare should have to see this.

We spent the night in the *enfermeria*, the small stone building beside the bullring where injured matadors are taken to be stitched up. It had water, a basin and an operating table to sleep on, and was perishingly cold. In the morning I felt ghastly; I'd developed a cold overnight and my head was full of catarrh. It was snowing heavily and all the water taps had frozen up. As I walked down the icy steps to the vets' offices, I prayed that all had gone smoothly with the blood test – if not we'd be making a quick dash to France to escape criminal prosecution. Thankfully all was well, although I had to wait another day for the correct paperwork and official certificates to come through.

Clare was astonishingly good-humoured about the way her 'summer holiday' was turning out. We spent the rest of the day shopping for warmer clothes and by the evening we looked ready for a polar expedition. I also bought a new camera and hoped that I would have more luck with it than the last one.

Bogey was worrying me. She seemed happy and much stronger than before, but she looked a funny shape. All the weight she had gained was around her middle and her nipples seemed swollen; I was terrified that she might be in pup, so when I went to the vets' the next morning for Bella's papers I took her with me. After much poking and prodding they told me she had a bad case of worms, which had bloated her stomach. They gave me a bottle of tablets to get rid of it and I heaved a huge sigh of relief.

We set off at two o'clock on Thursday afternoon, 27 April, finally leaving the town that I had entered eleven days earlier. I should have been 200 kilometres further north by now, but since Clare was with me I realized there was no point in worrying about distances; my friend was here on holiday and the primary objective of the next week and a half was to enjoy ourselves.

Some 4000 feet up on the desolate, scraggy hills of the Torre Miro, I began to regret leaving the safe walls of Morella. We could see for miles in all directions and it would have been beautiful if it hadn't been so cold. The wind hit us from all sides and the sky seemed very low. Where on earth were we going to spend the night?

Stuck on top of the moor we found a farm. It was utterly exposed and seemed an extraordinary place to choose to live. A rather dour couple agreed to let us camp and suggested that we put Bella inside the barn. Clare and I put the tent up and scrambled into our sleeping bags as quickly as possible: Bogey and George looked most put out that there was no longer enough room for them beside me, and they had to make do with the gap between the inner and outer tents. Clare elected to be chef and lay propped up on her elbows as she set about cooking while I tried to write the diary.

By most people's standards this would have been a nightmare, stuck in the middle of nowhere in a flimsy little tent with a gale force wind raging, but Clare just pulled her bobble hat further down over her ears and suggested that we brew up some glühwein, a great idea that worked wonders with my cold and sore throat. Chatting and laughing non-stop, she concocted a delicious meal of asparagus, tomato and cream cheese pasta, and acted as if she couldn't have asked for more from a holiday.

The wind howled all night and squalls of rain lashed down as if intent on washing us away. Neither of us could sleep. In the early morning it began hailing and I lay in the semi-darkness wondering what the hell we were going to do. A squall battered so hard against the side of the tent that we decided to take refuge inside the barn with Bella. We sat in a wooden pen which stank of chicken dung and drank endless cups of hot chocolate while our limbs grew gradually numb. I've never been so cold in my life.

The hail finally calmed to a horizontal drizzle and we decided that if we didn't start walking soon we'd freeze to death. The next village, Herbes, was fourteen kilometres away and 2000 feet down the mountain. We packed up a very reluctant Bella and slowly set off down to the Escalona valley, gritting our teeth against the wind and wrapping our scarves tightly round our heads. I have a price-less picture of Clare on the mountainside above Herbes looking utterly miserable, her face blue with cold, forcing her lips into a very unconvincing smile. The animals don't look any happier either. Those fourteen kilometres were the longest I have ever known; the wind never let up and just as we'd dried off from one squall of rain, another would hit us.

Our joy on reaching the village and finding the bar was indescribable. We found a man with a stable where Bella could stay for the night, but unfortunately there was nowhere for us; it was a bank holiday weekend, we were told, and there wasn't an empty bed in the whole village. However, it's amazing what a mixture of warmth and alcohol can do for the spirit. A few hours later we were camping on the school sports field, sheltered in the lee of the tennis wall. Clare's smiles returned and she made the best supper yet, a delicious mussel and prawn mush on a bed of rice. We sat up drinking far too much wine and discussing all the peculiarities and failings of Clare's current boyfriend – poor old Tom's ears must have been burning for hours.

I woke on Saturday morning aware that something was very different, but it was a few minutes before I realized what it was. As I pulled my outer jumper off, it suddenly clicked. I was warm! Clare and I clambered out of the tent to see clear blue skies, then practically skipped up through the village to have a wash at the bar. Our chattering attracted the attention of a nice-looking lady at an open window just above us, who invited us to come inside and use her washroom. She even had a proper loo, and we spent as long as we politely could in there. When we finally emerged she gave us bowls of milky coffee and biscuits, and I tried to answer her endless stream of questions. Her main concern was whether we were married, and when we said that no, we weren't, she yelled upstairs and brought forth her two sons from their beds.

'Marc is twenty-six,' she said, presenting the first, 'and Carl is twenty-four. Aren't they handsome?'

Clare started giggling uncontrollably and I tried not to catch the boys' eyes as I replied that yes, they were very handsome, but we weren't actually looking for husbands, thanks.

Bella had spent the night with a huge black mule and a bale of real hay, and was most reluctant to leave; the little old man refused to accept a penny for looking after her, and as we walked with her back to camp, I felt a great surge of warmth for the Spanish.

Disaster struck just as we were about to set off. George leapt off a wall and landed on a broken bottle, slicing one of the pads off her front right foot. There was blood everywhere. The pad was still attached by a thin flap of skin and I should probably have ripped it off, but couldn't, so I just shoved it back where it had come from to try to stop the incessant flow of blood. I then bandaged it up with my Murcian Tourist Board T-shirt, which soon turned bright red.

Throughout all this George didn't seem to be in any pain at all. As soon as I put her down on the ground she leapt about as usual, trying to make us throw sticks for her, occasionally glancing down at her foot with a baffled expression on her face. Nothing I could do would make her sit still, so we decided to set off and hoped we'd find bandages in Penarroya, the next village to the north.

Following the river Escalona down the valley, we noticed that the water had carved deep caves and basins into the steep sides, and the red layers of earth had eroded quicker than the grey, producing extraordinary, face-like protrusions, with large grey noses sprouting between sunken red eyes and gaping red mouths.

Our early morning rejoicing over the improved temperature had been premature. We saw the last of the sunshine at lunchtime and as we hastily packed up we saw rain clouds gathering in the distance. It began drizzling soon afterwards and our spirits fell even further. George had by now become aware of the pain in her foot and was lifting it up pathetically; the T-shirt was so sodden with blood that it would no longer stay on, so I ended up carrying her for the last few miles.

Penarroya de Testavins is a large village built on the side of a hill, its steep cobbled streets climbing up past quaint little timbered houses to a magnificent church at the top. We found a chemist's shop and bought bandages and plasters for George, but then our luck ran out, for all our enquiries about accommodation were either laughed at or rudely refused.

We ended up camping on a patch of grass sheltered between the walls of well-kept terraces of vegetables to the east of the village. I cleaned Georgie's foot and wrapped it up properly, using sanitary towels as padding, bandages to hold them on and a plastic bag on top to keep the whole thing dry. She still looked sorry for herself so we let her into the tent that night; Bogey was left between the inner and outer tents, but she found a way of pressing against me so that she ended up lying on more of my mat than I did. She was still a funny shape – those worming tablets didn't seem to have made any difference at all – but I was more concerned with George and since she seemed happy I didn't worry.

Sunday 30 April was the day we finally said goodbye to the bad weather. We headed northeast through well-kept orchards and vegetable plots down to the valley of Los Prados, then we climbed up through pine forests to gentle, gorse-covered hills. The view was magnificent; before us we saw range after range of harsh grey mountains: the Sierra de Miranda, the Sierra de Pandols and the

Sierra de Montsant. Somehow, over the next couple of weeks, we were going to have to cross them.

The Pantano de la Peña took our breath away. It's an old reservoir about five miles long, nestled among pine forests at the foot of the Perigañol mountains, a brilliant shade of turquoise. Clare was so carried away by it that she changed into her bikini, even though the water was still a good two miles below us.

We never actually had our swim, for by the time we found somewhere to camp, the sun had gone down and we were back in our jumpers. We put the tent up just twenty yards from the shore and were building a fire when two men drove past in a jeep and stopped to warn us that there were heavy fines for lighting fires here – the *Guardia Civil* would show us no mercy, they said. I hastily brought out the Calor gas instead.

We made our rioja and orange juice into *sangria* and sat on a large rock with our feet dangling into the lake, our spirits high. We somehow knew that the good weather was here to stay and that Clare's summer holiday was finally beginning.

We were hungry in the morning and finished off all the remnants of our food supplies – eggs, cheese and pâté, all mixed up together, piled on to fried stale bread. We had a beautiful walk along the Peña valley, past the huge dam at the mouth of the lake and down a steep, rocky track to the fertile Valderrobres plain. We gawped in wonder at the huge fields of poppies, carpets of bright red velvet billowing in the wind against a brilliant blue sky. After the cold grey of the past week, our senses were reeling.

I was fascinated by the way everyone spoke around here; I'd never heard Catalan before and was astonished by how un-Spanish it sounded: harsh and fast compared to the slurred lisping that I'd grown accustomed to over the past few months. I tried to pick up some of the words and the reaction when I attempted to use them over the next few weeks was extraordinary: the Catalans loved it and responded as if I'd paid them the most enormous compliment.

Tuesday's camp at Cretas was probably the most picturesque that I found in the whole of Spain. Outside the walled, medieval village is a small area of grassland jutting over the Calapata valley, not firm enough to build on so used only for pasture. An old farmer let us stay there and we sat watching the sun go down in a burning red sky. The morning was so beautiful that I couldn't bear to stay in bed and I explored the cobbled streets and stone archways of the village. Utterly intoxicated by the smell, I watched bread being baked in the huge, stone ovens of the bakery. It was flat and sweet, rather like Indian nan, and we managed to eat a loaf each. (Clare's appetite had soon caught up with mine; like me she was rather shocked by how hungry she always seemed to be, but meal-times were an important part of the day and we both felt so healthy that any talk of diets seemed ridiculous.)

Wednesday was hot, almost unbearably so, and Clare's sun lotion turned out to be of use after all. A week ago it had been snowing; now we had to rest in the shadow of the church at Lledo for three hours in the middle of the day for fear of sunstroke. Taking advantage of the well outside the church, we were at last able to wash our hair; the water was freezing, but the relief of rinsing out eleven days' worth of filth was worth it. We were both a good two shades lighter afterwards. We camped just outside a village at the foot of the Sierra de Pandols. Our next stop, the Santuario de Fontcalda, lay somewhere in the middle of those huge mountains; I wondered how on earth we were going to get through them.

On Thursday we joined our first *Grande Randonnée* (GR), a French long-distance footpath several of which extend into Catalonia. They are marked by red and white markers – Signal toothpaste signs, as Clare described them. I planned to use nothing but GRs in France and hoped I wouldn't be seeing much more tarmac until I reached Italy.

This first route was easy to follow for it simply led along a disused railway track. The tunnels were terrifying, some of them over a mile long, and without the torch I would never have dared venture through; cold water dripped down on us and the wind produced strange noises that I was sure were oncoming trains. I kept thinking of *The Railway Children*, when the boy breaks his leg in the tunnel and only just removes it from the track before the train comes.

We climbed higher and higher all day into some of the strangest mountains I'd ever seen. The gritty, dark rock was sheer and harsh, but would suddenly soften to form huge pools leading off from the fast-flowing river that we could see between the trees way down below us. How anyone had managed to build the railway line was beyond me.

There was a surprisingly large station for the Santuario de Fontcalda. The hot springs and church were once a very popular pilgrimage centre and apparently the healing powers of the water are famous. From the railway we had to wind our way slowly down the steep riverbank, which felt as though we were descending into a volcano. High peaks rose above us on all sides and the brilliant sunshine was soon a distant memory.

The sanctuary itself was disappointing. The church was firmly locked and there wasn't a soul about. Beside the church stood an ugly concrete building, which we decided was a youth hostel, and there was a modern picnic area with graffiti-covered tables and litter everywhere. It was a creepy place to spend the night, dark and dank, and I was pleased to set off early the next morning. We had a race on our hands, for Bella's *guia* had expired, and we were also out of money, so we had to reach both a bank and the *Oficina de Extensión Agraria* before two o'clock that afternoon. Gandesa was about fifteen kilometres and a mountain range away, and the clear blue sky was warning us that it was about to be the hottest day yet.

We made it with an hour to spare, but the last few miles were hell, as we passed huge factories and warehouses, madly barking dogs and leering lorry drivers. We didn't even have the energy to speak to each other.

The vet at the *Oficina de Extensión Agraria*, a kind-faced old man smoking a beautiful carved wooden pipe, looked at my papers in bewilderment; he'd never issued a *guia* for a *burro* in his life, he said, and was sure I didn't need one. After a few phone calls, however, he said I was right and quickly wrote one out, covered it in every stamp he could find – for the *Guardia Civil*, he winked – and gave it to me free of charge.

Clare and the animals were not happy when I came out. Apparently as soon as I'd left them Bella had shed sheer green liquid (all those poppies, no doubt) over the pavement, and Clare had been sworn at by passers-by; then children had poured from the school across the street, and all four of them were now being prodded by two dozen shrieking brats. Clare was obviously shaken and I looked round for somewhere to buy a drink to cheer her up. We found a restaurant, and blew half the money I'd cashed at the bank on a huge paella and a couple of bottles of wine; then some businessmen at the next table gave us a bottle of champagne. By the time we finally emerged at five o'clock we could hardly see straight. We staggered back through the town, which suddenly wasn't ugly at all but rather quaint.

We camped at the foot of the Sierra de Caballs, a massive amber block of hills on the other side of which lies the River Ebro. We wandered over the hills for hours the next day; the Signal toothpaste signs of the GR disappeared without trace and we got very lost. The sun grew hotter and hotter. Being above the tree-line we were without shade and we ran out of water; Bogey and Clare both looked ready to pass out by the time we found someone to ask for directions. A little bald man on a moped appeared out of nowhere, saying he could give us water and signalling along a track towards a small stone hut. We were too parched to feel suspicious, but as he took our bottles and swung open the hut doors, I suddenly felt revolted; the walls were lined with magazine centrefolds. There was something absolutely repulsive about seeing them here, in the middle of such beautiful unspoilt countryside. As Baldy reappeared with the water he gestured towards them and raised his eyebrows questioningly to us; we promptly said no and began walking away, and he just shrugged and turned back inside, as if he hadn't expected anything, but had thought it worth a try just in case.

We descended into the cool almond groves of the Cavall de la Torre, but we'd both had too much sun and our camp that evening was not a happy one. We felt sick and shivery, and for the first time since Clare had arrived neither of us could face a glass of wine.

Chapter 13
Bogey's Bladder

Bogey was very constipated the next morning and I was worried about her. She kept trying to go to the loo but nothing would come and she looked at me with a pained expression as if asking for help. Perhaps I shouldn't have given her all that seafood risotto last night, I thought, and I mentioned to Clare that in the morning we should find a vet. She didn't seem to want to lie down, so I saw no point in stopping, but we must have looked like a walking bunch of invalids – George on three legs, Bogey with chronic constipation, Bella still with diarrhoea, and Clare and me with beetroot sunburn.

As we entered Mora the church clock struck twelve. It was stiflingly hot – sweat was pouring down our faces and the shade of the town's buildings was blissfully cool. The Ebro was huge, dirty and industrial, nothing like the shady watering hole that I'd imagined. The only way across it was a four-laned road bridge, a great iron contraption at least 200 yards long. We took a deep breath and set off, promising ourselves a large beer at the first bar we found on the other side.

After about twenty yards scaffolding over the pedestrian section forced us out into the heavy traffic; Clare went ahead with the dogs while I walked behind with a nervous Bella.

'Help, Sophie!' Clare suddenly yelled. 'Come quickly! Bogey's bladder's hanging out!'

As fast as I could with Bella, I raced over. Bogey was hunched up, squeezing hard, and a slimy black thing was protruding from her backside. I bent down to look more closely.

'Oh my God, it's a puppy!'

Bogey gave a final heave and with a sudden rush it was out, a wet, black blob lying on the tarmac. Instinctively I broke through the sac round its mouth and nose and cleared away the mucus, willing it to breathe. Bogey turned round and began licking it; the blob moved, and I felt a rush of happiness as I watched the tiny creature coming to life.

We were causing a traffic jam; drivers were sitting on their horns behind us, and we had to move. In another twenty yards the scaffolding ended and we'd be able to return to the pavement, so I picked up the puppy, held it at a level with Bogey's nose, and ran there. We sat down at the edge of the bridge and we watched Bogey carefully licking and cleaning the puppy. I helped it to find a nipple and it began to feed. Lifting up its tail, I discovered it was a girl – born 7 May 1989, halfway across the River Ebro, ten minutes after midday on the hottest day of the year so far. What a way to arrive.

I couldn't believe what had happened. How could I not have known? How could I have been so stupid? Poor old Bogey, walking in this heat when she was about to give birth. My head was in turmoil, and I couldn't even begin to think about what I was going to do next. I just kept praying over and over again that there wouldn't be any more. One puppy would bring problems enough, but if there were a whole brood I wouldn't be able to cope.

After ten minutes, when there was no sign of any more puppies arriving, we began heading to a field of scrub about half a mile away. We'd just reached a filling station at the far side of the bridge when Bogey's abdomen began heaving again. She lay down in the shade of a petrol pump and within thirty seconds a little brown lump appeared, much smaller than the last. Bogey licked and licked at it, but it wouldn't move or breathe. It was beyond saving, cold and dead. I wrapped it up in some of the garage's hand towels and put it in a bin by the road, feeling terribly sad but also strangely relieved. Please God, don't let there be any more.

The black puppy was busy feeding and Bogey looked contented, but the men at the garage were getting angry, aggressively swearing at us to go away. The field I'd seen wasn't far away, so once again we moved on. It was incredible the way Bogey let me carry the puppy; she didn't so much as growl when I picked her up and seemed to trust me implicitly. We dumped all our stuff in the shade of some walls by the field and I made a bed for Bogey. I opened out a cardboard box to make a roof, and she lay on my sleeping mat, her puppy beside her.

Georgie was fascinated and kept running round and round Bogey, frantically wagging her tail and barking. I thought it would be best to leave mother and daughter alone together, so we tethered Bella a reasonable distance away and took George with us to a bar at the edge of the field.

I've rarely needed a brandy so much. I went to the loo and was shocked by my appearance: my face was streaked with blood and filth, and my eyes looked strange, the pupils so small they were hardly visible. We gulped down our drinks and tried to think constructively. I felt terribly guilty for not having known that Bogey was pregnant, and full of dread about what I should do next.

When I returned to the field to check on Bogey I thought I was hallucinating: next to the little black blob were three more. They were huge brown boys (Daddy definitely wasn't a Dobermann) feeding hungrily and trying to push the black one out. Bogey looked up at me with an expression of pride that took my breath away. She wagged her little stump and nudged at her babies, showing them off to me. I sat down beside her and burst into tears.

A few minutes later Bogey began heaving and another two brown puppies came out. As soon as she had cleaned them up I left her and returned to the bar. I knew I had some big decisions to make and I needed Clare's help.

I shall always feel ashamed and guilty for what I did that day, but I still feel that there was no other choice. I cursed British quarantine laws and wished that we could all just board a plane and go home, but it was impossible – I had to continue walking and there was no way of doing that with six puppies. Apart from that, I felt that Bogey was too weak to cope with six hungry mouths. I also had to admit that it would be very difficult to find homes for six mongrels.

The owner of the bar was very kind and managed to find a vet who was working on a Sunday. I rang him and he told me to bring the puppies at any time. After an hour, when I was convinced Bogey had finished giving birth, I went out with a box and took the five brown puppies from her.

I keep seeing Bogey's face, so proud and contented, as she suckled that row of soft velvet bodies. They screamed and screamed as I took them. Clare was sobbing uncontrollably as she held on to Bogey and I walked away as fast as I could. It took twenty minutes to walk to the vet's; the puppies cried the whole way there and my eyes were so full of tears I could hardly see where I was going. I loathed myself more than at almost any other time in my life.

The vet was a nice man. He gave them very quick injections and they quietly fell asleep, never to wake up again. I stayed to see it done, I wanted to make sure that they didn't suffer, but when the last one was gone I broke down completely. The vet was very kind and let me sit in a corner of his waiting room with a box of tissues until I'd calmed down. He refused to accept any money from me and I walked back to Clare in a daze of mixed emotions – guilt and sadness, and a sickening relief that it was over.

Clare was silently watching Bogey with her one remaining puppy. I hadn't been able to take them all away; it would have broken her spirit and I could never have forgiven myself for that. I'd left her with the first one, the little girl born over the Ebro. She was the spitting image of her mother, black with tan markings on her feet, chest and face, and with the beautifully long ears and tail that Bogey must have been born with too. I named her Dido after the queen of Carthage immortalized in the *Aeneid* who was my favourite character in history, and who was also a relative of Hannibal's. George was becoming very jealous, so Clare and I took her back to the bar where we proceeded to get very drunk. I needed to blot out the memory of what I'd just done.

At around half past nine Bogey started walking round and round in circles. She was restless and looked as though she were in pain. Her stomach began straining again and she pushed so hard that I thought her eyes would pop out. It must be the afterbirth, I thought, and tried to see what was coming out.

It was a brown tail about two inches long! There was obviously a puppy wedged in there, stuck upside down: it was now seven hours since the last one had come out, so I didn't think it could possibly be alive. I was just washing my hands to help pull it out when Bogey gave a massive groan and suddenly it arrived, the biggest puppy of them all. A few seconds later it began a frantic wailing, a clamouring for attention extraordinarily loud for such a tiny animal. Bogey seemed astonished, but happily cleaned it up, and the puppy hungrily started feeding beside its sister.

I was surprised to find that the new arrival was a girl, for her head was unbelievably wide. Her strength of character and will to live amazed me; it was as if she'd known what would have happened to her if she'd come out earlier. You win, I thought, and named her Cleopatra after another of my favourite heroines; it suited her demanding nature and went well with Dido.

'It's strange how holidays are never quite how one imagined,' Clare said, which must be one of the understatements of all time. She was leaving the next day – back to her normal friends doing sensible jobs, back to her man, back to her well-behaved Norwich terriers. But as I thought about London and all that I was missing, I realized that I didn't want to go back with her. Despite all that had gone wrong, despite not knowing what the hell I was going to do with two new-born puppies on my hands, I wanted to finish this crazy journey of mine.

Chapter 14
Peregrine with a Monkey

On Monday 8 May Clare's coach rumbled off towards Barcelona, leaving me sad and deflated as I walked back to town. I got over it with a frenetic round of activity, searching Mora la Nova for the equipment necessary for mobile puppy-rearing. I had surprising success, returning to camp two hours later with a lidded basket, two new towels, two sheets of cotton, a bottle of multi-vitamins, a food supplement for lactating mothers and a kilo of liver. We rested till four, then I started packing up. We couldn't stay here; we were too low, too close to the river, the heat and flies were unbearable and I wanted to escape to the cooler hills. I planned to take the next few weeks slowly and see how Bogey coped. Mileages no longer seemed important; as long as we reached Montserrat by the end of the month I'd be happy.

I tied the basket on top of the saddle bags, padded it with a towel, put the puppies in and shut the lid; they didn't even cry. Bogey looked worried, so I lifted her up and showed her where they were, which seemed to calm her. Then we all set off, walking slowly along the road to Garcia. Bella's steady pace gently rocked the basket and the two puppies were soon fast asleep. Bogey walked at Bella's side and was surprisingly happy, as if pleased to have a break. If anyone approached us she would start growling and barking furiously; I realized that as long as I kept the puppies near me I couldn't be safer. We camped down by the river, where Bogey took her babies into the middle of a hollow tree. She was a wonderful mother, and I was beginning to discover that the puppies were the biggest time-wasters in the world: they were so beautiful I could sit and watch them for hours.

The next morning I joined the GR route again, and began my discovery of the Sierra de Montsant, a beautifully unspoilt area with some of the friendliest people I've ever met. We spent the first night in La Figuera, perched at the top of the fertile Tormo valley, and Bogey brought her puppies inside the tent. Luckily she no longer minded George being near her, and it was very funny seeing the smaller dog with the puppies. She tried to play with them, but soon grew impatient and bored when they failed to respond.

On Wednesday we walked to Cabaces, a long, thin village built on the side of the valley like a terrace. I became convinced that the only other person to have walked on this GR route was the man with the giant tube of Signal toothpaste, for there was no path at all. Often I would have to leave the animals at the last sign and scour the surrounding area for up to twenty minutes before I found the next; progress was painfully slow. Much of it was also too steep for a fully laden donkey, so I frequently had to carry half of Bella's load. If GRs were like this in France, there was no way I'd reach Rome by October.

On Thursday I crossed the desolate sierra and found La Morera de Montsant, an ancient walled village shadowed by an extraordinary line of towering grey rock. The bar was at the bottom of the old mayor's house, and I sat outside in the courtyard drinking my Coke and being quizzed by the old ladies in their beautiful black lace. They admired the puppies, and came to the conclusion, from the look of Cleopatra, that the father was a German Shepherd.

The next day we wound our way down to the old medieval town of Cornudella de Montsant in the flat green Siurana valley. I stopped to buy a baby's bottle and some powdered milk because Bogey had hardly any milk at all and the puppies were making her nipples sore. Cleopatra took to the plastic teat immediately, but Dido just couldn't get the hang of it, so at feeding times Bogey and I took a puppy each. They were growing incredibly fast; Dido was petite and fine-boned, with smooth, short hair and a placid temperament; Cleopatra had longer, fluffy hair and was broader and heavier. She was astonishingly boisterous and bossy for a little animal whose eyes weren't even open yet.

I'd just set up camp on Friday evening when a storm hit us so fiercely that the tent fell down. The rain was coming down like bullets and we were drenched in seconds. A huge bolt of lightning split the sky apart over our heads and Bella went berserk, pulling her tether from the ground and careering off towards Cornudella. I ran after her and luckily she came back to me when I called; she was terrified, her heart pounding like the Charge of the Light Brigade. When we returned to the remains of the camp, by now almost awash, only George and a wailing Cleopatra remained; Bogey had taken Dido off somewhere. I yelled and yelled, but there was no sign of them.

We took shelter in a small barn, then I called for Bogey till I was nearly hoarse. At last she appeared, leaping into the cart where I'd put Cleo, but there was no sign of Dido.

The storm was becoming worse and the rain was torrential; if I didn't find Dido soon she'd be dead. I set off with George and searched the thick grass and rough undergrowth. Georgie seemed to think we were going shooting and began delightedly putting up birds, and I cursed myself for owning the two most stupid dogs in the world. Ten minutes later I was still searching, tears streaking my wet cheeks, desperately calling Dido's name. I'd practically given up hope, but then I saw George pawing at something in the undergrowth. It was Dido, looking like a drowned rat but still alive and squealing.

My diary entry that evening still makes me smile when I read it: 'I'm sitting in a rickety old cart surrounded by my saucepans, strategically positioned to catch all the water leaking through the roof of this tumbledown barn. A huge white pig is grunting at me over the top of what I hope is a strong partition; he's very smelly, but there again, he's probably thinking the same about me. The dogs are lying at my feet, all of them asleep. Am I crazy to be feeling so incredibly happy?'

I was woken on Saturday by a man's face leaning over the side of the pigsty and asking me what the hell I was doing. Trying to speak Spanish first thing in the morning while clutching a murderously defensive Bogey and with two pigs oinking hungrily three feet away was nearly impossible, but eventually he seemed to understand and said I was welcome to stay as long as I liked. He gave Bella some pig food, which she loved, and came back in his car half an hour later with two bottles of drinking water for me. It was still raining, so I settled down to read the trashiest of the books that Clare had brought – Jilly Cooper's *Rivals*.

The heavens didn't close until late afternoon, when we set off again and slowly climbed up the valley to the extraordinary hamlet of Albarca. It sits perched on top of a hillside and consists of just four or five beautifully restored stone houses. As I approached, a man of about fifty rushed out with a camera exclaiming what a wonderful sight we were. He insisted I come into his house and drink some pink champagne, and he gave me bread and salami as he chattered non-stop about how great he thought the English are because we treat animals properly. I suddenly heard a furious growling and dashed outside to find Bogey intent on killing one of his Pekingeses. That didn't go down too well and he opened a bottle of Vin Santo afterwards to calm his nerves.

I spent the night in his garden and set off early across high, heathered moorland towards Prades, where I sat down in the huge square by the church and cooked up liver and eggs for the dogs on my gas stove, while tourists took pictures of us and old men inspected Bella's hooves. We were quite a sight, I suppose; I felt as though I were leading a travelling circus and wished I could make charges for each performance.

As we were leaving Prades I saw a secluded restaurant and decided to treat myself to Sunday lunch. As I drank my coffee I felt confident enough to write the article that Mum had been pestering me to send to the local papers at home.

Writing about my journey made me realize how different I was feeling now compared with those first few terrifying weeks with Emu. That cold, sickening fear of the unknown had disappeared, thank God; my stomach muscles were no longer continually tense, my thoughts not always suspicious when I met people. There were many reasons for my new confidence, I suppose; Bogey certainly had much to do with it, especially now with the puppies. I knew that she would fight to the death to protect them. Clare had made a difference as well, for she hadn't been frightened at all and had made me realize that most of the dangers lay in my imagination. I was also travelling in a much safer part of Spain now. Catalonia seemed much more civilized, somehow – more prosperous, more concerned with art and religion, with beauty and song. Here I noticed a pride in the past, a respect for things old that had been horribly missing in the south.

But the main reason why I was no longer continually frightened, I realized, was because I was now so much better at what I was doing. Surviving, I supposed, was the only word to describe it; living from day to day without being robbed, raped or murdered, moving from place to place without getting lost or injured, caring for my animals and keeping myself clean and respectable. And enjoying it too. For the first time in years I was excelling and it felt marvellous.

We were now only eighty miles from France and soon I would have to start looking for a home for Bella. I was growing increasingly worried about this; it was ages since I'd seen any donkeys working in the fields and I was no longer continually asked if my *burra* was for sale. The closer you are to France, I was told, the more donkeys are used for meat: the thought filled me with horror. I decided to aim for Montserrat; it's an important pilgrimage centre and seemed an appropriate place to finish the Spanish leg of my journey.

From Prades we wound our way down the thickly forested slopes of the Tossal de la Baltasana to the huge, flat Francoli plain. We descended over 2000 feet in three hours and I had to carry the puppies because the road was so steep they would have fallen out of the basket on Bella's back.

106

Feeling hungry for culture, I made a detour to visit the monastery at Poblet. It was a magnificent place made of honey-coloured stone. Coachloads of tourists were arriving and I saw with dismay that there was an entrance fee of 400 pesetas. I emptied all my bags but could find no more than thirty-five; the nearest town with a bank was three miles further north and I couldn't face walking all the way there and back. I sat down at the fountain outside the gates and tried to decide what to do.

Why not? I thought. I left the animals in a nearby field, changed into my cleanest clothes behind a hedge, then walked up to the ticket office and said I wanted to speak to the abbot.

'Why?' asked a snotty woman at the desk.

'Because I'm a pilgrim on my way to Rome with my donkey,' I replied, hoping my nose wouldn't grow too long.

She looked me up and down in horror, then picked up a phone and spoke to someone in Catalan. A monk appeared and ushered me through a heavy wooden door into a large, bare room, where he asked me to wait.

Five minutes later a tall, old man wearing a cream-coloured habit entered the room and greeted me in perfect English, introducing himself as Father Benedict. While I was waiting I'd been trying to think of a reason I could give for asking to see him, but he acted as if it were the most natural thing in the world that a girl on her way to Rome should stop to meet him and demanded no explanation.

He was a lovely man, exceptionally well informed, and he spoke English better than anyone else I'd met in Spain, if a little quirkily. He referred to me as a 'peregrine' – I kept thinking of falcons – and to Bella as my 'monkey'. When I asked whether the monks sang much, he instantly burst into song; he had a deep soft voice that echoed all round the room.

The official monastery tours were in Spanish, Catalan, French and German, so Father Benedict insisted on showing me round himself. There was a fantastic library, but most of all I liked the gardens. They were so peaceful, I could just imagine the monks of old wandering around in silent contemplation.

When I asked Father Benedict how he would advise me to reach Montserrat by foot, he brought out some beautiful old maps of the area. He couldn't promise that all the tracks still existed, he said, but he devised a route that would take me past two deserted castles and give me one of the best views in Catalonia.

The next day's walk through the cornfields and huge vineyards of the Francoli plain should have been tedious but somehow wasn't. After the painfully slow progress of the last week it was great to see the miles roll by so quickly, and the village where I camped that evening was one of the loveliest I found on my entire walk. It had the ugly name of Piles, but was home to the nicest children in Spain. They led me to a small hill above the village where I could camp, then crowded round and chatted while I put the tent up and cooked my supper. They told me there was a market in Santa Coloma the next day so I passed through the town in the morning on my way to the Queralt mountains. Here I managed to buy things I'd been needing for ages: tent pegs, hair conditioner and proper crepe bandages. I tried to find a vet for Bogey, who was eating like a horse but not putting on any weight. No luck, though. At least when we get to France, I thought, she'll be able to have a proper rest while I search for a donkey.

In the afternoon I climbed up through the hidden village of Bellprat to Queralt castle, a romantic tumbledown ruin. As Father Benedict had promised, the view from the top of the tower was breathtaking. In the distance was Montserrat, its extraordinary pinnacles making a striking landmark. To the south was the shimmering Mediterranean and behind me I could just make out the monastery at Poblet. I felt marvellously free, miles from anyone, and I'm still not sure what came over me but to celebrate I climbed on to the highest piece of wall, pulled down my shorts and knickers and did a moony to the world.

The next day I stopped for a siesta at the pretty village of Santa Margarida de Montbui, and we camped in the shadow of Claramunt castle. In the morning we began the ascent of Montserrat.

I was back on a long-distance footpath again, although Signal had now been replaced by Aquafresh, so I had to look out for blue-and-white-striped signs. We gradually climbed higher and higher on to steep and rocky moorland, frequently losing our way and walking round in circles until I realized that there were at least three different footpaths marked with blue and white stripes. We camped at the foot of the great crown of Montserrat and in the morning walked on the road up to the monastery, set on a ledge in the sheer white rock that reaches up like fingers into the sky.

The crowds were horrendous and the heat unbearable as I walked the final mile to the camp site. Later I realized I should have brought out my MENCAP tin and collected money from the hundreds of tourists who prodded at me and took photos of us; I was hot and bad-tempered by the time we reached the camp site, and even more so when they wouldn't let us in. I wished I'd never decided to come here. However, we eventually found a perfect spot way up above the monastery on a grassy ledge which caught the breeze and gave me a far better view than any from the town below.

We'd made it! As I looked down on the distant lights of Barcelona that evening I felt very proud of myself; the Spanish part of my journey was as good as done. I spent a blissful, lazy weekend reading *Rebecca* and playing with the puppies, not venturing down to the crowds until Sunday afternoon when I dutifully toured the monastery. The black Virgin and child were as beautiful as I'd been told, and there were some fascinating oil paintings, but I couldn't stand the endless stream of noisy people and soon returned to the peace of my camp. I thought of how much I was looking forward to a week's holiday in France while I searched for a new donkey, and hoped that I'd find a home for Bella soon. We could all do with a rest. Little did I suspect that a nightmare was about to begin.

Chapter 15
Hell Without a Donkey

On Monday morning we slithered down to Monistrol, the village at the northern foot of Montserrat. I stopped to ask the old men at one of the bars if they knew of anyone who wanted a donkey; I'd been doing this for about a week now in every village I passed, but with no luck so far. One of the men was a timber merchant, he said, and used mules to pull trees down the mountain – would my donkey be any good at that kind of work?

I'd always known I'd have to leave Bella, but my mind and my heart were in turmoil. I'd dreamed of finding a family who wanted her as a pet, but as I hadn't seen a non-working donkey since I left England I knew there was little chance of this. Maybe pulling logs down from Montserrat wouldn't be such a bad life, and she'd be with other mules for company.

But she was so small, and if he was used to mules he'd be bound to overwork her. And he didn't want to pay more than 5000 pesetas. I'd been told I wouldn't get more than 10,000 even at market, but while the money wasn't really important, I didn't want to practically give her away unless I was sure. Eventually I decided against it. France was still a week's walk away – there was no need to jump at the very first offer.

When I returned to the bar a man of about forty approached and offered me a drink. Was I the girl with the donkey, he asked. If I was selling it for just 5000 pesetas, he'd like to buy it for his children; he ran a restaurant at the edge of the village and there was a field behind where the donkey could live.

I couldn't believe my ears: this was a dream come true. His wife arrived with a little boy in a push-chair and asked whether Bella would need much looking after – that such a thought could even cross the mind of a Spaniard made me jump for joy. I talked to them for a few minutes, then suddenly it was done – the papers exchanged, 5000 pesetas in my hand. One of the other men at the bar was driving into Barcelona and agreed to give me and the dogs a lift to the railway station from where we could catch a train to France.

111

'I'm leaving in five minutes,' he said, and went to pay his bill. I loaded my bags into the back of his van, then walked over to Bella who was happily grazing fifty yards away. As I sank my face into her soft brown fur and she nuzzled her nose into my stomach just as she always did, the tears began rolling down my cheeks. Bella trusted me, she had done all she could for me over the past three months and now I was leaving her in the hands of strangers. Even if this family treated her well, I knew there was no way I could safe-guard her entire future. I'd found the best home for her that I could, but it didn't make saying goodbye any easier. My heart was in my throat and I couldn't stop crying.

The man giving me the lift was honking his horn at me to hurry up. I looked round and saw a group of little girls were watching as I sobbed.

'Don't worry,' they said. 'We'll make sure she's all right. We're going to help look after her; she'll be happy here.'

I tried to thank them as I took a deep breath and hugged my donkey for the last time. I climbed into the van, and lots of people waved as we drove away. 'If you need me, just call my name' was playing on the radio, and I cried the whole way to Barcelona.

'How could you be so stupid as to think you could take dogs like those on a train?' the man in the ticket office shouted at me. 'No, of course you can't put them in the guard's van! The guard doesn't want to be ravaged by a Dobermann any more than anyone else, does he? They must be in a crate, and sent as cargo. No, of course we haven't got any crates! You must buy the crate yourself. Where can you find such a crate? How should I know?'

'And it mustn't be some flimsy thing, you know, that those beasts can break out of,' joined in the woman from the next desk. 'It must be of iron or very strong wood.'

'Now get out of this station, or I shall call the *Guardia Civil*. What? I don't care if you've nowhere to go to, this is a railway station, not a charity . . .'

No hotel in Barcelona would accept the dogs so we spent a miser-able night just inside the station gates. In the morning I trudged round every pet shop and department store in the city. The closest I found to a crate was a wire cage that George could just about squeeze into, price £80, but there was nothing for Bogey. I would have to have one made, they told me at the biggest department store, and gave me the addresses of three carpenters. The first said he was busy all week, but could perhaps do it on Friday; the second said he could make one by tomorrow, but it would cost me £250. The third was all locked up and no one answered the door.

I was so desperate I even tried the British Consulate: 'We are

112

here to help people with real problems, miss, not those who don't want to pay 50,000 pesetas for a crate.'

The puppies were screaming so I stopped at a bar to feed them. As Cleo finished her bottle she crapped down the front of my dress and I let out a wail of self-pity. It was all so crazy. We had to travel only fifty miles and I would have to throw the damned crate away as soon as we reached France.

Initiative was called for, I decided. I headed back to the station, took the pack saddle and bags to the cargo office and organized to have them sent to Portbou without me. The dogs and I then walked four miles out of Barcelona to the autostrada, I took a slug of neat whisky and stuck my thumb out.

'I hope I never lose this piece of paper. When I'm back at home, telling everyone what a marvellous time I had, someone please force me to read this page. I don't think I've ever felt so miserable and I can't stop crying. I hate men, I never want to have sex again in my whole life, they're disgusting, horrible, I hate them, all of them . . .'

24 May 1989

It took me over twenty-four hours to reach France. Spanish lorry drivers, I discovered, meant business. I've often hitchhiked before, with very little trouble, but for some reason I was now attracting every pervert on the highway.

My first lift was in a large, modern lorry driven by a nice-looking guy of about thirty. He was going to Gerona, and I felt pleased that I'd be two-thirds of the way to France by dusk. I'd brought my tent with me and planned to spend the night in a camp site.

Jaime, he said his name was. He was perfectly charming at first, chatting inconsequentially, offering me cigarettes, admiring the puppies, and I, happy and relieved to be finally leaving Barcelona, smiled and chatted back. It was five minutes before he began the 'What beautiful eyes you have' routine, but I've heard this so often that I wasn't worried until he pulled open the curtains behind him to show me his bed.

He tried almost everything; he declared undying love, promised to take me all the way to France, offered money, even said a blow-job would be good enough. It was fifteen minutes before he finally realized that my 'no' really did mean 'no'. He then became angry and aggressive, hurling abuse at me before pulling over to the side of the road and demanding that I either have sex, give head or get out.

I got out, swearing that I wouldn't travel in a lorry again and would only get into a car if there was a woman in it. Two hours

113

later, however, when no one had stopped, I realized I was in no position to be choosy. When a lorry driver pulled up and said he was driving to Marseilles, I threw caution to the wind and climbed in. The chance of reaching France in one go was too tempting to refuse.

This one was the silent type. He was fat, a huge belly oozing from the gap between a dirty yellow T-shirt and blue canvas trousers, and he was surprisingly blond for a Spaniard. He seemed uninterested in me and didn't even ask my name; I thanked God and dozed off.

The sound of changing gears woke me and I looked up to find we were pulling into a lay-by. Turning to me without a trace of emotion, the driver simply said, 'Let's do it now'.

I sprang away as he grabbed my upper arm and I began hitting his hand to be free of him, but abruptly stopped when his fist sent my chin flying and I knocked my head against the window. He stared at me with steely eyes as, with his free hand, he began undoing his belt.

Bogey was asleep in the footwell beneath me; I screamed her name and reached down for one of the puppies. I clutched Dido to my chest and Bogey leapt up on to the seat, growling at she wasn't sure who, but it had the right effect and the driver let go of me.

'If you touch me again,' I said, my voice sounding very strange to me, 'I'll tell my dog to kill you.'

Holding tightly on to both puppies I slowly opened my door, threw my bags down and climbed out.

'Bitch!' he called as he drove away. 'You don't really expect to have a ride for nothing, do you?'

The sun was going down, and I didn't dare stick my thumb out again, so I started walking. I was still shaking, yet I felt angry rather than frightened. I wished that I *had* been able to order Bogey to kill the bastard.

After about half an hour I found a café where the owners let me wash in their bathroom and camp in their garden. Luckily I was so exhausted I slept well, and the next day had renewed courage. Whenever a male driver stopped I decided to make it clear before getting in that I did not want sex, and to my fury all but two immediately drove off without me.

I did have some enjoyable lifts, however. A lovely lady schoolteacher from Figueras took me about fifteen kilometres, I squeezed next to the beautiful blond children of a Dutch family in a campervan, and two young guys in a jeep took me the final ten kilometres to Portbou. George was sick on the back seat – I could have killed her. She's always been a hopeless judge of character.

My luggage was waiting at Portbou, and I found it hard not to give the French guard a hug as he helped me on to the train and told me what beautiful dogs I had. We got off at Banyuls, the second town from the border, and in very shaky French I asked at the ticket office where I could find the camp site.

'About a mile up the hill, away from the town.'

We set off, the dogs straining on their leads, the puppies squirming and me struggling to hold on to them, as well as the six saddle bags and the pack saddle. We were about halfway there when a police car drove up behind me. Two stern-looking men in blue uniform called to me to stop, and the one in the passenger seat got out and approached me, demanding my passport. I could see him taking in my enormous amount of luggage, my filthy clothes, my bruised face, my swollen eyes.

'I'm going to the camp site, I'll have to leave my passport at the office there,' I told him. '*Please* could you possibly check it later?'

To my surprise he agreed and they crawled along behind me in the car. In exasperation I turned to them.

'If you're going to follow me to the camp site, would you mind taking some of my luggage for me, please? I'm tired and it's heavy, I'd be very grateful.'

'We are not a taxi service, mademoiselle; we are here to inspect your passport, not carry your luggage.'

It was the only time I've ever called a policeman a bastard to his face.

At last we reached the 'Camping Municipal', an enormous place, almost empty. A stocky, grey-haired man came out of the office and looked at me warily; I stuck my nose in the air and decided that from now on I was going to force people to treat me well. Within two minutes I'd told him that I was on a walk in aid of charity, that my brother was handicapped (it's amazing the effect this has on people – they change their tone of voice and put a sort of caring look into their eyes), that my father was a very important politician and that I was a qualified lawyer. Writing about it now I feel ashamed of myself, but at the time I was desperate. I'd suffered such humiliation over the past two days, I was prepared to do anything to be treated with respect. And it worked. He showed me to one of the best camping spaces, charged me less than half the proper price for staying there and over the next two weeks he gave me numerous lifts to the station, acted as my secretary and let me have free use of his telephone.

That evening I walked into Banyuls with the dogs; it was an old-fashioned seaside resort, small and uncrowded, with cafés and restaurants lining the sea front. I sat down at one of the outside tables, and asked the waiter if it was all right having the dogs with me.

'Of course,' came the reply. 'Would you like me to bring some scraps of food for them?'

With that sentence I fell in love with the French. I looked out to sea and raised my glass to France. The nightmare of the past few days was over, and a new episode of my journey was beginning; I suddenly felt full of hope.

Now all I had to do was find a donkey.

After a day's recovery, spent sleeping and sunbathing on the beach, I began scouring the French Pyrenees for donkeys. I badgered the local paper in Perpignan into writing an article about me, which produced a few leads, and I hitched from village to village asking if anyone had an *âne* for sale. My eyesight let me down more than once and I nearly persuaded an old farmer to sell me a light brown cow grazing on a hillside which I was convinced was a donkey.

I was appalled by how bad my French was. I'd spent ten years at school studying it, but now I could hardly string a sentence together. I kept thinking in Spanish, and after being almost fluent I found the struggle to make myself understood horribly frustrating.

After a week I was beginning to despair of ever finding a suitable donkey. The only ones I'd seen were under four or over twenty, in foal or unbroken stallions. I couldn't believe the prices – none were being sold for less than 2,500 francs, £250. I'd almost decided to buy a stocky little roan pony instead, when I received a phone call from a man in Mosset, a village about thirty kilometres inland. He had a Poitou, a rare type of donkey from southwest France, traditionally used for heavy work but now rapidly dying out. Mrs Svendsen at the Donkey Sanctuary had told me I'd be very lucky to find a Poitou.

Monsieur Perpigna was a funny little man of about seventy, very sweet but rather gaga. It took half an hour of explaining my journey before he even agreed to show me his Poitou; he wasn't going to sell Balthazare to just *anybody*. He'd been trying to find a new home for him for nearly a year, but no one so far had been good enough. Finally I seemed to pass muster and we went out to the field behind the house.

'Balthazare!' called M. Perpigna, and in a sudden flurry of hooves and mud appeared the most magnificent donkey I'd ever seen. He was enormous, a good twelve hands, and had ears double the size of Bella's. He was covered in a thick blackish-brown coat, with a furry white belly and a white nose, and he gave out such an aura of strength and good health that I could do nothing but stand and admire him. It was love at first sight.

I returned to Banyuls that evening overjoyed with the thought that tomorrow I'd be able to resume my journey, to find Bogey shaking and weak, with a raging temperature. She wouldn't eat and in the morning the side of her head had swollen to the size of a football. She could open only one of her eyes and her gums were bleeding. It was terrifying – I'd never seen anything like it. The camp site manager drove us to an animal clinic where the vet took Bogey's temperature, felt her ribs and examined her eyes, then gloomily shook his head. She had a very serious infection, he said. If it was what he thought, it would probably kill her. He advised that she be put to sleep to save her from suffering.

I sat down in shock. Bogey couldn't die now, not after all we'd been through. Perhaps I should have taken the vet's advice, but after my experience of vets in Spain I was loath to trust him. At my insistence he gave her some injections and a course of tablets; he told me to keep the puppies away from her and to return in a few days.

Over the next two days Bogey's weight dropped off until she was as thin as when I'd first found her. Her head was so swollen she could hardly drink, let alone eat, and she couldn't even get up to go to the loo. I continually washed her down to keep her cool, but she hardly seemed to recognize me as the fever raged inside her.

Somehow she managed to sweat it out of her system and when, on the fourth day, she began to take an interest in the puppies again, I knew she was going to be OK. I took her back to the vet's for more injections, paid his 400 franc bill and then, two weeks to the day after my arrival, I packed up and set off for Mosset to collect my donkey.

Balthazare cost me 3000 francs and as I counted out the notes I shivered, thinking of the state of my bank balance at home. It took hours to leave Monsieur Perpigna's house; he made me promise to feed Balthazare two loaves of bread every morning, to brush his ears upwards, not downwards, to put a special ointment on his willy to stop the horseflies biting it, and dozens of other crazy little things that I knew I'd forget. At last we went out to saddle him up, but Balthazare's girth was nearly six inches wider than Bella's and the bags lay awkwardly, high up on his back. His hair was so long and soft that the whole lot kept slipping and I nearly despaired, gritting my teeth and trying to remind myself of all the trouble I'd had with Bella at the beginning.

Finally we were off. Balthazare walked so fast I could hardly keep up and his great heavy strides threw the puppies from one side of their box to the other with such force that I had to take them out and carry them myself – not easy while I was also desperately holding the pack saddle steady and trying to stop Balthazare swerving into the thickly-grassed verges. I wondered what on earth I'd let myself in for; at this rate we'd reach Rome in a fortnight.

France

Chapter 16
Hannibal Leads the Way

I just couldn't get the hang of the name. Balthazare. It always came out wrong and anything I tried to shorten it to sounded silly. As I sat outside my tent that evening sewing extra straps on to the saddle bags and making a sheet into a sling for the puppies, I decided to change his name completely. Thus, beside a stream at the foot of the Roc de l'Hirondelle, Hannibal was christened. He was so big and strong and handsome that it suited him well.

As we twisted up to the Roque Jalere the next morning, I thought how great it felt to be on the move – just my animals and me. It was all very different from before, though. A new donkey, a new language, a new country – I felt as though I were beginning all over again. I kept calling Hannibal Bella and found it difficult to like him at first; compared to my sweet little Bella, he was a stubborn bastard. If he didn't want to go somewhere, he was so strong that there was nothing I could do to force him, so *he* was usually the one who chose our resting places and picnic spots. I was also fast learning the disadvantages of travelling with an animal who'd spent his whole life on an isolated Pyrenean mountainside: as we passed through the beautiful little villages of Sournia, Prats and le Vivier, I discovered that he was terrified of lines on the road, of drains, of telegraph wires, of anything unfamiliar at all. We had to make huge detours to pass them and I prayed that his confidence would improve before we reached any bigger towns.

The main problem, however, was the pack saddle. Despite my alterations it was practically useless and continually slipped off Hannibal's huge back. On Thursday evening I saw that it was beginning to give him sores, so on Friday I carried two of the bags myself. The weather was humid and close, and I felt tired and bad-tempered. Cleo yelled all day; she only shut up if I took her out of the sling and held her by the scruff of her neck, as her mother carried her, but she was too heavy for me to do this all the time. Dido, on the other hand, was an angel. She usually slept between feeds, or propped her feet over the edge of the sling and looked out.

Someone had told me there was a blacksmith in St Martin, so on

Friday afternoon I took a detour through the tiny village. Hannibal's feet were desperately in need of shoes and if I didn't find a farrier soon I'd be in trouble.

I discovered that the blacksmith had died twelve years ago; rain began falling so I decided to hurry on and camp in the first free patch of land I could find.

Hannibal, however, had other ideas. He refused to budge an inch and just stood in the middle of the street getting wet. Not even bribes of peppermints – a sure winner with Bella – made any difference. As the storm began in earnest I gave up, tying him to a railing and running off to pitch my tent next to the cemetery. I peeled off my wet clothes and huddled inside with the dogs. When Hannibal began braying I plucked up the courage to go and rescue him; this time he walked with me gladly and an old man said I could put him in one of his sheds on the other side of the village.

I'd only meant to be quick so I'd just put on my boots and my waterproof jacket over my bra and knickers. As I led Hannibal past what felt like a hundred faces curiously peering out of windows, I frantically tugged down my jacket in a hopeless attempt to cover my bottom; I was wearing the very skimpy Tom and Jerry briefs that Clare had given me for my birthday, and I was terrified that they'd turn see-through when they were wet.

I had to be ill sometime, I suppose. That night my temperature soared and I thrashed around in the tent, feeling at death's door. My limbs ached and my eyes couldn't bear the morning light; for the first time since I left home I couldn't face breakfast. I tethered Hannibal nearby and lay down in the shade of the cemetery wall, utterly miserable.

It was a rotten weekend, one of the worst. The villagers wandered down every now and then to stare at me, but I didn't even have the energy to talk to them. On Sunday afternoon I rang home, but found it very difficult not to cry as I tried to convince my parents that I was having a marvellous time. I felt weak and exhausted, drained of all enthusiasm for what I was doing. I would have given anything to have gone home.

On Monday morning, thank God, my temperature had gone down. I'd had enough of St Martin and I desperately needed more food for the dogs, so I packed up and got going as quickly as possible. I still felt groggy, but it was a relief to be on the move again and the scenery was glorious, becoming craggy and mountainous, reminding me of the fells at home. I even sang, which I hadn't done for weeks.

We reached the Agly valley very quickly, and as we crossed the bridge and joined the main road to St Paul-de-Fenouillet a car stopped beside me and a funny-looking white-haired man began speaking to me in atrociously bad French. I discovered that he was English, staying with his French wife at his in-laws in St Paul; he was very friendly and insisted that I come to the house when I reached the village.

I liked St Paul. Its position was stunning, surrounded by steep mountain ranges on all sides. Edward's wife Georgette energetically set about finding a farrier and arranged for me to stay at a nearby camp site. It was great having someone else sorting out my problems, and since I was still feeling shaky after my flu I welcomed the thought of staying here for a couple of days.

Jean-Paul, the camp site owner, was a big, friendly chap who drove me to Perpignan in search of a new pack saddle. I had no luck, though, and returned feeling disheartened and poor; the saddleries had treated me as though I were mad and just tried to flog me ridiculously expensive pieces of leather-covered foam padding.

The next morning Jean-Paul drove me out to see Joseph Gau, the farrier, who revealed that he no longer smithed. I could have screamed, but it was impossible to be upset for long. Françoise, his wife, sat me down with a glass of wine while Joseph began phoning every farrier he knew. After the fourth negative reply he turned to me and explained the problem: farriers rarely make their own shoes nowadays and none of them had anything small enough for a donkey. Joseph had an idea, though. He took me out to the barn, where there was the most enormous collection of equine junk, rummaged about for twenty minutes and finally produced a set of mule shoes. They were too long, but their width looked right and we decided it was worth a try. Joseph rang the farriers again, saying he had the shoes and just needed someone to put them on, and he persuaded one of them to come to the camp site the next day.

Over lunch I mentioned to the Gaus my pack saddle problems, whereupon Joseph's eyes lit up. He dug out an old French army mule pack, an incredible wooden contraption held together with iron hinges and hooks. The straps needed a few alterations, but the basic pack fitted perfectly and my bags could have been made for it. There were even hooks for my washing up bowl and tethering rope. I was overjoyed and wished there was some way I could thank him adequately; he wouldn't let me pay anything for it and my donation of Bella's old saddle to his junk collection seemed pathetic in comparison.

The farrier arrived at the camp site the next morning with his portable furnace in the back of his jeep. I was appalled by the way he put the shoes on; he made no effort to bash them to the right size and didn't even cut the extra length off. To add insult to injury, he charged me 350 francs. Still, at least Hannibal was shod.

It took us two hours just to reach the Gaus' due to Hannibal's first encounter with a zebra crossing. Françoise showed me a place to camp by the river, beneath a laden wild cherry tree where Hannibal and I gorged in ecstasy. I got so sticky with the juice that I forced myself to swim in the river, which was freezing but exhilarating. At last I'd fully recovered from my flu, and I luxuriated in feeling healthy, swimming down to the bottom, climbing the rocks and sliding down the waterfalls. Afterwards I felt a little crazy and on my Calor gas stove I made some cherry jam, fishing the stones out with my penknife. It was too runny but tasted delicious.

The next stage of the journey took me along the GR36, but it wasn't well marked. As I approached the mountains and saw the valley I'd have to climb, I almost felt ill again. It was virtually sheer, the peak towering 2000 feet above me.

With Bella the walk up the narrow path would have been simple, if slow, but with Hannibal it was almost impossible. He wasn't nearly as sure-footed as Bella and was frightened of even small steps or branches across the track. He kept stopping and on the steepest stretches I had to unpack him and carry the bags myself. It took hours and my patience was sorely tried; it was nearly midday by the time we reached the tree line, and I sat down to have a rest in the last bit of shade. Hannibal was busy eating so I didn't bother to tie him, but a minute later I regretted it, when suddenly he tossed his head and set off down the path at breakneck speed.

'You bastard, come back here!' I screamed as I sprang up. He was already out of sight and frantically I ran after him; the dogs joined in, thinking it was a great game, but the only effect we had was to make him run even faster. The path zigzagged down the mountainside, so I began hurtling straight down through the undergrowth to try to overtake him. Brambles and briars snatched at me in my hot pursuit but Hannibal was always too quick for me. I don't think I've ever hated an animal so much. We were soon down in the valley – in less than ten minutes we'd descended what had taken two hours to climb – and Hannibal was heading for the main road.

I ran faster than ever in my life. To my surprise I found that I was catching up with him and as I got closer I saw that his lead had caught round one of the shoes on his back feet, so he could manage nothing more than a fast trot. At last I reached him and grabbed on to his halter; I seemed to take him by surprise and he abruptly stopped. My boot briefly made contact with his rump, but I was too relieved to be angry for long.

A passing motorist stopped to ask me if I was all right. I looked at him, confused.

'Have you been attacked?' he asked, his face full of concern. I looked down and realized that my shirt was ripped and my arms and legs were covered in blood. The undergrowth had scratched and torn at my skin and my hair was full of burs and twigs; I must have looked quite a sight.

With his help, I prised Hannibal's lead from where it had jammed between his hoof and the shoe, blessing the farrier for doing such a bad job; if he'd cut off the extra length on the shoes as I'd asked, Hannibal would probably have disappeared forever in a cloud of dust.

We reached the top by four o'clock, and the morning's nightmare soon became a memory as we walked down through green meadowland to the Riben valley. Hannibal was now walking happily and I was astonished at the speed we were travelling. The pack saddle was perfect; it never slid off, even down quite steep slopes.

We camped below the ruins of the Château de Peyrepertuse. I opened out my map and realized that we would have to get a move on to reach Italy by August. In eight days we'd only walked fifty kilometres. The problem, however, was Bogey. She just didn't seem to be getting better. If only she were smaller, then I could carry her; her feet were swollen and painful, and she seemed to be constantly tired. All I could do was feed her as much as possible, but she was still as fussy as ever.

We were now crossing the Corbière mountains, and my love affair with Languedoc-Roussillon was beginning. This was château country, with medieval ruins on almost every skyline; the fertile vineyards of the valleys gave way to thickly gorsed hillsides carpeted with pungent yellow flowers and sheer, thickly wooded slopes. The simple beauty of the villages took my breath away; Rouffiac and Massac, Laroque-de-Fa and Termes, Mayronnes and Caunettes, tiny settlements tucked into the valleys, with no modern buildings and very little traffic. The people, however, were obviously used to tourists – I was no longer the oddity that I'd been in rural Spain. Here I was just another foreigner, albeit one travelling in a way they approved of.

With the weather being warmer I spent my first night in my hammock and slept surprisingly well. It was so much cooler than the tent and saved a lot of time in the morning – I was packed up and away in ten minutes.

My journey continued down the steep-sided Sou valley, and as I was singing *Take that Look off Your Face* to the puppies at the top of my voice, I noticed a group of people working in the garden of an almost-built house not far from the road. They turned out to be English and I was intoxicated by their friendliness. They lived out here; the four girls had just begun their school holidays, and there was such an atmosphere of relaxed fun that when they said I was welcome to spend the day with them, I couldn't resist it. I realized that what I was missing more than anything was family life – and this was one of the loveliest families I've ever come across. We bathed in the river at the bottom of the garden, teaching the puppies how to swim, and in the evening we all dressed up and went to a guitar recital in Montjoi, where I met Thierry, a family friend who said he'd be interested in taking one of the puppies. Dido and Cleo were now six weeks old, both big and strong and becoming uncomfortably heavy in the sling round my neck. They were draining Bogey of all energy and she no longer enjoyed them as she had when they were little; she was still agonizingly thin and seemed to have a temperature again. I realized the time had come to find the puppies new homes.

Thierry and his girlfriend, Catherine, were nervous about taking on a Dobermann half-breed; in France, as in England, fierce breeds had been getting a bad press. Against my advice, they took Cleo rather than Dido because she looked nothing like a Dobermann, ignoring my warnings about her boisterous character. They very generously gave me 200 francs, saying that this was what they would have paid at an animal rescue home, and drove away with Cleo nestled on Catherine's lap.

I felt strange after she'd gone – rather guilty for not shedding any tears. That night I camped on the local football pitch; I strung my hammock between the goal posts, and Hannibal grazed around the edge of the field. Dido slept on my lap; she seemed lonely without her sister, and kept crying for her, but luckily Bogey didn't seem too upset.

It was after I found a home for Dido two days later that the loss of both puppies hit me. I'd stopped in a village called Puicheric, on the River Aude halfway between Carcassonne and Narbonne. A scruffy lady of about fifty approached me as I was unloading Hannibal and asked if I'd like some hay for him. I accepted gratefully and moments later she invited me in to breakfast. Annie's house was full of animals. 'I just can't turn them away,' she explained, 'and now people keep bringing them to me.'

Over breakfast she told me that she worked at a home for handicapped children nearby, where they keep two old donkeys. She was fascinated by what I was doing and suggested I stop at a town called Lamalou on the River Orbe, where there were many centres for the disabled. Annie then told me she knew some people who'd love that puppy of mine, so I agreed to meet them.

The butcher and his wife seemed nice enough; they wanted Dido half as a guard dog and half as a pet, they said. I felt that if anyone were going to feed a dog properly, it would be a butcher, and I trusted Annie not to recommend anyone who wouldn't treat an animal well. It was all over horribly quickly; I kissed Dido goodbye and handed her over. The butcher gave me a huge bag of meat as payment and Annie ushered me out of the shop as I began to cry. Two minutes later I rushed back and made them promise not to dock her tail or cut her ears, then I packed up Hannibal and walked out of the village, with Annie riding beside me on a bicycle.

Bogey was surprisingly untroubled – much less so than me – and walked quietly as we headed for the Canal du Midi. Annie led me down to the towpath on the southern bank and then said goodbye, telling me not to worry, she'd make sure the dog was all right.

I felt terrible. There was nothing hanging round my neck, no furry bodies doing kamikaze jumps out of a basket on the donkey's back, no one screaming for a feed; we were now a very small and subdued party of travellers.

Chapter 17
Summer Feeding

My daily routine was becoming a little unorthodox, but it was the only way I could survive in the stifling heat that descended upon France in June and July. The dogs were incapable of walking between eleven and five; their feet swelled up from the heat of the ground and they were utterly miserable. Consequently we did most of our walking in the early morning and the evening. I began setting off as soon as it became light, at about five o'clock, which meant I'd been walking for up to three hours before the morning's bread was on sale, by which time I was famished.

Unlike Spain, where every village had its own little store which sold everything, I found that villagers here relied on mobile bakers, butchers, greengrocers and fishmongers. The prices were extortionate, but the quality of the food was so good that it was difficult to complain. Without exception the shopkeepers were friendly, and generous with their leftovers: the bakers usually gave Hannibal their stale bread and I had a constant supply of bones for the dogs from the butchers.

The vans delivered in the morning and I soon discovered that meat or fish had only to sit in my bags for a couple of hours before going bad, so breakfast soon became my main meal of the day. Once I was used to it, I could happily consume up to two loaves of bread stuffed with concoctions of ham, cheese, eggs, salad, even steak if I was feeling rich. My appetite was phenomenal; occasionally I'd feel guilty and try to cut down, but then I'd become tetchy and irritable, so I decided it was better to be fat and happy.

I'd become alarmingly strong; hauling Hannibal out of verges was far more effective than pumping iron and I reckoned that if a man attacked me now, he'd be in for a shock. My hands looked like a builder's; they were so hard and coarse that I couldn't even stretch my fingers out straight.

I was uncharacteristically abstemious with alcohol at this time. Gone were the long evenings spent drinking litre after litre of wine by the camp fire; now I walked until the sun went down and was so tired that I went to sleep as soon as I'd put up the hammock. I drank at least two litres of milk a day; my body seemed to crave for it and I no longer minded the UHT taste. After my siesta I'd have 'tea' – milk, bread and honey, fruit and cheese, a healthy meal that lasted me till breakfast the next day.

The dogs were now having two meals a day at the same time as me; in the morning they'd have a kilogram of liver and offal, and in the evening they had a tin of dog food. English Pedigree Chum was the only one they would eat, or else Kit-e-Kat, mixed with a loaf of bread, a litre of milk and half a dozen eggs. Yet neither of them carried an ounce of fat and I constantly felt guilty because they looked so thin.

After the puppies left, Bogey's health improved quickly. She began putting on weight and seemed happier, no longer permanently anxious. Her ears began to heal (the puppies used to chew at them and their rims were a mass of bloody scabs that I'd been helpless to protect) and her energy slowly returned. She used to try and sleep with me in the hammock, which was impossible; one of us barely had to move an inch in our sleep and the whole contraption would turn upside down, dumping us both on top of a very disgruntled George lying underneath.

During these weeks in Languedoc I also began to grow fond of Hannibal, mainly because I finally stopped comparing him to Bella. He was a much more complex character – some days he would walk like a dream, on others he would need constant reassurance and persuasion, and sometimes he made me so angry I wanted to kill him. He constantly tried to eat from the roadsides, and he found vineyards irresistible. Like me, he adored wild cherries. He would take a huge mouthful, mush them up between his teeth and suck in the juice, then with great care spit out all the pips.

He hated going uphill and stopped every few yards if I let him. It took all my strength to drag him up some of those mountains and my patience was tried as never before in my life. Often I ended up carrying the bags myself, making three journeys to the top while he rested; even then he would *still* make a fuss when I led him up on his own.

Downhill, however, he was fearless. He loved sliding and would do a strange jump-and-whoosh routine through pine forests and on slippery paths. I nearly killed myself trying to keep up with him, but since his great escape attempt I didn't trust him on his own. I dreaded meeting anyone coming in the other direction, but luckily the French seemed about as keen on walking as the Spanish, and during my whole time in France I came across only two other hikers, and they were German.

Many of Hannibal's habits and characteristics would have been adorable in ordinary circumstances. He was incessantly nosy: he had only to catch a glimpse of a car moving on the horizon, or hear a voice echoing across a valley and he would stop, prick up his ears and refuse to move on until he had worked out what it was. Children's voices had a particularly strong effect; as we passed through villages this used to drive me nutty, for children would rush to their windows and call out to us, and if Hannibal had his way we would have spent an hour in every village talking to them all. Instead, I would end up dragging him away, feeling like a wicked old witch as the children called out, '*Ah, le pauvre petit âne! Il ne veut pas marcher! Il est fatigué!*'

Children adored him and he let them clamber all over him; the sticks and stones of Spain seemed a world away.

I loved the people of the Languedoc. They were almost always friendly to me, and seemed pleased when I said I was English; most of the tourists round here are German, they told me. This had been Maquis country, where bands of young men and women had taken to the hills during the War and the villagers had done their best to protect them. In almost every village is a plaque commemorating those who had died fighting the Nazis and there were always fresh flowers alongside.

Old people told me stories about the war – of brothers and husbands, of wasted youth and living hatred. In human terms France's occupation had never meant anything to me before; now I found myself fascinated by it, and I wondered how the German tourists felt when they saw the plaques. Whenever I saw them approaching in their big Mercedes and BMW cars along the narrow lanes, I had a crazy urge to run and hide.

The beauty of the Haut Languedoc stunned me. It was easy to imagine the Maquis hiding in the thickly forested mountains; apparently it is prime wild boar country, although I never saw one. Each village seemed more picturesque and unspoilt than the last and as we walked from St Jean-de-Minervois to Lamalou, through Euphène and Pardailhan, Riussec and Pousselières, la Fraise and Escagnes, I felt privileged to be seeing such places as they are meant to be seen, with time to fall in love with them. I still feel that if I could live anywhere in France this is where I would choose – in the range of mountains between the Rivers Aude and Orbe.

I did actually meet some English people living out here, a retired couple from Putney called Pat and John. They invited me to have lunch with them in their beautiful little house in Mézeilles. We had meatballs, potatoes, carrots and gravy, and it tasted so deliciously of home that I had thirds. In the afternoon we sat outside and Pat cut my hair; she was a hairdresser and was horrified by the state mine was in. She gave me some special conditioner and told me to soak my hair in olive oil to try to stop it drying up in the sun.

They gave me some more paperback novels and directed me on my way, and as I climbed out of the village I remember feeling very happy. A friend who was supposed to be joining me had let me down, but I was enjoying my own company. My grandmother would be coming out for a week at the end of July, so I had that to look forward to.

It's a shame that the best bits of my journey – the quiet evenings lolling along deserted lanes as the sun went down, the perfect days when I didn't have to shout at Hannibal even once – are also the most boring to describe. No one was horrible to me, no disasters occurred, I was never frightened, never short of food and the sun never stopped shining. This was the life I'd originally dreamed of, back in November, and I couldn't think of anything in the world I'd rather be doing.

Chapter 18
Polly, Polly and Rose

On Sunday 25 June I reached the old spa town of Lamalou-les-Bains on the River Orbe. Annie and others had told me about its centres for the handicapped, but nothing had prepared me for the shock of being almost the only able-bodied visitor in the whole town.

On Sunday evening I changed into my best frock and wandered along the main street looking for a cheap place to eat. I was fascinated to see that the shops, restaurants, hotels and pavements were all specially adapted for the disabled. It was a true spa town that has continued in its original purpose of caring for the sick. It had a turn-of-the-century air to it, rather how I imagine Edwardian Brighton might have been. I passed an old boy in what looked like an antique wheelchair – it was wooden, with three wheels and huge handlebars. When I asked him if I could take a photograph he gave me a huge grin and said I'd have to pay a franc for the privilege; I so admired his nerve I gave him two.

When a group of men in wheelchairs invited me to join their table, I readily accepted and soon began quizzing them about the place. Philippe, Tomas, Jean-Paul and Yves were from a rehabilitation centre just outside the town; they were all paralysed from the waist down, three from motorbike accidents and Yves from a falling tree. Apart from Yves, who was nearly forty, they were tragically young, just a little older than me, and they'd all been under twenty-one when their accidents happened.

Tomas had been a blacksmith in the Cevennes; he told me that they used to shoe the *cows* there because they walked such a long way to pasture! Yves had been a lumberjack; in fact, all of them had been doing very physical jobs and their paralysis meant they had also lost their livelihoods.

They were full of praise for Lamalou and were very surprised when I said there was nowhere similar in England. The facilities meant they could live relatively normal lives and because there were so many handicapped people here they never stood out as oddities. In fact it was I who felt out of place.

133

I agreed to meet Philippe, Tomas and Jean-Paul at lunchtime the next day for a drink. They brought half a dozen friends along – all men – and they were embarrassingly complimentary to me. They had very sophisticated wheelchairs and I had great fun trying them out – the speed they could reach was terrifying. We had races up and down the street and I suggested they try for the Disabled Olympics.

They insisted that I have supper with them again and against my better judgement I agreed. This time, however, it was a disaster. They each began to tell me how attractive they found me, how they hadn't been able to sleep last night, how they couldn't stop thinking about me and proceeded to describe exactly what they were capable of sexually. They were still men with men's desires, they said, and they *all* wanted to take me to bed. I tried to be light-hearted and jokey, but it was difficult and they knew just how to play on my guilt. Underneath it all I was just like the rest, they said; I couldn't see beyond the wheelchair.

If they hadn't been disabled I would have told them to bugger off, that I simply didn't find them attractive. But I was so frightened of offending them that I spent most of the meal trying to reassure them that they *were* attractive, but that I wasn't that sort of girl.

I left feeling very depressed; here I was, trying to raise money for the mentally handicapped, spouting their cause to everyone I met, and I couldn't even cope with spending an evening with some men who'd lost the use of their legs. But later I realized they were right: I *had* thought they were different from other men because of their wheelchairs. I'd stupidly presumed that their disabilities automatically made them nicer, safer people.

I meant to leave early the next morning, but it was market day and I couldn't resist it. I bought a pot of rosemary honey, treated myself to some sunglasses – little John Lennon ones that wouldn't give me panda eyes – and bought a new lead for Hannibal, hoping that leather would be kinder to my hands than rope.

I felt great as I climbed up out of the town on the small road to Bardejean. The hills were beautiful and the air was filled with the scent of gorse flowers. An old man asked me where I was going with my '*petit âne*' (everyone called Hannibal little, even though he was the biggest donkey I'd ever seen) and I stopped to explain my journey. Saying that he'd like to give some money for '*les pauvres enfants handicapés*' he went to his van by the side of the road. I wasn't really concentrating as he produced two 100-franc notes and shoved them down the front of my shirt. Holding on to me, breathing heavily, his face red and his eyes bulging, he said there would be more for the little children if I had sex with him, and he tried to force my hand down on to his crotch. I started kicking him and screamed for Bogey, who ran up immediately and he let go. With Bogey at my side I took the money out of my shirt and ripped it up in front of him, calling him every filthy name I could think of, trying not to cry. All he did was laugh as I walked on up the hill. I wished I didn't feel so hurt; similar things had happened so often I should have been immune to them by now. I'd always regarded old people as my allies, but this one had shattered that trust.

I didn't cheer up until I found the perfectly preserved medieval village of Boussagues on the other side of Mount Coudour that evening. I wandered the deserted streets, staring up at the huge, thick walls and tiny windows, and later sat writing my diary in the beautiful old cemetery.

I don't know why, but I put up the tent that evening, for the first time in weeks. In the night it rained and as the dogs curled up beside me I smiled – I did have a guardian angel after all.

Wednesday 28 June. The cool after the rain allowed us to cover a huge distance the next day – up the Vernoubre valley and over the Col de la Merquière. The view from the top was glorious: wooded hills, a sudden escarpment of rich red earth, and funny circular hills rising from the rich agricultural land on the plain below. In the distance I could just make out the town of Clermont l'Hérault. Stopping in the little farming village of Brenas to fill my water bottles at the fountain, I got talking to an old man sitting nearby.

'German are you?' he asked.

'No, I'm English.'

'Just as bad. They all come, the Germans, the Dutch, the Scandinavians, in their enormous great cars, with their enormous great cameras and their ugly blond children. I have no time for them. How much do you want for your donkey?'

I walked on and gradually descended the Marette valley until I rounded a corner and saw the Lac du Salagou. It was an extraordinary sight: a bright green, perfectly conical hill rose up in the middle of the lake to over 1000 feet. The surrounding land was a strange mixture of rough, parched heath and impeccably neat vineyards. Beside the lake I could see clusters of little villages and I set off towards the largest of these, Octon, hoping as I heard the church clock strike seven that the shops would still be open.

As I reached the grocer's in the square a fat man standing by the door began making loud braying noises and thought himself very funny.

'*Très drôle, monsieur,*' I called. '*Mais qui est le vrai âne?*'

Sitting at one of the tables outside the café were three very pretty girls of about twenty, talking and laughing. I eyed them enviously – their clothes looked so clean and feminine, their hair shone in the sun, their hands were smooth and delicate – they were what I wished I looked like. I felt filthy and ugly in comparison, in my torn shirt held together by sticking plaster, my cut-off jeans and clomping heavy boots. One of them leapt up with a camera when she saw me and began snapping madly; I was too tired to mind or feel embarrassed and walked on past.

As I was tying Hannibal in the shade at the far side of the square the same girl approached me and asked in rather peculiar Italian whether I spoke English. She came from London, she said, and was out here on holiday with her friends; would I like to join them for a drink?

Polly, Polly and Rose they were called. They had just finished their 'A' levels and were in France recovering, staying at Polly's father's house a few miles away. I readily accepted their supper invitation: the promise of a shower, a bed, a glass of Pimms and music from a real stereo was almost too much for me.

I found somewhere for Hannibal to spend the night and drove back with them in their clapped-out old Mazda to a tiny hamlet called le Mas Canet. I fell in love with the house; it was a ramshackle old schoolhouse built round a small courtyard, with outdoor stone staircases creeping up the sides of the walls, and every door and window at different levels. I still dream of living in such a place.

I stayed for two days, unable to resist the chance of being utterly carefree and silly for a while. Polly-whose-house-it-was let me put all my clothes through the washing-machine and lent me stuff of her own to wear. She was lovely and reminded me of Emu – tall, slim and beautiful, and slightly scatty. Photographer Polly was a nut after my own heart. She was very enthusiastic about my journey and is one of the few people I've met whom I can imagine doing something similar. She was also a brilliant cook. Rose was quieter; she had the most fantastic gingery-blonde hair that fell in great thick curls halfway down her back.

We spent the day swimming and sunbathing at the stunning Gorges de l'Hérault and the girls filled me in on what had been happening in *Neighbours* and *EastEnders*. That evening we sat up late playing dirty-word-only Scrabble and listening to music, and gradually I remembered how I used to spend my time in those good old days when I was normal. In the supermarket we spotted an exquisite-looking young man and followed him for miles in the car – the poor guy was probably terrified, but it felt great to be the pursuer for a change!

I could happily have stayed for weeks, but by Friday the woman looking after Hannibal was complaining about the noise, so I sadly packed my bags and said goodbye to Polly, Polly and Rose. I walked along the track to the lake and at midday stopped at the shore, where I discovered that Hannibal adored bamboo. I left him stuffing himself while the dogs and I went for a swim and then, since no one was about, I stripped down to my knickers and sunbathed. I'd only meant to stay for twenty minutes or so, but I fell asleep and must have been there for hours, for when I woke my back and the tops of my thighs were in agony.

I slowly opened my eyes and nearly died of shock. Lying on his back beside me was a man with no clothes on! He must have been about forty, with a pot belly and a hollow chest and a deep all-over sun tan.

'Hello,' he said. 'Would you like a cigarette?'

'No, thank you,' I replied, trying desperately to look anywhere but *there*. 'I'm just leaving.'

I tried to crawl up the beach to my clothes without revealing my boobs, while he continued chatting gaily to me about how he used to live in England twenty years ago and why was Mrs 'Tachair' so anti-Europe? I made vague responses to his questions as I packed up the saddle bags, but now he was sitting cross-legged and facing me so it wasn't easy. I've never met anyone so completely uninhibited.

'Good luck,' he called as I left. 'By the way, what's your name?'

'Erica!' I shouted back, and laughed.

We walked cross-country round the back of Clermont l'Hérault, crossed the busy N9 and headed for the village of Ceyras. Near the river I passed a gypsy camp and a stream of scruffy but very pretty children rushed out to quiz me. I felt exhausted and didn't have the energy to answer their endless questions, but Hannibal wouldn't leave them so I asked them to show me the best way across the river. They led me to a ford where the water was about two feet deep, saying it was the shallowest point this side of the main bridge, but Hannibal refused to put even his toe in. The village was just twenty yards away on the other side of the river, but I knew that nothing would change his mind; I'd have to find somewhere to camp nearby.

The children ran home to get someone called Pepe – he'd know exactly where to go. A few minutes later they returned with a nice-looking man of about thirty whose eyes lit up when I said I'd come from Spain: he was Spanish, he said, and began bombarding me with questions, asking me exactly where I'd been. It was about a mile before we found the camping ground; the river bed widened and there was a huge shingle beach where I spread the ground-sheet of my tent. There was very little for Hannibal to eat, though, and Pepe said he'd bring me some hay. I said goodnight to the children and as they left I began to brew some tea.

As darkness fell and I waited for Pepe to return, I began to panic. I was in the middle of nowhere and no one but some gypsies knew I was here. If I was killed I wouldn't be found for months. I'd practically invited a strong young man to come and get me; what an idiot I'd been. I was so paranoid that when Pepe returned I had my knife in my hand and Bogey firmly at my side and I was actually surprised when he didn't attack me.

I soon felt very guilty for my suspicions. He'd carried a whole bale of hay all the way here and just wanted to chat to someone who could speak Spanish. We shared a saucepan of tea and when I told him I was tired and wanted to go to sleep, he was a perfect gentleman and left immediately.

In the morning I felt terrible. I wanted to be sick, I had a head-ache, I was sweating and shivering – it had to be sunstroke. The weather was close and thundery so I had to start walking, but I did not enjoy that day. The land was flat and dull with no trees to give any shade, just mile after mile of vineyards. At Jonquières the wea-ther broke and I sheltered from the rain in a café, where I was served the strangest tea I'd ever tasted – a microwaved cup of milk with a Lipton's tea-bag in it.

The storm passed after a couple of hours and as I walked on towards the hills of the Cevennes, my spirits lifted. Ahead of me the land suddenly rose by 2000 feet, promising a breeze and some grass for Hannibal. It was like entering another world as I twisted higher and higher into the rugged, scraggy hills. This was *chèvres* country; the grass was nibbled to the ground and the clanging of bells drew my eyes to small clusters of brown goats roaming wild.

Deep black clouds were appearing from the north and the wind had whipped up so I stopped at a farm and asked the young woman inside if I could camp in the shelter of one of their barns. She gave me a huge grin and called outside for her husband, who came run-ning up and greeted me like a long lost friend. Their accents were so strong that it took me a while to understand what they were saying, but at last the penny dropped. They had converted one of their barns to a *gîte*, and I was the very first guest!

It was very impressive. Downstairs was one enormous room, with a kitchen at one end, an eating area in the middle and chairs and sofas by the far wall. Upstairs were four shower rooms and comfy bunk beds to sleep twelve. To me it seemed like a five-star hotel, yet they charged just fifteen francs – much less than the camp sites.

For the first time in months I had both luxury and privacy, and it was bliss. I had a fantastic night's sleep and woke feeling refreshed and fully recovered from my sunstroke.

After breakfast I spread my maps out to have a serious think about my route. Today was 2 July; I'd planned to be across the Rhône by now but I was 200 miles behind schedule. The distance I'd covered over the past month was pathetic, and there was no way I could now cross the Alps and still be in Italy by August. Bearing in mind too that Hannibal was useless at walking uphill, I decided to keep as close as I could to the French coast, while avoiding the tangle of main roads and motorways. I hoped the GR6 would see me through.

From now on my target was twenty-five kilometres a day; I was determined to make my sacrifice of the Alps worthwhile by reaching Italy as soon as I could, so that when my parents and younger brother joined me in August I'd have time to enjoy myself. Bogey was now strong enough to cope with this and I knew Hannibal would have no problem; the main trouble would be fitting the walking into daylight hours.

With renewed zest I set off across the wild moorland, reaching a cluster of houses called les Lavagnes at teatime. Just beyond the village I stopped dead in my tracks – before me a steep-sided gorge dropped away beneath my feet and thickly forested mountains stretched to the horizon. I understood immediately why Robert Louis Stevenson had been so crazy about the Cevennes; this was spectacular, a land of fairy tales and adventures. I was sorely tempted to scrap my plans for Rome there and then.

I let Hannibal drag me down the valley at top speed, past the lovely village of Pegairolles and down along the side of the river. An English Dormobile drove past and I waved so frantically that it stopped. The couple inside put some money in my MENCAP tin and attempted to assuage my homesickness by giving me a *Daily Telegraph*, a box of jelly babies and a tin of *Heinz baked beans*! Words cannot describe what I felt at seeing such goodies.

A couple of hours later, camped by the river, I lay in my hammock devouring every inch of the newspaper, even the financial pages and the royal engagements, with the tin of beans sitting on my chest. I rationed myself to one spoonful every five minutes to try to make the ecstasy last, but even so I reached the bottom far too soon.

Chapter 19
A Taste of Romance

I reached St Jean a day late, Monday 3 July. Ribbons and balloons littered the ground, scraps of food were scattered over long wooden trestle tables and I realized I'd missed the fiesta. Since no one was about I scavenged for leftovers and my animals ended up having a feast: bread, fruit and pastries for the donkey, pizza and salami for the dogs.

Hannibal sank his head into the fountain for a drink, then nearly gave me a heart attack as he abruptly reared and careered over to the other side of the square, sending the packs flying and me sprawling to the ground as I tried to keep hold of his lead. What had frightened him? I tried to lead him back to the fountain, but he wouldn't take even a step in that direction. I tied him and returned alone, peered into the water and a few seconds later I was creased with laughter – goldfish! The little red flashes darting about in the water had given my big strong donkey the shock of his life! I gave him a hug and tried to calm him, but as we left the square and walked out of the village, he kept peering anxiously behind him, as if he expected something to jump out and chase him.

We set off through a pass in the shadow of the Montagne de la Seranne; later the road descended steeply to cross a stream, on the banks of which I found the hamlet of Papet. In its midst was a bright blue, imitation castle, straight out of *Chitty Chitty Bang Bang*; it looked as if it were made of marzipan, with little turrets and towers, even a miniature swimming pool.

By now it was swelteringly hot, but I wanted to reach St Bauzille-de-Putois by midday. I planned to visit the Grotte des Demoiselles, a massive underground cave that I'd read about; I felt like being a tourist for a while. On the way we passed a turf farm where, as an advertising gimmick, the owner had covered his Citroën 2CV with turfs. It was an extraordinary sight – just grass, windows and four wheels; but even more amazing was the fact that the car worked – he even gave us a demonstration. Hannibal then caused much hilarity by eating it, which I thought was a much better advert for his turf.

141

Finally we reached St Bauzille. I swam in the river, then left the animals in the shade while I hitched a lift to the Grotte des Demoiselles. The largest cave was called the cathedral; massive organ pipes lined the walls and in the middle was a stalagmite that looked breathtakingly like the Virgin and Child. The cathedral's name also came from the effect it had on a singing voice; it made even me sound like Aled Jones, when I finally plucked up my courage, since no one else in the party would, and sang the first verse of *Loch Lomond*.

I returned to the animals feeling rather overwhelmed, had a cup of tea and set off once more. The walking wasn't hard, but Hannibal was being difficult and I was tired from having missed my usual siesta, so when I saw a sign saying *'Camping à la ferme'* I called it a day. An elderly man with fluffy grey hair and a welcoming smile came out of the house and asked if he could help me. Of course I could stay at the camp site, he said.

'My son is in charge of the camping and the site's beside his house. There are showers and everything. If you carry on along the drive, it won't take you long.'

I groaned. I just couldn't face walking a whole mile in the wrong direction. The old man looked hurt, insisting that it wasn't very far, that the water would be hot in the showers, that there would be plenty of grass for my donkey. I stood wavering, not knowing what to do.

Just then a tractor entered the yard and my mind was suddenly jolted from its lethargic indecision as I watched the most beautiful man coming towards me. He looked about twenty-eight and was tall, with short, dark hair. He was wearing nothing but cut-off jeans and fell boots, and he had the most fantastic body – broad-shouldered, smooth-chested, tanned almost mahogany. As his brilliant blue eyes smiled at me I felt like a heroine from a Barbara Cartland novel. I couldn't remember when I'd last felt like this.

His father introduced us.

'Guy,' he said, 'this young lady would like to stay at the camp site tonight. Do you think the donkey would be all right tethered to one of the trees?'

'Yes, that'd be great! We've no one up there at the moment, we need a bit of excitement. Has my father told you where to go?' He gave me a huge smile and I swooned. I was definitely staying, so I called the dogs and set off along the track, suddenly wide awake, my spirits soaring.

'Hang on a minute!' called Guy, running up to me. 'You must be exhausted. Why don't you drive up to the camp site with your luggage? I can walk up with the donkey.' He began lifting the

142

saddle bags off Hannibal and indicated a Fiat Uno parked outside the house. 'Can you drive?'

'Yes, that would be marvellous,' I replied, wishing I could think of something better to say.

We packed the car up with my stuff and Bogey sat beside me while I drove across the valley, leaving Adonis to bring Hannibal and George.

It wasn't really a camp site, just a grassy area outside a small stone house, with a shower block and some water taps. I dumped my stuff beside some trees that were perfect for my hammock and began making Bogey's supper. Two men came out of the house and introduced themselves as Gérard and Laurence, friends of Guy's who were here on holiday, and they offered me a vodka and tonic. I hadn't drunk anything so sophisticated in months. A short while later Guy arrived.

'Your donkey's an absolute bastard,' he said, but smiled as he tethered him in the best patch of grass and gave him a bucket of water. He came over and poured himself a drink, then turned to me and said, 'You must have supper with us. We're not much good at cooking, but we've plenty to drink, and I want to hear all about your adventure.'

I gulped down my drink, hoping that the alcohol would free me of my sudden shyness; I felt as if I were thirteen again. God, his eyes are beautiful, I thought, as I mumbled that I must go and have a shower. I scrambled around in my bags for a clean shirt, wishing that my clothes were more flattering; I couldn't find any clean knickers so went without. After my shower I spent ages putting on make-up, then scrubbed it all off again – far too obvious. This is crazy, I kept saying to myself; you've spent the last four months dreading men finding you attractive and hating them for being such randy bastards. Now look at you – wishing you were thinner, trying to hide the shine on your nose, and praying to God to make him like you.

I took a deep breath and walked out to join the men at the table on the terrace.

'Tell me what you think of the wine,' said Guy. 'It's from the farm.'

It was a sweet rosé, surprisingly good, and Guy told me it was made from a special type of grape grown only in the Cevennes. We sat watching the sun go down and I listened as they told me about the area. I learnt the names of the best spots for hang-gliding, the best mountains to climb, the best rivers to canoe . . . I felt the wine mellowing me and I relaxed, gradually joining in the conversation. They were easy guys to get on with. Gérard was bespectacled and rather earnest, eager to please, like a little terrier. Laurence was older and more sophisticated, from Paris, and talked to me about law and what I did at home. Guy was simply perfect. He was one of those people who inject such enthusiasm into whatever they are describing that they make anything seem interesting; and he listened in the same way, as if the speaker were the most fascinating person in the world. I wished he'd put his shirt on so that I could concentrate properly when I was talking to him.

Then someone remembered supper and they all ran inside to fetch it. They'd been right about their lack of culinary skills – when I saw their offerings of burnt hamburgers, soggy rice and tomato ketchup, I wished I'd offered to cook, but we were all hungry so it didn't really matter.

My enquiries about vine-growing sparked off an impromptu wine-tasting. They taught me how to do it properly, swirling it round my glass, sniffing it, and gurgling the air through the wine in my mouth which was marvellously intoxicating. We tried four different bottles and I realized as I went to the loo that I was absolutely smashed. I could hardly walk straight; I leant against the wall and grinned from ear to ear. I felt marvellous. I found some aftershave and put a little on my wrists and neck, and then I backcombed my hair. 'Go for it, Sophie,' I remember saying to my reflection in the mirror. 'You deserve it.'

I returned to the table and we sat talking for hours. Gradually the conversation slowed down, so I got up and bade everyone goodnight. Guy offered to help me put up my hammock and as we walked outside my heart leapt to my throat. Please, please make something happen, I thought, as I tried to take as long as possible tying the hammock strings to the tree, but it was finished all too quickly and Guy turned back towards the house, saying he would check on Hannibal. My heart sank. I'd been as forward as I dared, so I admitted defeat. Typical, I thought; I've been chased by every ugly lecher in the Mediterranean, but when I meet a man whom *I* find attractive, he doesn't even look twice. I unrolled my sleeping bag, found the T-shirt I used as a nightie and waited for him to go inside before I changed.

But he didn't go straight inside, he came back towards me.

'The donkey's fine,' he said. 'Are you sure you're OK out here? Are you sure you don't want to come inside?'

I insisted that I was fine. 'Goodnight then,' he said, and kissed my cheek. I couldn't move away and we stood there for an interminable moment, almost touching. The moon was full and I could just see his face; what the hell, I thought, I've nothing to lose, and I looked up at him with what I hoped was pure, uninhibited lust in

Diane Palmer helps the blacksmith fit Hannibal with some new shoes

Standing on the Franco-Italian border

Clare takes over as head chef

Raising money in Italy

Hannibal joins Stevie and Ted for lunch

Trying to convince mum of Hannibal's charms

Dad and Stevie *(Photo: Bob Collier)*

Lost with the
animals in
Riomaggiore, Italy

George helps Tim plan the route

Feeling shattered in the mountains above Camaiore, Italy

Meeting some lost goats on the Luccan plain, Italy

The final steps to Rome

my eyes, pleading with him to make the first move. He smiled at me for a moment, then his arms came up around me and he kissed me. Thank you, thank you, thank you, I thought, as I kissed him back with all the passion that only four months of sensual deprivation can produce.

Chapter 20
Up a Creek Without a Donkey

I set off early in the morning on 4 July, before anyone else had woken. I never have been any good at goodbyes and I had a rotten hangover. I didn't want Guy to see me green-faced and puffy-eyed.

Despite my head, however, I couldn't keep the smile from my face as I walked into the morning sun towards St Hippolyte-du-Fort. It had been *so* good to meet some young men who weren't frightening or threatening, who didn't want anything from me, whom I could talk to as friends. It was also reassuring to know that I could still find a man desirable; I was afraid that all those bastards I'd come across might have turned me into a real man-hater, terrified of anything physical. But no, Sophie was still as capable as ever of falling in love – and it felt fantastic.

I celebrated by buying a cheap little radio from a tiny electrical shop in the centre of St Hippolyte, and then treated myself to breakfast at one of the streetside cafés. Numerous people asked me if I was following the Stevenson trail, and were suitably impressed when I replied no, I was on my way to Rome.

I decided to get some distance under my belt by walking along the main road to Durfort; the traffic wasn't bad and the scenery more than made up for the tarmac. We were surrounded by thickly forested hills of established trees, not newly planted pines, and to the north I could see mountains stretching into the distance. We walked for about four miles, by which time it was midday and I couldn't stand the heat any longer, so I found a suitable spot for a siesta, and within ten minutes I was asleep.

I woke about two hours later when the sun took my shade away. I slowly came to and began scrummaging about in my bags for some water; as I did so, however, I felt horribly aware that something was wrong. I looked at the dogs, still asleep beside me, then scanned the bushes to see if someone was lurking.

'Oh my God!' I screamed. 'Hannibal!'

He'd disappeared. I ran over to his tether and found that it had simply snapped. I screamed his name; my mind was a panic-stricken blank, and I had no idea where to start looking.

Tying the dogs to the tree, I ran half a mile back down the road to where I'd passed some workmen. Luckily they were still at their machines. I yelled at them to stop and frantically asked whether they'd seen a donkey.

'A dark brown one, was it?' they replied blandly, as if it happened every day. 'With a white nose? Yes, it ran past about half an hour ago, heading towards St Hippo. Quite a speed it was going, too.'

Oh Jesus, I thought, he's going to cause an accident, and I started running again. At least I now knew vaguely where he was, which was a relief, and I hoped that I'd be able to catch up with him. Where the hell was a car when I needed one? It felt like an eternity before at last a blue Citroën appeared heading in the right direction. I stood in the middle of the road waving my hands at it to stop, then jumped in and screamed at the driver that it was an emergency and he must drive to St Hippolyte as quickly as possible. He did as I asked, but he was very rude when I told him the exact nature of the emergency, saying that the only good donkey is one that's sliced on a plate.

There was no sign of Hannibal en route. On reaching the town I leapt out and ran round frantically asking pedestrians and shopkeepers if they'd seen a donkey. They simply looked at me as if I'd lost my marbles, so I was soon convinced that he hadn't entered St Hippolyte.

I returned to the main road, calling Hannibal's name into the hills on either side as I ran back towards where we'd camped, scanning the dust for hoof marks and yelling into the trees. There was no sign of him at all and by four I was back with the dogs, who thought they'd been deserted and leapt all over me in delight.

Feeling desperate, I decided to ring Guy; he knew the area like the back of his hand and he might at least be able to lend me a car. I approached the nearest farmhouse and knocked at the front door. It was opened by a tall, slim lady with glasses, who invited me inside as I gasped out my story. Anne, as I later learned she was called, listened intently, then sat me down and poured me a drink. She told me not to worry, she'd help me find my donkey, and she began by phoning the police station in St Hippolyte.

They'd seen him! He was in the town! Anne smiled at me and did a thumbs-up sign, and I leapt up to try and hear what was being said.

'Can you tell us exactly where he is,' Anne was asking, 'so that we can come and fetch him?'

Then her face dropped and I knew something was wrong. She called someone an idiot, put the phone down and turned to me; they had seen me walking through the town with Hannibal that morning – which was why they'd said he was there. No one had seen a donkey that afternoon.

'Never mind,' she said, 'we'll find him ourselves. He's most likely to head for water; if you continue down this track you'll find the Vidourle, and then I suggest you follow it west towards St Hippo. Meanwhile, I'll ring all our neighbours and tell them to be on the lookout.'

I set off again feeling much more positive. I ran through fields of neatly planted vegetables down to a dried-up riverbed, then turned right as Anne had told me. I screamed and yelled Hannibal's name and wished my eyesight were better as I scanned the sides of the valley for a sign of him. I passed the ruins of an old castle and jumped from rock to rock along the empty riverbed as it twisted towards the town roughly parallel to the road.

I had dozens of false hopes, imagining that I heard something moving in the bushes, seeing shadows in the trees. But two hours later I was back at the farm, feeling hoarse and miserable – I'd found nothing at all. Anne told me to come with her in the car and we drove along the main road again, stopping at all the tracks, searching for hoof marks, calling into the hills again and again. We drove down some of the tracks to houses and farms where Anne spoke with the owners, but all of them just shook their heads and offered their sympathies. Anne was marvellous, she wouldn't let me cry and kept thinking of new places to look.

Then I had an idea: I asked Anne if she knew of anyone who kept horses, or perhaps even donkeys, nearby; if Hannibal heard or smelt other equines I felt sure he'd go to them. It was probably a long shot but she'd heard of a man who kept donkeys about twelve kilometres away; perhaps Hannibal had heard them braying and gone to them. Returning to the house, I met Anne's husband, Robert, a huge, bearded man with a booming voice who said he'd just rung the police station again to tell them how important this was. Anne rang her donkey man, but he'd seen nothing. By now it was nearly nine o'clock; it would be dark in an hour. I couldn't stop shaking.

'Don't worry,' Anne tried to reassure me. 'He'll soon be thirsty or hungry, or perhaps just lonely, and he'll turn up somewhere.'

But I remembered the friend of my parents who'd driven into a horse on the road at night; the horse was killed and the friend could have been too. I kept picturing terrible accidents, and all because I'd bought that stupid leather lead to save my precious hands.

I couldn't just sit round doing nothing, so I checked on the dogs and set off down the main road again, desperately calling into the trees. What if I never found him? What a way for my journey to end, I thought, with my donkey lost in the Cevennes.

When I reached the outskirts of the town I gave up. It was becoming difficult to see and I'd be run over myself soon if I wasn't careful. I stuck my thumb out and climbed into a blue van driving in the direction of my camp. We'd gone about two kilometres when I saw a group of people gathered on the other side of the road. I asked the man to stop and I got out, hoping against hope.

As I crossed the road I saw him.

'Hannibal!'

He looked up, and I'll never forget the expression on his face as he charged towards me, nearly knocking me flying.

'You bastard,' I said as I held on to him, 'You've put twenty years on me.'

He rammed his head into my stomach, a familiar gesture that he thinks is affectionate, then looked at me and stamped his foot. I couldn't believe it – anyone would have thought *I* had been the one to run away. I wanted to kill him for what he'd put me through, yet he was so obviously pleased to see me that it was difficult to hate him.

The young people with him had seen him standing by the side of the road five minutes earlier. They'd easily caught him and had stayed with him while the girl driving their car had gone to the police station.

I thanked them all and started walking Hannibal back to camp. I was so tired that I jumped on his back; he didn't seem to mind and didn't even need to be guided. About a mile from the farm I met Anne and Robert driving towards St Hippolyte – they'd just been informed by the police that Hannibal had been found and were coming to fetch him. I must come inside for some supper when I got back Anne called as they turned round.

Half an hour later I fed the ever-patient dogs, tied Hannibal to a tree with the most elaborate set of knots imaginable and then stumbled up to the farm. It was only now that I properly realized that Anne had given up her whole afternoon and evening to help me and she didn't know me from Adam. Yet again I wished that I had some way of repaying kindness.

As I lay in my hammock later, with both dogs balanced precariously in my lap, my mind wouldn't relax. What if Hannibal had been killed? What if he'd been lost forever? I'd had more luck than I deserved, and being suddenly back to normal felt strange and uncomfortable.

The next week was my quick dash across the Rhône valley. I enjoyed it more than I'd expected to; I'd had enough excitement in my life for a while and because the land was flatter I could usually use tracks and paths instead of roads. The prosperity of the region was reflected in beautiful houses and farms, and many of the villages were lovely: Canaules-et-Argentières, where I met a farrier in action (but he didn't have any shoes to fit Hannibal); Nozières, where I found a perfect camping ground by the cemetery; Sanilhac, where I rang Granny and arranged to meet her at the railway station in La Grasse in two weeks' time. We passed many equestrian centres, a source of fascination for Hannibal, who always insisted on stopping to rub noses. Horses seemed to confuse him; he would look from them to me as if asking, 'Is that what I look like? Something's not quite the same, I'm sure . . .'

Hannibal and I had never eaten so well. This was fruit country and it was picking time; as we crossed the fields of peaches and nectarines, melons and apricots, we were given crates of whatever wasn't good enough to send to the shops. The pickers always had a cheerful greeting and a smile, and they used to tease me about my singing because I usually didn't notice them till it was too late and they'd already heard.

I found I could pick up the BBC World Service on my radio first thing in the morning and it was great to get up to that bracing theme tune and the newsreader telling me in his impeccable accent that it was 3 a.m. GMT, which made me feel very virtuous. At siesta time I tuned into the European music channels and discovered that there were some beautiful songs in the charts – Gloria Estefan's *I Don't Want To Lose You Now*, Bette Midler's *Wind Beneath My Wings* and the Bangles' *Eternal Flame*. I learnt all the words and Hannibal soon became the most serenaded donkey in history.

But then we met the Rhône, and the journey very nearly came to an abrupt halt. Hannibal was absolutely terrified of it; he'd never seen such a vast expanse of water and he had no intention of going anywhere near it. As a secondary deterrent, all the modern bridges crossing the Rhône had narrow lines of guttering stretching across them at twenty-yard intervals to make sure they drained properly. Hannibal refused to walk over these, no matter how well I tried to hide them by covering them with grass or bamboo.

I'd had to leave my *Grande Randonnée* route after Hannibal refused to cross the Pont du Gard, so the first bridge we tried was further north than originally planned, near Aramon. I wasn't too worried at this stage, but when he also refused the small, quiet bridge south of Comps, I began to realize how serious the problem could be. Sticking to old bridges would take me miles out of my way.

How the hell had I managed to find such a bloody stupid donkey? How can an animal that weighs half a ton be so frightened of falling down a two-inch gutter? I tried every type of bribery imaginable – peaches, Mars bars, honey – but it didn't make the slightest difference. I stood behind him and whacked him, much harder than I like to remember, but he wouldn't budge an inch.

The glare of the sun on the water was making my eyes hurt so I stopped to look for my sunglasses and had an idea. A blindfold! It was worth a try. I found my towel and carefully wrapped it round Hannibal's eyes, blocking out every ray of light. Then I tried to lead him forward, reassuring him in as hopeful a voice as I could muster. But he just dug his heels in more firmly than ever and began tossing his head about in a frantic effort to rid himself of the towel, which he soon managed.

But I wouldn't give up on the idea. Perhaps total darkness wasn't right; I tried to think of how I could make the equivalent of sunglasses, so that he would still know vaguely where he was going.

I ripped the cotton chiffon lining out of my skirt and held it up against my eyes. It was perfect, removing the glare from the water, the gutters from the road and even the dust from the air, but I could still see the basics of my surroundings. If this didn't work, nothing would.

He didn't try to shake it off, yet neither would he cross the bridge. I jumped to the optimistic conclusion that it was because we'd been standing beside this bridge for nearly half an hour and nothing would make him forget it, so we set off back to the second one at Comps. He walked well with the chiffon over his eyes, hardly seeming aware of it, and as we approached the bridge I began to pray.

There were hardly any cars on it; conditions were perfect. I started singing to try and fool Hannibal that there was nothing in the vicinity to worry about, and to my joy he stepped over the first gutter. I wanted to hug him and kiss him and tell him how clever he was, but I was so terrified of putting him off or reminding him where we were that I just kept on going, singing the same song over and over again. We reached the island in the middle of the river and I relaxed a little, thinking that if he refused the next bridge, he'd end up spending the rest of his life here. I needn't have worried; Hannibal was now well in his stride and walked across without a care in the world. When we reached the far side I flung my arms round his neck and yahooed. I shall always count that river-crossing as one of my greatest achievements.

Heading for the hills of Provence through the wilderness of les Alpilles (the 'little Alps'), I walked through the strange, twisted rocks of the eroded limestone peaks to Les Baux, an ancient fortified village perched on the mountain ridge, where I had my first taste of Provençal tourists. The steep, narrow streets led to dozens of 'olde worlde' cafés and souvenir shops, and I had to pay twenty francs to see the castle. But no amount of tourists could ruin the spectacular views; I saw the Mediterranean for the first time since Banyuls. The comtes des Baux were notoriously cruel and sadistic, and used to hurl their prisoners from the top of the fortress to the sharp white rocks 1000 feet below.

Above the village of Maussane I found an unusually clear and fast-flowing stream, so I washed my laundry and hair while cheering Edberg through the Wimbledon final on my radio. It was the hottest day yet and I had to force myself to set off again at five o'clock, heading eastwards along the foot of the Alpilles.

After a couple of miles the track cut through a very smart golf course behind the Servanne château. I stared in longing at the many ponds and artificial lakes as I felt the sweat dribbling down my back; we passed a bunker and Hannibal must have felt the same for he strained towards it, longing for a roll. Finally I could stand the temptation no longer and when I reached a spot where no golfers were in sight, I quickly unpacked Hannibal and took off my boots. We raced towards our respective oases and flung ourselves in; the water was cool and surprisingly deep, and judging by the ecstasy in Hannibal's groans, his sand-pit was perfect. All I could see were four legs stretching upwards, and a cloud of sand as he tossed from side to side.

My hopes of going unnoticed were in vain, and before I had time to climb out of the water we'd attracted a small crowd. I feared I was going to be in trouble, but luckily they had a sense of humour and as I clambered out, trying not to look too obscene in my wet T-shirt, some of them even clapped. I borrowed a rake and tried to hide the hoof marks in the bunker, extracted a golf ball from George's mouth and tried to look cool as I waved and walked away.

My mountain break was short, for the next day (10 July) I was down in the plain. Salon was the largest town so far on my route, but I thought the quickest way past it would be to plough straight through the centre. It wasn't as bad as I'd feared and as we walked up the main street Hannibal provided me with the best entertainment I'd had in weeks.

There was a commotion behind us and an ambulance came hurtling past, sirens blazing. Hannibal stood stock still as he heard it, ears forward and eyes bright as he tried to identify the sound. Suddenly he took off after it, eeyoring incredibly loudly apparently convinced that the ambulance was a donkey – or perhaps he thought there was a donkey trapped inside. Even the dangers of Hanny hurtling down a main road dragging me and the dogs behind him couldn't stop me laughing. Luckily the ambulance soon disappeared and Hannibal gave up.

On my way out of town I stopped at a large supermarket and to my astonishment found some genuine Alpen. Ignoring the price labels (over £2 for a small box), I bought three and splashed out on a litre of fresh milk as well. Five minutes later I was back with the animals in the car park. After opening a tin of Pedigree Chum for the dogs, I sat down on the tarmac, poured myself a huge bowl of cereal, and for the third time in twenty-four hours, a crowd of people gathered round to stare at me. This time, however, I was too content to care.

Chapter 21
Storming the Bastille

Pelissanne frightened me. It was much bigger than I'd expected and seemed to be inhabited almost entirely by Arabs. Though the centre was very pretty, the sidestreets stank of poverty; filthy children stared at me from open doorways and the bars were full of men whose dark eyes followed me as I passed. There was a large area of rough ground by the river, but I was afraid to camp here. I wished it weren't so late as I stopped at the ornate fountain in the main street to water the animals and tried to decide what to do.

A beautiful Arab lady from one of the nearby houses came out to speak to me; her English, apparently learned from the BBC World Service, was excellent. She invited me to join her family for dinner; I wished I could accept, but I didn't dare spend the night outside in this place. With about an hour of daylight left, I decided to continue on my route away from the village and stop at the first farm I came to.

As I set off over the bridge out of Pelissanne a man of about thirty approached me. He had longish black hair and a moustache, a dark Eastern skin and was wearing a strange kind of gold embroidered waistcoat. He asked if I was looking for somewhere to stay.

'No,' I said, and tried to quicken my pace.

He followed, calling out to me, 'I own a field, not far from here. It would be perfect for you. Don't worry, it would be very safe, no one would know you were there.'

I ignored him and kept going, Bogey by my side, but he followed me out of the village, talking continually.

'Wait, mademoiselle, please! Where are you going to spend the night? You are vulnerable, out here on your own. There are many dangerous people round here, they might come and hurt you. You do not know this area like I do, you would not know where to run to . . .'

I considered turning back, but thought that if I continued ignoring him he was bound to get bored and go away. Thank God for Bogey – I kept hold of her collar the whole time, confident that she wouldn't let him hurt me. George, however, I wanted to murder;

155

she was busy bringing him sticks to throw and seemed to think she'd found a lifelong friend.

The man went on and on, and I was beginning to get very frightened. He'd been following me for about two miles; I could imagine myself having to walk all night by torchlight, with him just a few feet behind me. Where the hell was a house? I decided my silence was doing no good at all, so at last I turned to him.

'Please, monsieur, leave me alone. I am quite all right, I have no need of any help. I have my Dobermann to protect me and I just want to be alone. Please go away.'

'But why do you want to be alone?' he replied. 'It is not natural for a woman to be on her own. Everyone needs friends, it is good to have friends, and I want to be your friend, I want to help you. Why are you being so horrible to me?'

I wished that I could order Bogey to tear him to pieces. At last I saw some houses up the hill to the left. I turned to my pursuer and tried again.

'Go away! I don't want you with me. I don't want your help! Don't follow me any more, or I'll get very angry and I'll set my dog on you.'

He stood at the bottom of the track with a horrible smile on his face as I walked up to the houses, then he turned and began to walk back towards Pelissanne. I felt relieved and looked around for the entrances, noticing children's toys in one of the gardens – always a good sign.

However, as I looked in through the high wire fencing surrounding each house, it slowly dawned on me that no one was at home. Oh God, I'd have to return to the road. I hung around for a while, wanting to leave enough time for the man to be far enough away not to notice me, but darkness was falling quickly, so after a few minutes I descended the track again as quietly as possible.

I saw a shadow moving on the road; Georgie gave out a yelp of excitement and rushed off towards it. The man appeared from the bushes.

'I could have told you no one was there,' he said. 'They're just holiday houses, empty during the week. It's all right, though, I know somewhere you can stay.'

This time I snapped.

'Bugger off you bastard! Just leave! Go! I don't want to see you again! If you dare lay a finger on me, you'll regret it. *George,* you idiot, *come here!*'

I set off along the road again practically running now, but he was still following, this time about ten yards behind.

'No, I want to come with you,' he was saying. 'It is not safe for a young woman like you to be on her own. You need protection.'

I kept screaming at him to fuck off, in the vague hope that someone might hear and come to my rescue. It was almost completely dark now and I was beginning to panic.

After about five minutes I saw some lights ahead of me and made out two houses by the side of the road. I rushed towards them, but discovered that the first one was just a caravan; the second was a proper house with a large garden and a tall wire fence round it. I ran up to the gate and frantically rang the bell, attracting the noisy attention of a very large Alsatian. I looked behind me; there was no sign of him.

At last a woman's head appeared from an upstairs window.

'What do you want?'

'Please, madame, please help me. I need somewhere safe to spend the night. A man is following me and I am frightened; I am all alone with my animals. Please could you let me in?'

'I have nowhere for you to stay,' she said and closed the window.

I couldn't believe it. As I looked behind me into the dark shadows, I felt utterly vulnerable. I rang and rang at the bell again and this time a man appeared at the window.

'Go away!' he shouted.

'Please, monsieur, I'm frightened!' As quickly as possible I tried to explain who I was, that I was on a pilgrimage(!) to Rome, that I was raising money for charity, that I needed help, but my voice was shaking so much that he probably didn't understand half of it.

'But we have nowhere for you to stay,' he protested.

'Could you put your dog inside your house and let me sleep in the garden?' I pleaded. 'I could leave the donkey out by the road, but please, monsieur, let me inside your gates.'

'I am sorry, mademoiselle, but we cannot help you.' He shut the window again and firmly drew the curtain.

I set the bell clanging again until the man appeared once more, shouting at me to go away.

'Please, monsieur, could you ring the police for me?' I called back. 'Could you tell them that I need help, that I'm being followed by a man and I'm frightened that he intends to hurt me? Could you tell them to send a car out along this road? Could you do that for me, please?'

'All right, mademoiselle, I shall ring the police. Goodnight.'

And again he shut the window.

The caravan was my last chance, so I ran back along the road to it, expecting a dark figure to jump out at me at any moment. I hammered on the door, almost hysterical by now, and was taken aback when it was opened so quickly. A man of about fifty stood in front of me; he wore blue canvas trousers and a string vest, his hair was greased back from his forehead, and his appearance at first frightened me. But his face was kind and he listened carefully to what I was saying, and for God knows what reason I trusted him. I knew that I was going to be OK.

He suggested that I camp just outside and he would leave his door unlocked in case I had any trouble. Hannibal could go in the field at the back; it had just been harvested and there would be plenty of wheat among the straw. He brought a bucket of water for me to wash with and I laid my tent out on the ground at the back of the caravan.

'Goodnight,' he said. 'If you're at all frightened, just come in or call me.' And he disappeared up the steps again.

I lay awake for hours, hugging Bogey and listening to the radio blasting from inside the caravan. No police car appeared and I cursed the owners of the house up the road. But perhaps I'd just become too used to people being kind and generous, I thought; perhaps I was wrong to expect them to open their doors to a stranger. There was no reason, I supposed, why they should have let me in; I looked like a scruffy tramp and with Bogey at my side, they were probably frightened of *us*.

I had a troubled night's sleep and was relieved to see the light of day. I was up and away in five minutes, leaving a note of thanks on the caravan steps.

A few hours later a police car pulled up beside me. Four policemen got out and demanded to see my passport and the dogs' rabies vaccine certificates. They spent ages looking through them and reading out the details over their car phone. When I asked them why they were doing this, the one in charge replied,

'Oh, we had a phone call last night from some people who said they were being bothered by a gypsy girl, so we thought we'd come and check you out.'

To reach Aix quickly I made the mistake of following an old Roman road – mile after mile along a straight, flat line. I thought I'd go mad. However, I did cover an impressive distance, reaching the outskirts of town by six in the evening. I found a large, impressive house with a beautiful green field in front of it and decided to ask if I could stay there – Hannibal hadn't had a good feed for ages.

A very sophisticated-looking woman in her late twenties astonished me by agreeing to my request. Her brother-in-law owned the land, she said, but the field wasn't being used for anything, so as far as she was concerned I was welcome to stay.

The field was covered with a network of pipes and sprinklers, and I hadn't seen such good grass since the Pyrenees. Hannibal didn't know where to start and ran round snorting in excitement while I put the tent up in as discreet a position as I could find. I was just making the dogs' supper when the lady from the house walked down to me with two little boys of about six at her side.

'Would you like to join us for dinner?' she asked. 'It's my nanny's day off and I would be very grateful for a hand with the children if you'd like to come up to the house. You're welcome to wash in the bathroom, too, if you like.'

This seemed like an excellent bargain, so I quickly brushed my hair and tried to smarten myself up before following her. I had a great evening; there were four children – two of hers plus a niece and a nephew – and we had a delicious meal out on the front terrace. The children wanted rides on Hannibal, but he was furious to be interrupted from his eating session and refused to walk an inch.

The town of Aix-en-Provence is wonderful – tall, elegant houses, narrow, cobbled streets and ornate fountains in every square. As the streets slowly came to life and shops opened, I sang *Who will Buy*? from *Oliver!* and felt blissfully happy.

Rounding a corner into one of the biggest squares, we discovered it was market day and saw the most superb display of fruit and vegetables. Hannibal went wild and I thought I'd never get him out of there. We were given so much fruit that I thought he'd be ill, but I finally managed to drag him away.

The countryside I climbed up into that afternoon was spectacular. Before me was the Montagne Sainte-Victoire, a steeply ridged range over 3000 feet high, whose limestone peaks seemed to change colour before my eyes. I realized too late that this was heralding a thunderstorm, but luckily managed to find shelter at a camp site near Baurecueil. I wimped out of climbing the mountain the next day, following the road along its southern edge instead, but was thus probably better able to enjoy its beauty. I'd heard about Sainte-Victoire before; Cézanne painted it over 100 times, believing it epitomized all that was beautiful in Provence. This was *Jean de Florette* country, too, which made me notice how dry the soil was despite the previous night's storm. The grass was parched and dead, and I felt pleased that Hannibal had eaten so well at Aix – there was little nourishment to be found here.

On Thursday evening we reached Puyloubier, at the eastern foot of Sainte-Victoire, and I found a village under transformation. The square was festooned with red, white and blue ribbons, tables were being carried about and balloons being blown up; old men were getting annoyed at intrusive ladders disturbing their boules games and the bars were full of those already making merry. I asked what was going on and a dozen faces turned to me in astonishment. Didn't I know about the Bicentenary?

There had been a gradual build-up of excitement over the past few weeks about the Bastille Day celebrations – and tonight was the 13th, 'la Grande Fête', the start of it all.

A man in a track suit suggested that I take Hannibal out to the football pitch a couple of kilometres from the village; there would be fireworks tonight, he said, and he might be frightened if he were any closer. The dogs and I would be able to stay at the *gîte* in the centre of the village.

We did as recommended, but the *gîte* was dark and dingy, with an outdoor loo that stank and a cooker that gave me an electric shock. It was also expensive, but the woman in charge didn't mind the dogs, and I wanted to be in the centre of the village for the celebrations, so I agreed to stay. I changed into my party dress, put on some make-up and went off to join in the fun.

The children were beautifully dressed up as red, white and blue peasants, and a stage was set up on the steps of the town hall for a pantomime that I was told would start in a few minutes. I was given a paper lantern with a candle inside and the lady from the grocer's gave me a cup of wine and a fruit tart. The village policeman insisted on telling me the history of the Revolution – being English, I couldn't possibly have been taught it truthfully, he said – as the pantomime began.

The king, Marie-Antoinette, Robespierre and various other characters, whom the policeman wasn't much better than me at identifying, acted out a wonderful show and we then chased them all round the village, in and out of buildings. 'Ghosts' and 'murderers' and shrieking women sprang out from every dark corner, fireworks kept going off in odd places and there were frequent stops for drinks along the way. We finally caught the characters back on the steps of the town hall, where there was a trial. The king was given a chance to defend himself, Marie-Antoinette gave her 'Let them eat cake' contribution and then there was a vote of execution. About 100 children thrust their arms in the air in a unanimous decision to kill their monarchs and I had a sudden urge to do a Scarlet Pimpernel rescue attempt.

Moments later the policeman grabbed my arm and took me to the other side of the square to see the storming of the Bastille, alias the wine cooperative. The thinnest people in the village were inside pretending to be starving prisoners and we all cheered as the building was stormed by some rather dubious sound-effects and red, white and blue smoke billowed out of the windows. Everyone sang the *Marseillaise,* then we all crowded round the centre of the square to watch the fireworks.

I somehow found myself seated next to the mayor, who told me he was honoured that an English girl should be joining their celebrations and he insisted that I take photographs of every Catherine wheel. The display was frighteningly amateur; the fireworks had been sent from central government in Paris and no one seemed sure how they worked. When one was lit but failed to go off, the mayor walked ceremoniously over to help and came within a fraction of having his head blown off. Apart from me, no one else seemed perturbed by the incident, and now the real merriment started.

The square was cleared for a dance floor and the king and a by now very male Marie-Antoinette miraculously turned themselves into a band. Grannies and children were all dancing together, free wine was being served at the bars and it was impossible not to be carried away by it all. I was asked to dance by men ranging in age from six to seventy-two. It was a night I'll never forget; every party since has felt flat in comparison.

During the night my drunken sleep was disturbed by what I thought were squidgy mosquitoes. Climbing off the bunk, I turned the light on and stared at my bed in horror. It was crawling with vile little beetle-like creatures wriggling in and out of the mattress. My skin began itching all over as I thought of having lain on that writhing mass and I ran out to the shower room and sprayed myself down with cold water, wishing that it was morning so that I could leave. I spent the rest of the night lying on the tiled floor of the hall and left as soon as it was light, feeling itchy, exhausted and hungover.

I was interested in seeing the festivities of a larger town, so I headed for the medieval pilgrimage centre of St Maximin-la-Ste-Baume. On the way I bought two dozen red, white and blue balloons and tied them to Hannibal's pack saddle, which aroused many hoots and cheers as cars passed us.

Pushed for time, I walked the last few miles along the N7; it was the busiest road I joined on my entire trip and it was terrifying. All three of my animals seemed to have a simultaneous death wish, straining out into the middle of the road as if intent upon being run over, and I felt drained by the time we reached St Maximin.

Unfortunately the nearest camp site was two kilometres away in the wrong direction. It was very frustrating; I was determined to see the celebrations, and needed to go back to town to find some food for the dogs, but short of camping on the pavement I didn't know how I was going to do it.

I was beginning to despair of finding somewhere suitable when I found a patch of rough land between two houses. The owner, apparently, lived in Marseilles, but the neighbours took us to their hearts. Monsieur Albert insisted that he look after Hannibal in his garden and some other people invited me and the dogs to spend the night in theirs. I was overjoyed – Cinderella could go to the ball after all.

That evening in St Maximin was very special because it allowed me to be anonymous; for a few hours I was just an ordinary tourist, not 'The Girl with the Donkey'. For once I could be the spectator, watching people other than me make fools of themselves, and I loved it.

The festivities were rather disappointing, just a small fireworks display and a disco, but I had a great meal at one of the outdoor restaurants in the square. I longed to take a photo of the waitress – she was fiftyish and rather large, but had truly dressed for the occasion. She had somehow poured herself into a blue and white stripy boob tube, a red mini-skirt, red and white stripy tights and red high-heeled shoes.

As I walked back to my camp, I thought how lucky I was to have been in France during this time. The Bicentenary hadn't crossed my mind when I'd been organizing my journey, and now I had participated in it all.

Chapter 22
Raising Hopes on the Côte d'Azur

The devastation left in poor Monsieur Albert's garden! Despite my advice, he had lengthened Hannibal's tether and my voracious donkey had systematically chomped his way through two flower beds and pruned every leaf and shoot from three young cherry trees. Fortunately Monsieur Albert was remarkably good-humoured about it; he even seemed to have grown quite fond of Hannibal, tickling his ears and stroking his nose as he gave me detailed directions for walking by track to the village of Bras (the name still makes me laugh!) up in the hills to the northeast of St Maximin.

I had a lovely morning's walk, although it was oppressively hot when I reached Bras at eleven. I left the animals by the river while I found a telephone box in the village; it was over a week since I'd rung home and I was feeling guilty. My father answered and I knew something was wrong because he didn't instantly hand the phone over to Mum.

'Try not to get upset,' he was saying, and my heart leapt to my throat, terrible possibilities flashing through my mind. 'Granny had an accident in her car on Monday . . .'

He proceeded to tell me that she had been driving on the motor-way near Sedbergh and for no apparent reason her car had gone over the edge and rolled down the bank. She was in the intensive care unit at Lancaster Hospital with severe head and neck injuries; her condition was stable, but it was still uncertain whether she'd pull through. Mum and Jo were visiting her at the moment, so if I rang again that evening they could tell me more. I put the phone down, walked to the nearest bar and ordered a whisky. I was deeply shocked; I'd lived with my grandmother for a year, and I'd had to bully her every day into putting on her seat-belt. I sat in a daze, praying that she'd be all right.

I'd been so looking forward to meeting up with Granny in La Grasse. At eighty she was still capable of handstands and cart-wheels, she still went off on walking holidays, her marbles and her muscles both in perfect form. There had always seemed to be something immortal about her; I couldn't conceive of her not being around.

I found my paints and spent the afternoon making a card for her. It was a picture of us – a fat brown donkey, a fierce black Dobermann, a tail-wagging George and a much-slimmer-than-life me walking along a country lane. In the evening I rang home again and spoke to Mum. Granny was much improved today, she said; she was over the worst. No one knew how serious the effects of the head injuries would be, only time would tell, but she was well enough to recognize and shout at Mum, so it sounded as if she'd soon be back on form.

Now that Granny wasn't joining me, I felt slightly lost and aimless. I was dying to reach Italy; July was not the right time to be in Provence – there were tourists everywhere and the heat was almost unbearable. But the Alpes Maritimes lay ahead and I knew it would take nearly two weeks to cover the next 100 kilometres.

I did my best to keep off the beaten track and had a good walk the next day down the Ribeirotte and Carami valleys. My camp that night was at a beautiful old farm near the Lac de Carces. It was run by a lady of about fifty, who invited me inside and gave me a glass of wine while she sold me some eggs and a (dead) chicken. She told me that her son used to go out with a girl called Sally from Cleveland – did I know Cleveland? – and would my donkey like some hay? She gave me a whole bale for Hannibal and showed me a place to camp down by the river, underneath a huge tree where I hung my hammock. For once I had time to cook a proper meal, but it turned out to be the dogs' lucky night – my Calor gas ran out before I'd even added the meat to the pan, so they got the whole chicken.

The next day was the hottest yet. I breakfasted at the tiny village of le Thoronet and longed to stop but was tempted on by the promise of a swim in the Argens, just a couple of miles away; I hadn't had a proper wash since Thursday and I smelt terrible. I dunked my head in the village fountain and walked on, reminding myself to buy a new hat when I was next in a town – Hannibal had eaten so much of mine that it was virtually useless.

When I reached the river I groaned. It was green and stagnant and stank even more than I did. I walked down the small road that ran alongside it, hoping at least for a cool spot for a siesta, and pulled over to the edge as I heard a car approaching behind us. As it passed I saw a GB sticker on its boot and I waved madly as I always did when I saw a British car. About 100 yards in front of me it turned left up a steep drive and disappeared.

Sweat was dribbling down my back and my legs stuck together as I walked. What the hell, I thought, they can only say no. I tied Hannibal and walked up the drive, wondering if I'd lost all sense of decency as I knocked on the door of a smart stone house. It was opened by a nice-looking man of about forty, who looked at me expectantly. Here goes, I thought.

'I'm very sorry to bother you, but my name is Sophie Thurnham and I'm English and I'm on my way to Rome with my donkey and my dogs and I'm collecting money for MENCAP, and have you got a shower that I could use for five minutes please?'

He looked completely astounded, but to my surprise said yes and invited me inside. The bathroom was the most luxurious five square yards I'd seen for months; it even had a real bath. I longed to soak in it for hours, but I'd promised to be quick so thought I'd better just have a shower. It was bliss as the heat drained out of me and I saw the water running down the plughole gradually turn from brown to clear. I came out feeling refreshed and grateful.

They were a kind and unpretentious family, and when they asked me to stay for lunch I gladly accepted. In the afternoon we swam in the pool and I even sunbathed for a while, feeling acutely conscious of my snow-white stomach and thighs; they looked so silly next to the mahogany brown of my legs and arms.

Leaving the Argens valley, I headed up into the Malvoisin, the forested hills behind Fréjus, reaching the pretty hilltop village of Bagnols-en-Forêt on Wednesday 19 July. After watering the animals, I went into an ironmonger's shop to ask if they sold camping gas.

'Are you English?' asked the tall, thin, grey-haired gentleman behind the counter in a very smart colonial accent. It took me by surprise – you don't expect ironmongers in small French villages to be English. We chatted for a while and he told me that there were quite a few English people living in the village.

I then went to the baker's and discovered the best bread in France. The oven was a huge black cavern in the wall and I stood watching in fascination as the baker pulled the bread in and out on long poles, stoked up the fire and pushed in more wood from a pile at the back of the room. When he noticed me, he shook my hands and welcomed me inside, insisting that I taste the batch of bread that he'd just brought out of the oven. Some more people arrived, all villagers and friends of his; he introduced them to me and then produced a tray of pâté and cheese. As he asked me about what I was doing and I told everyone the story of my travels, he opened a bottle of delicious red wine and we all sat round drinking and tucking into the food. No one seemed to have anything else to do and they acted as if I was the most interesting person in the world.

An hour and two bottles of wine later I finally said goodbye. It was too hot to walk any further till the sun began to go down, so I put Hannibal in a sheltered grassy area below the village, then returned up the hill with my diary to sit in one of the cafés for a few hours.

As I passed a knick-knack shop, I bumped into the English man I'd met earlier.

'Oh, hello again! Still here?' he said. 'We were just going for a drink; would you like to join us?'

Behind him was a large man with bright blue eyes and a friendly face, who looked vaguely familiar.

'That would be lovely,' I said, and we walked up to the square. I kept looking surreptitiously at his friend; I was sure I'd met him before somewhere, but couldn't begin to think where. He was English too and spoke with a slight Lancashire accent; who could he be?

He asked me where I came from, and when I said Crook in Cumbria, he stopped and looked at me in astonishment.

'What's your name?' he asked. As I was about to reply, it suddenly clicked.

'Mr Hindle!' I cried, and rushed up and gave him a kiss.

For many years Peter Hindle had been the landlord of the Sun Inn at Crook, about half a mile away from where we lived. My first-ever job was in his kitchen, washing up while my elder sister helped with the cooking. About three years ago Mrs Hindle died suddenly and Mr Hindle went to France, needing time and space to come to terms with his loss. We'd heard the odd word of him through his children, but no one really seemed to know where he was or what he was doing.

Now I'd found him!

The last ten days of July I look back on as a time of complete madness, but I probably wouldn't change a thing if I had to do it all again. Mr Hindle and Bruce somehow persuaded me to undertake a massive MENCAP money-raising campaign along the Côte d'Azur. The coast was the shortest and quickest way to reach Italy, and I decided that if I was going to suffer the huge number of tourists that such a route would entail, I might as well get some money out of them.

I spent three days in Bagnols organizing the plans and enjoying Mr Hindle's hospitality. He spoilt me, taking me out to excellent restaurants and driving me for miles around the area as we devised my route and tried to find camping places for the week ahead. He suggested I ring Radio Riviera, the English-speaking station that operates from Monte Carlo. They were very enthusiastic and agreed to give me coverage every morning to let listeners know where I would be if they wanted to give donations, and they invited me to come for a proper interview when I reached Monaco.

We made two large white placards to tie on each side of Hannibal, explaining in brightly painted letters what I was raising money for. Mr Hindle found some small plastic buckets for putting coins into and bought balloons and ribbons to add to the festive spirit.

We checked with the police about the legality of my plans and discovered that I needed proof of authenticity regarding the charity I was collecting for. I rummaged through my papers, but was told nothing I had was good enough – it had to be in *French,* they said. So I rang MENCAP, who immediately faxed a bilingual letter of authorization out to me.

I also went to a veterinary clinic in Fréjus to check on regulations for the border crossing into Italy. They confirmed what I'd been told back in February by the Ministry of Agriculture in Paris – that all I needed for Hannibal was a certificate of good health obtainable from a registered vet at any of the towns near the border.

On Sunday morning I set off as early as possible to avoid the traffic and reached Mandelieu by eleven. This was as close to Cannes as I wanted to camp, so I set about looking for somewhere to stay, putting on my MENCAP slogans and placards to attract sympathy. But I was unprepared for the hostility I provoked; the first two sites gave a definite 'no' to my request, even though both were advertising vacancies, and the second said that his reaction was because I was collecting for charity – his campers didn't want to be 'begged at' by the likes of me.

I stiffened the old upper lip and headed for the hills instead. On the northern edge of the town I came across a huge camp site that was barely half full, and I tried again. Tying the animals outside the office, I was about to enter when an old man stormed to the doorway, furiously shouting at me.

'Get out! Go away!' he yelled. 'I do not allow any animals here!'
'But I'm . . .'
He didn't wait to listen and slammed the door in my face. I turned and walked away, feeling hot and miserable, but after I'd gone about thirty yards I heard a voice calling me.

'*Mademoiselle! Arrêtez-vous, s'il vous plaît!*' A pretty blonde woman of about thirty was running towards me from the direction of the office. When she reached me she apologized for the behaviour of the owner, saying he was a stupid old man whom none of them liked. If I promised to be discreet, she could show me somewhere to camp. She led me to a large area of rough ground hidden behind trees and bushes, showing me a large gap in the

167

fence where we could all climb through. It was a perfect camp – there was water, privacy, even grazing for Hannibal, and I didn't have to pay a penny for it.

I woke up to a cold grey Monday morning and set off for Cannes, but I was rather behind schedule when I eventually found a phone to call Riviera Radio for my five minutes on air. In the meantime, I missed my rendezvous with Mr Hindle, who'd driven over with all the money-raising equipment – placards, buckets and balloons. There was chaos while he called out the police to look for a missing girl with a donkey. Finally we found each other and by ten o'clock we were ready to go. I was wearing my brightest clothes and biggest smile, and was determined to raise at least £100 before the day was out. We set off, calling out cheery greetings to passers-by, shaking our buckets and MENCAP tins, pointing out the placards and the banners.

I'd never collected money on the street before; the closest I'd come to it was electioneering for my father, which was a doddle in comparison. A few people crossed the street to get away from us; a few showed some interest, then turned away when they'd read the placard; and a few, just a few, came up with smiles and greetings and put coins in our buckets. The vast majority, however, simply ignored us. I couldn't believe it. For nearly five months I'd been longing for people to ignore me and act as if I was nothing out of the ordinary; but now, the one time when I was making a special effort to make an exhibition of myself, when I actually *wanted* crowds round me asking where I was going and what I was doing, I'd become invisible.

I was determined not to be depressed by it and as we made our way across the Croisette, something happened which cheered me up enormously. I saw a very good-looking young man come running in our direction and suddenly realized that it was me he was heading for.

'Are you called Sophie?' he asked. As I nodded, he told me that he was Pete, Polly Anderson's boyfriend, and he'd heard all about me from Polly, Polly and Rose. He'd just come off the train from Lodève, and when he saw me he'd thought there couldn't possibly be *two* girls wandering round France with a donkey. He was gorgeous; I now understood all those sighs of Polly's and wished I didn't have to say goodbye so soon.

As Mr Hindle and I continued along the Croisette, it began to drizzle. No one was about and the paint on my beautiful placards was dribbling, so we decided to call it a day. Mr Hindle took the placards in his car and we agreed to meet at Golfe-Juan for an afternoon fund-raising session on the beaches.

By the time I reached Golfe-Juan it was raining hard. The beaches and promenades were deserted. Hanny and the dogs were looking miserable, so I found a field just off the main road and left the animals sheltering under a huge oak tree while Mr Hindle and I did the only thing possible in the circumstances – sat down for a huge meal on the sea front. It cost far more than what we'd collected for MENCAP that morning, but it raised my spirits.

There was a thunderstorm during the night, but I felt safe under the oak tree, the dogs and donkey by my side, and not a drop of rain touched me. The morning was bright and sunny, and I set off with renewed vigour, determined to make up for yesterday's disaster. I had a surprising amount of success and by the end of the day my MENCAP tin was full. Nevertheless, the majority of people treated me like a leper. It's horrible remembering the filthy looks I was given as I shook my tin, the comments of, 'How do we know you're not going to just spend the money on yourself?', the accusations of cruelly abusing my animals. The worst were those with video cameras who spent up to five minutes filming us with their expensive equipment, but wouldn't put a penny in my bucket.

I was stopped by the police, once in Golfe-Juan and twice in Antibes, and they were horrible, appearing almost disappointed when I produced my letter of authorization. Usually beggars are locked up for the night, they said.

Yet the donations I did receive made up a million times for all the nastiness. I can't describe how good it felt when people came up with a large sum of money and told me they thought what I was doing was wonderful. The children and young people were always the best, and the British I met were almost always encouraging and generous; I'll never forget the group of inter-railers from Lancashire who gave me their entire evening's beer money. It seemed an enormous sacrifice when the bars alongside us were brimming with far wealthier tourists, who happily paid 100 francs for a gin and tonic but told me to bugger off and stop spoiling their view when I asked for contributions.

The best place was the beach at Antibes. I went there in the hope that Hannibal might give donkey rides, but all he did was roll over and over in the sand. He attracted a huge crowd of children, though, who were lovely and ran back to their parents for money to put in the buckets. I also met an English photographer who took numerous pictures of us and gave me the address of the farm where he was staying. They trained trotting horses there, so he was sure they'd either let me stay or know where I could go. This was a great relief, and as the sun began to sink I put away my paraphernalia and set off up the pebbled beach of the Baie des Anges.

The photographer's friends were a great couple, an English girl and a French guy whose father owned the farm. They invited me inside for supper and insisted I have a real bed for the night. They were the first people I'd come across for ages who didn't treat me as if I was mad; they just thought that what I was doing sounded fun and gave me all the help they could. We sat up for hours counting the day's gatherings, finding far more centimes than francs, but even so it was a rewarding amount, almost £100, and I felt very pleased.

It was unbearably hot on Wednesday as we walked on the main road up to Cagnes-sur-Mer. The dogs were unhappy at being on leads all day and I wished I'd never started on this coastal route. The only one of us who seemed to be enjoying himself was Hannibal, who practically trotted along the flat roads and loved all the attention he was getting from passers-by.

Shortly after we stopped for a rest at midday a car pulled up and two men from *Nice Matin*, the local paper, introduced themselves; I needed as much publicity as possible, so I spent quite an amusing half hour answering their questions and posing with Hannibal for the camera. Soon afterwards two ladies in a smart car stopped beside me and came out to fuss over the animals. I suppose they meant well, but at the time I found their behaviour very insulting. They were animal-lovers of a type I thought were exclusive to England – convinced that every animal other than their own is badly treated.

'Poor little things! Have you nowhere to live?' they asked me. 'How terrible! You just walk all day? How awful for you!'

They told me they both owned horses and knew how much animals suffered from the heat at this time of year. After about ten minutes they shut up long enough for me to ask them the way to the Hippodrome where I'd been told I could find a farrier.

The younger lady went over to Hannibal, picked up one of his front hooves and gasped.

'Oh yes,' she said. 'They are in a terrible state. We must take him to a vet at once.'

I panicked. Poor Hannibal – I hadn't even noticed anything was wrong. For that matter nor had anyone who'd looked at his feet at the horse farm last night, but I was too worried to remember that. The younger one offered to accompany me while the older lady drove the long way round in her car.

The Hippodrome was a massive stadium that stables hundreds of horses, situated right by the sea. It was three o'clock, so few people or horses were about. We walked down the shaded road leading towards the hospital block and tried to chat. When we were nearly there, she suddenly asked me how long Hannibal's foot had been bleeding.

'Bleeding?' I replied in horror, stopping to look at his feet.

I suppose it was cruel of me, but I laughed for a long time at the silly cow who had made me feel so guilty. That morning we had walked past some orchards and Hannibal had walked along grabbing at the fruit rotting on the road. As I now inspected his hoof, I saw that a deep-red plum had got stuck to the sole. This woman must have presumed it was a bloody sore.

I felt indescribably relieved and my confidence suddenly returned. My animals were well treated and I swore no one would intimidate me like that again.

Chapter 23
Donkey Smuggling

There are two full-time vets at the Hippodrome in Cagnes-sur-Mer; both were in the middle of a crisis when I arrived on 26 July, trying to save the life of a very valuable horse with colic, so they told me to put Hanny in one of the three stables next to the surgery and wait. One of them returned briefly at about eight in the evening, saying I was welcome to stay the night there and he'd try to find me a farrier in the morning.

All the Hippodrome farriers, however, proved to be either too busy or unwilling to come and shoe a donkey, and it was the Palmers who found one for me. I met Nicky Palmer and her mother, Diane, when they came to visit Nicky's pony, Nana, who was in the stable next to Hannibal having tests. Diane reminded me of my own mother ten years earlier, spending the entire summer holidays ferrying her children about in different directions – Jonathan to windsurfing, Nicky to her ponies and now me in and out of Cagnes-sur-Mer.

When, two days later, I was still waiting with a barefoot Hannibal, Diane arranged for their own blacksmith to come the next morning. He made the most beautiful little shoes I've ever seen and he wouldn't let me pay anything for them.

By now, however, I'd discovered I had a major problem to overcome. The French Ministry of Agriculture, the Italian Embassy in London and the vet I'd seen in Fréjus had all failed to inform me of two vital requirements in order to get a certificate of good health for Hannibal to enter Italy: the donkey must have had a blood test for equine anaemia not more than one month prior to departure, and it must have spent the previous month at a specific address known to be free of any animal with equine anaemia.

In other words, there was no way I could legally travel by foot through France to Italy with an equine. I was devastated – all my plans and my dreams were suddenly in jeopardy.

Everyone at the Hippodrome rallied round and some were even prepared to put their jobs on the line by faking papers for me. Many said they would certify that I'd been staying on their land for a month, but the problem lay in the blood test – it can only be done in Paris and took about three weeks at that time of year. The stable boys advised me to cross into Italy through the mountains. They marked on my map the routes where I wouldn't meet a soul, recommending that as soon as I was in Italy I should tell everyone that Hannibal was an Italian donkey and that we'd been travelling through the mountains from Turin.

During the days when these plans were taking shape, the Palmers ferried me about, fed me, let me sleep in their spare room and wash in their shower – they gave me a beautiful taste of family life.

On Saturday I rather reluctantly resumed my journey. I had to reach the other side of Nice before I could stop to camp and it was the hottest day of the whole summer; sweat poured off me and I felt tired and irritable, longing to jump into the sea just a few yards to my right; but I couldn't leave the animals and I didn't have time.

After about an hour of walking, a horrible, little French man of about fifty began following me, saying, 'You're cruel and your donkey is going to die. The sun is too strong. He's going to die. You are horrible and ignorant, your donkey is going to die.'

I thought I was going to go mad. I kept screaming at him to leave me alone, but he wouldn't. I felt hotter and hotter and more and more angry. Hanny was the one who *could* cope with the heat (I knew that if he wasn't happy he wouldn't be walking so well beside me); it was the dogs and I who were about to collapse.

I stupidly tried to cross the main road to get away from him, but Hanny didn't like the idea and we brought two lanes of traffic to a standstill as he suddenly decided he was frightened and wasn't going to walk another inch. The horrible man came and stood with us in the middle of the road and we must have made a farcical scene. He was still telling me my donkey was dying and what a bitch I was, while I screamed at him to go away, simultaneously trying to cajole Hanny into moving to the side of the road.

A car hooted very loudly and Hannibal leapt into action, shedding his pack all over the road as he jumped on to the pavement and sending two stands of postcards flying in opposite directions. It was a nightmare; the chorus of disapproval yelling at me now included the furious shopkeeper and his wife, plus the drivers I was blocking, and the horrible man who'd driven me into this fiasco.

Once again the English community proved to be my saviours. The London-born owners of a restaurant-bar on the sea front came to my rescue, letting me tie Hanny in the shade of their terrace and insisting that the dogs and I come inside. They fed and watered us all, and gave me the mental and physical boost I needed to get through the afternoon. We continued along the main road, past Nice airport, where Hannibal was surprisingly calm and brave, then along the Promenade des Anglais, where I was stopped by the police three times for 'begging'.

We climbed up on to the Cap de Nice as darkness fell, camping in rough ground below Mont Boron. I remember sinking my teeth into a banana and chocolate spread sandwich and deciding no supper had ever tasted so good. The sooner I returned to the hills again, the better. We had a hell of a night, caused by the huge flashing light of the Cap Ferrat lighthouse that swept constantly across the bay and sent Hannibal into something close to a fit. There was nowhere I could take him where he couldn't see it, so I kept having to get up and calm him. This was one of the rare times when I was scared of him, for he was too frightened to know what he was doing and kept rearing up on me.

Sunday's walk was better; east of Nice is nothing like as developed and the villages we passed still retained something of their traditional character. We stopped for the night at Eze-sur-Mer, where a group of locals told me that I would never be allowed into Monaco the next day.

'They simply don't let undesirables in,' they said. 'Tramps, beggars, hippies, scruffy students . . . They certainly won't let a donkey soil their precious streets.'

The alternative to following the coast through Monaco meant climbing thousands of feet up on to the rock above – three days' walk instead of one – but apart from that, I *wanted* to go to Monaco. I was meant to be giving an interview at the radio station in Monte Carlo and I hoped to collect a fortune for MENCAP by standing outside the casino for a few hours.

Determined that no one would be able to describe me as an undesirable, I spent Sunday evening transforming our image. I plaited some coloured ribbons into new dog leads and a halter for Hannibal; I took the saddle bags into the sea and scrubbed and scrubbed at them until they looked cleaner than they had for months. In the morning I brushed Hannibal's and the dogs' coats and my own hair until we all shone; I put on my best dress and some make-up, and tied my hair back with a big red ribbon. We set off looking as if we were entering a best-dressed-pets competition.

Sure enough, we were descended upon by six policemen as soon as we'd crossed the Monaco border and with their hands on their guns they told me I must turn back. I stood my ground and made such a fuss that they eventually relented. I threw everyone's name at them that I could think of: the Queen Mother was supporting my journey (she's patron of MENCAP, so it was almost true), Maggie Thatcher would hear of this (well, she might have done), and I demanded to see Prince Rainier before I'd let them take me away. After ten minutes they said I could carry on, as long as I walked straight through and didn't try to collect money. Two of them came with me, one on each side, to make sure I did as I was told.

They let me take a detour to Monte Carlo Radio for my interview, but said I couldn't leave the animals outside the building, so I had to speak into a tape recorder on the pavement.

Monaco was disappointing. It was full of rather grotty apartment blocks with most of their shutters closed. The shops were no more chic and glamorous than those of Cannes and Nice, and it had considerably less character. I looked up at the Pink Palace and decided that Prince Albert could find another wife.

We reached France again in less than two hours (Monaco is *tiny*) and the policemen wished me well. I'd been angry at first when they wouldn't let me shake my MENCAP tin at everyone we passed, but once I'd put it away they were friendly and helpful, clearing traffic for me to cross the roads and showing me the best way through the town. They told me that no one is allowed to collect money without permission from the Prince; I wished I'd known earlier and I would have tried to get it.

I spent the night at a camp site in Cap Martin and on Tuesday climbed up behind Menton into the hills, immediately realizing how quick coastal walking had been, despite all its faults. We camped by the graveyard in Castellar, a beautiful Provençal village, where I bought my last supplies of lavender water and felt sad that I'd be leaving this country the next day. France had surprised me; I'd never expected to feel such an affinity for it.

I set off early on Wednesday, up a steep tarmac track to the farm by the St Bernard chapel, then along a well-used path through cool, shaded woods to the Col d'Albarée. It was bliss to feel so alone, to be away from the crowds at last. We reached meadowland, grazed by alpine cows with huge bells round their necks, and parted company with the main path as we turned east towards Mont Grammont and the Col de Treitore. As we struggled up the final climb I looked at the figures on the map and realized that this pass, the first way across the Alps after the Mediterranean, was already higher than Ben Nevis and I felt very proud of myself.

We finally reached the top at about four o'clock and I stood on what I reckoned must be the border and looked before me in amazement – a vast, mountainous wilderness stretched on and on for what seemed like hundreds of miles. I tried to pick out the route I'd planned, but as I scanned my surroundings I noticed something else that made my hair stand on end: forest fires. I could see three of them – one in front, one behind and one further inland. None were very close, but they terrified me.

I'd heard about recent forest fire problems on the radio; apparently, most of the planes were fighting huge fires in Corsica, leaving too few to cope with the Riviera's blazes. I looked at the three around me and there was no doubt in my mind: I was heading back to the coast. The thought of getting caught up in a forest fire with the animals was too horrific to contemplate.

In usual Hannibal style we charged down the Italian side of Grammondo at top speed. The first sign I had to confirm that we really were on Italian soil was a large notice from the Regional Tourist Board of Liguria informing me that all hunting and shooting was strictly prohibited. It was full of bullet holes!

We camped on the path, since there was nowhere else flat enough, and I sat listening to the Italian channels on my radio, trying to remember the language and wishing that I could stop thinking in French. A wasp flew into my bottle of wine without my noticing and stung me when I next took a swig. Luckily, I didn't swallow it, but it got me on the inside of my bottom lip and the next morning I could hardly talk; it was agony and I looked extraordinarily ugly.

The path pitched steeply and suddenly down towards the village of Torri and I began to feel very nervous, sure that a customs officer would be waiting for me. We passed some farms and pretty little cottages, then hit the concrete road leading to the village; some people called out to me in greeting and I waved back, trying not to look as guilty as I felt. Suddenly I panicked: I saw a man in blue uniform coming up the road towards me on a motorbike. This was it, I thought; someone's reported me. I stood still and tried to think of a defence, my heart in my mouth.

As he rode past, and as I saw the letters and parcels in the basket at the back of his bike I felt very stupid. Trying to calm down, I reasoned that I was in Italy now, so theoretically no one could prove that Hanny wasn't Italian. Even so, I kept my mouth shut as I walked through the village, deciding it was better just to smile and pretend I couldn't speak Italian rather than lie.

We walked down the Bevera valley, through Calvo and past quarries and marshy bamboo fields, then followed the Roia River down towards Ventimiglia. I wished there was a way I could hit the coast further away from the border, but there was no bridge across the river so I had no choice. As we approached the motorway I made out a building, and as I realized what it was I wanted to curl up and die; the customs stopping point was directly above where my little road went underneath the motorway. We were miles from the border and I hadn't expected this at all. My heart was beating nineteen to the dozen as we came into full view of the building; I was convinced that someone would come down to check my papers. I tried to make myself look as Italian and peasant-like as possible, covering my legs with one of Hannibal's hessian sacks and hiding all my fair hair well under my hat. To my enormous surprise, no one called out to me to stop and as we walked out of sight on the other side I felt euphoric, as if I'd just got away with murder.

The owner of a camp site near the sea at Bordighera allowed me to stay in his own private garden. The dogs and I went for a swim, then I sat on the beach, having my last look at France and enjoying the feel of Italian sand beneath my feet. For a while I'd thought I'd never get here; not only that, but it was 3 August and despite the delays of the past few days I was on schedule. I'd rung home from the camp site and discovered that Clare was coming out to join me again in a week's time; this news made me feel incredibly happy, for I'd feared that Clare had hated her trip to Spain. If she was willing to take a second dose of punishment, she must have enjoyed it, and I couldn't wait to see her again.

My donkey was shod, my dogs were well and I was about to start the final stage of my journey. Apart from the great lump on my mouth, life could not have been better.

Italy

Chapter 24
Rivieras and Revederes

I didn't mean to, but I stuck to the coast for nearly a week and found I was enjoying myself. I was able to cover an enormous distance each day by keeping away from the mountains, and it was addictive to see the inches on the map slip by so fast.

I find it hard to explain why I loved the atmosphere of the Italian Riviera. The crowds were just as thick as those in Nice and Monaco, but their make up was different; I'd left behind the international jet-set of the Côte d'Azur and found myself among ordinary Italian families.

We kept mainly to the Via Aurelia, the busy road that follows the coast, although there were often pedestrian promenades closer to the shore where the dogs could walk free. The coastal towns and villages have been developed relentlessly and if I'd been driving through in ordinary circumstances, I would probably have thought it tragically spoilt by concrete apartment blocks and countless cheap bistros. But in my present circumstances those bistros meant affordable bowls of delicious seafood spaghetti and handsome waiters tirelessly chatting me up; those grotty flats meant children waving out of open windows, then running down on to the street and demanding that I stop to give them rides on my *asino*. The qualities of the people more than made up for the ugliness of the buildings around them.

Contrary to my expectations, these people proved to be far more generous than the affluent crowds on the French Riviera. Suddenly, the average contribution leapt from one franc to 2000 lire; but more importantly, I found little of the depressing scepticism that I'd encountered in France. I no longer felt like a beggar; even the police smiled at me and helped me across road junctions in a way that had never happened in France.

Perhaps it was because I wasn't trying so hard. I wanted to cover as much distance as possible before Clare's arrival, so I wasn't concentrating on raising money and it upset me less when people ignored me. In fact, I smiled more, which I'd already learned was by far the best way to open purses. Maybe Hannibal's new Italian placards helped; they were created by a group of children I'd met at a camp site and were phrased less formally than the ones I'd used in France. *'La Grande Promenade à l'Ane de l'Espagne à Rome pour aider MENCAP'* gave way to *'Sto andando a Roma da cinque mesi con i miei tre amici per aiutare i portatori di handicap – per favore, aiutarme ad aiutarli'* (I've been walking to Rome for five months with my three friends to help the handicapped – please help me to help them), and it seemed to strike the right note. I was made to feel proud of what I was doing.

Everyone had warned me that Italian men would be the worst of all, yet with a few exceptions I found myself rather enjoying the attention. Italian lechery wore a smile on its face, and it was difficult to take offence; *'Ciao, bella,* I think you are absolutely beautiful and I want to go to bed with you' was meant as a compliment, not a threat, and none of them seemed to expect me to say yes. I felt safe with so many people everywhere and could occasionally afford to flirt back, which was great. Their taste was appalling, though – just a few yards away on the beaches were beautiful women wandering round in G-strings. I was just a big smelly girl in fell boots.

Since everyone else was baring flesh, I felt that I could safely bare more of myself to the sun without being considered provocative. I ripped the back out of my MENCAP T-shirt so that I could wear it as a halter-neck and my back and shoulders soon turned as brown as the rest of me. I began taking a pride in my looks again and spent more time and effort than usual in making sure that my clothes were clean and my hair was brushed; I even bothered to put a bit of make-up on in the morning. It probably all sweated off within a few hours, but at least I tried.

I have some lovely memories of this time and it stands out as being very different from any other part of my walk. The larger towns we passed through, San Remo and Imperia, Albenga and Alassio, I liked; their historical centres had been well preserved and the hotels and parks had a smart, turn-of-the-century air. The stretches between the towns were filled with huge glasshouses of flowers; not an inch of flat land between the mountains and the sea was wasted, and everything was colourful – even the grass in the parks was a brighter green than anything I'd seen before. It grew in strange, thick blades and Hannibal hated it.

Hannibal walked very well on the whole – he always preferred roads to mountain tracks – and on the straights the dogs took it in turns to ride on his back. This was too tricky an operation to manage on a slope, but with nothing else to worry about as we plodded along the Via Aurelia it was rather fun and gave George and Bogey's feet a rest from the hot tarmac. Hanny didn't seem to mind the dogs' extra weight, because I was eating out more often and he had fewer supplies to carry.

I managed to find shops selling hay, so feeding him wasn't too much of a problem, and bakeries were usually very generous with their stale bread. Italian dog food, however, was rather peculiar; the most common kind consisted of macaroni with dried pieces of meat, but George and Bogey just stared at their bowls in horror and refused even to try it. Fresh meat cost a fortune – liver was more than £3 a pound – so I was forced to buy tinned stuff, but according to my two-dog testing panel it tasted even worse than the French brands.

At night we stayed at camp sites which, although fully booked, never turned us away and never charged me. The tents were always tightly jammed together, with barely a foot between them, but the atmosphere was fantastic. The sites were family-centred, having excellent restaurants, shops and bars, plus evening entertainments where grannies and teenagers bopped together to Kylie and Jason.

Most of the people I met asked the usual questions: where did I come from, what was I doing, why was I doing it. Usually I gave my stock set of answers, but a few conversations stick in my mind. While I was eating my lunch in the central gardens in San Remo an old lady came to talk to me. She was greatly concerned at my not being married and jumped to the conclusion that I was walking through Europe in order to find myself a husband. 'Don't you like English men?' she asked.

Italians especially seemed to find it impossible to understand my enjoyment of solitude. From the men this was partly a joke – how could I possibly go for so long without a boyfriend? they asked, insisting that after five months I must be *desperate* for it – but many people simply thought I must be mad to be travelling voluntarily on my own, thousands of miles from friends and family. Perhaps this partly explains why the MENCAP donations here were so much greater: they thought I was making an enormous sacrifice solely to raise money, for they could think of no other reason for wanting to walk 3000 kilometres alone.

This Italian interlude wasn't without its disasters. In Imperia we caused a terrible traffic jam when a policeman blew his whistle and caused Hannibal to come to a sudden stop in the middle of a major junction. Cars hooted their horns, men swore at us, women screamed, and Hannibal grew more and more terrified; then the traffic simultaneously decided it had had enough and charged round us, leaving us stuck in the middle. We were there for five minutes before the policeman summoned three colleagues to stop the cars long enough for me to persuade Hannibal to walk to the pavement.

Tunnels were a constant problem and one that blindfolds could not solve. It was the strange echoes that frightened Hannibal, and short of putting in ear plugs, there was little I could do to help him. With constant reassurance he would eventually and nervously walk through them, usually without mishap – until we met the lorry.

I'd become used to traffic honking their horns at us – neither the Spanish, the French, nor the Italians seemed to have any idea of the nervousness of equines, and cars constantly hooted in friendly greeting. It was pointless getting annoyed and usually I just waved back, while thanking God that neither of my donkeys reacted to it. Until the tunnel, that is.

It was a huge tanker that did the damage. The driver yelled something I couldn't understand through his open window and hit the horn. The effect even frightened *me:* it was a long tunnel and the noise reverberated deafeningly. Hannibal reared, the pack saddle flew off his back into the middle of the road and he careered forwards, dragging me and the dogs after him to the tunnel's end. The saddle bags were blocking the road and a chorus of hoots behind us only terrified him more. Luckily, he calmed down once he was in the open air. I tied him to a tree near the road and ran back for the bags, receiving a torrent of abuse from a queue of about thirty waiting cars.

On Tuesday 8 August I headed inland. Clare was flying out the next day and I'd arranged to meet her at four o'clock at the railway station in Altare, about twenty kilometres west of Savona.

As soon as I began climbing into the steep, thickly wooded mountains I wondered why on earth I'd stayed at the coast for so long. The concrete apartments and cramped camp sites were replaced by unspoilt countryside dotted with tiny old villages. Many of the houses were holiday homes and at this time of year the villages turned into thriving, friendly communities – in winter it was dead, the young people told me.

In the first village I reached, Verrezzi, an old lady invited me to join her family for lunch. I followed her into a tiny house full of people of all ages. They were all vaguely related, they told me, and lived in different parts of northern Italy, but each year as many of them as could fit would escape the heat of the cities and come to this house which their family had owned for generations. The old lady's parents had lived here, but now it was used only in the summer; its facilities were very basic, but they said that a sink on the balcony and a loo shared with the house next door were all they needed for such a short time.

We had a deliciously simple lunch – spaghetti, plainly cooked, with rosemary-flavoured olive oil and garlic which we added ourselves, followed by baked onions, salami, tomatoes, bread, fruit . . . We ate slowly and lazily, and children came and went as they pleased. I felt greatly envious of this relaxed culture; I just couldn't imagine it happening in England.

The family wanted to take a photo of me with my animals and brought out a contraption that looked as if it was made in the last century; you had to look into it from above and push shutters in and out; I couldn't believe it really worked. Then the old lady ordered one of the younger men to lead me along an ancient, stone-stepped path from the village to an old church at the top of the mountain. From there he showed me a short cut to Eze, down in the next valley.

The gradients were exhausting and I began to worry about reaching Clare by four o'clock the next day. I didn't stop walking till it was dark and set off again as soon as I could in the morning, climbing up the steep road from Carbuta to the Pian di Corsi and hoping I'd reach the top before it became too hot.

The mountains were so beautiful that they took my breath away; ridge after ridge stretched to the horizon, covered in ancient forest of chestnut and pine that smelt delicious and shielded us from the sun. The dogs were in heaven, for we passed only one car all day, but Hannibal was being difficult; he was furious to find that climbing uphill was not a thing of the past after all and was pursuing his old 'six steps' policy, demanding a rest every three yards. As before, I ended up carrying half the bags.

The ridge-top road marked on my map from the Pian di Corsi to Monte Alto didn't exist. I searched and searched for it, but there was nothing, so I had no option but to walk the long way round via the Bormida valley – an extra fifteen kilometres. Despite Hannibal's speedy downhill trot, I knew there was no way I'd be at Altare by four, for it was already past two by the time we reached the tiny village of Pian Soprano, with eighteen kilometres still to go.

Finding a bus stop, to my enormous relief I saw that there was a bus due at half past three direct to Altare, arriving at five minutes past four – perfect. I looked around for somewhere to leave the animals and decided to ask at the big, smart house I'd first passed at the top of the village, which had a barn below it; and hopefully it owned some of the meadowland by the river. The old lady who answered my knock seemed very flustered by us; she told me to wait while she fetched someone and came back with Valeria, a girl of my age from the village, who could speak English. With Valeria as interpreter, she told me it was fine to leave my dogs in the barn and my donkey tethered by the river while I went down to Altare to meet my friend.

Valeria invited me to have lunch with her family while I was waiting for the bus. After the meal we began talking about my meeting with Clare and Valeria asked me how my friend was reaching Altare.

'By train from Savona,' I replied, but one look at Valeria's face told me that all was not well with my plans.

'But there are only two trains a day from Savona to Altare,' she said, 'one in the morning and one at about eight o'clock in the evening. To reach Altare by four she would have to go all the way to San Giuseppe and then catch a stopping train in the other direction.'

Oh, no! On the map it had looked like a major line, so I'd presumed there'd be a train every few hours. Clare couldn't speak Italian and would never be able to work out the San Giuseppe route, and it would take hours even if she did. Valeria saved the day; we'd drive to Savona, she said, and meet Clare's train from Genova.

We stopped at Altare on the way but there was no sign of Clare, so we hurtled on to Savona and ran to the information office to ask if an English girl had been enquiring about connections to Altare. No, they said, so I set about meeting every train from Genova. Clare wasn't on any of them and as the clock ticked its way round past five I grew increasingly worried. At last I phoned Altare station to ask if there was a Miss Clare Turnbull waiting; I wasn't particularly hopeful, but I suddenly heard a rather nervous, confused voice saying, 'Hello?'

'Clare! Are you all right?' I screamed.

'Of course I'm all right!' she said. 'Where the hell are you?'

She'd taken a taxi (a practical solution that hadn't even crossed my mind) and had reached Altare at exactly four o'clock.

Two hours later I arrived back at Altare and found Clare sitting under a tree outside the station, looking blonde and beautiful in a pink cotton dress and espadrilles. I rushed up to greet her, realizing too late how incredibly smelly I was – I hadn't washed for two days and I'd climbed 5000 feet in the meantime. She recoiled with her hand over her nose, then burst into laughter as she looked at me.

'Sophie!' she screamed. 'How can you possibly go round with legs like that!'

I hadn't shaved my legs since I was in Majorca in April and fifteen weeks had produced a thick, golden fuzz on my calves that I had grown rather fond of. Few Italian women shaved, and at least mine wasn't black, but over the next week Clare was never able to look at my lower legs without breaking into hysterics.

This second visit was much more the holiday that she had dreamed of when she'd come out the first time. Ever optimistic, she'd again brought a bottle of champagne and some smoked salmon, and this time we really *did* drink and eat with our feet dangling in a sparkling stream as the sun went down over the distant mountains.

Her rucksack was filled with goodies: real Pedigree Chum for the dogs, Polo mints for Hannibal, and for me a huge tin of Ambrosia custard, a much-needed tube of Germolene, some new inners for my Brasher boots and half a dozen Agatha Christies, which were to fill all the week's free moments. Not that there were many – we chatted constantly and I realized how much I'd missed human company. It was good to be able to talk about the sorrow of leaving Bella and the puppies behind, and discussing the more frightening moments of the past months helped me to see the funny side of it all.

Clare was the perfect travelling companion; we'd had our first cooking jobs together in Italy and she went to great lengths reconcocting some of the recipes we'd learned four summers before. We ate like kings, and it was during this time that I rediscovered the joys of wine after two months of relative abstinence in France.

We had a great week, taking life slowly as we walked from village to village, not worrying too much about mileages, concentrating on eating well and finding good places to sunbathe. Altare marked the beginning of the Apennines, the range of mountains that stretches the whole way down to the toe of Italy and which, since I'd wimped out of my attempt to cross the Alps, presented the most challenging walking of my wholé trip. With Clare, though, I wasn't too ambitious and we stuck mainly to small roads, for their gradients were exhausting enough; Hannibal, with two people's supplies, was carrying more weight than usual so it would have been both unfair and unrealistic to have expected any great feats of mountaineering out of him.

Hannibal and Clare took an instant dislike to each other. I think he was jealous that I was spending my time talking and singing with someone else; Clare thought he was lazy and brutish. They brought out the worst in each other – Hannibal kept trying to bite Clare and I hardly dared leave them alone together. It was a complete clash of wills.

Chapter 25
Holiday Highlights

All our camps that week were memorable and we received an extraordinary amount of kindness from the local people, especially the farmers. The farms were tiny and primitive, often consisting of just half a dozen cows. Everyone kept chickens and rabbits, and the villages gave out an air of extreme industriousness, with every inch of available flat land being used. Hay had been cut and gathered by hand and was stored in high, round stacks at regular intervals on the hillsides; considering the effort that had gone into making it, I was astonished by how readily the farmers gave me great sackloads for Hannibal and always refused to accept any payment.

We spent Clare's second night in a barn on a relatively large farm in the softer hills to the north of Altare. We were given not only hay, but a huge bucketful of warm, fresh milk and a litre of home-made wine, which was bright pink and fizzy. It helped dispel my visions of being savaged by wild boars – the farmer told me that '*cinghiali*' were the cause of the ploughed earth outside the barn.

We crossed Montenotte the next day, Friday 11 August, and camped under some huge horse chestnut trees on smooth, well-grazed meadowland above Pontinvrea. I persuaded Clare for the first time to sleep under the stars; it was a hot night and it seemed crazy to put the tent up, so we spread the ground-sheet out to keep our sleeping-bags dry, and sprayed repellent all over ourselves to ward off the insects.

All went well at first and we were just dozing off when Clare suddenly jumped up and swore that something had landed on her – a huge spider, she thought. I told her to stop being so paranoid, but a minute later something fell on me too. I heard movement in the trees above us, then there was a sudden deluge of what felt like little pieces of wood falling down on us. I grabbed the torch and shone it upwards, beginning to laugh as the beam fell on a thick bushy tail. Clare's spiders were little pieces of chestnut shell that an industrious squirrel had been laboriously chipping off his dinner.

At the market in Pontinvrea I bought luxuries like tin-openers, cork insoles and new socks. At lunchtime we had a hairwashing and laundry session in the Rio del Giovo and we looked vaguely clean and respectable as we entered the busy tourist town of Sassello later in the afternoon.

Sassello is a ski resort in winter and the modern, chalet-style houses on the outskirts looked rather out of place. The town itself was beautiful, though, with its steep red roofs and green shutters, cobbled streets and huge church towers. We left the animals by the river and had a drink in one of the cafés in the square, reading the brochure we'd found in the tourist information office. Apparently 'a lot of wallknown peuple' had lived here and many 'ortistic works', such as 'the important pointing of the Croxifission', were 'presewed' in the Perrando Museum. I was interested to discover that England was to blame for the high level of emigration from the region in the last century: 'With the invasion of the bast furnace, the English iron was imposed to the merchants, so people who worked in mines were obliged to leave their jobs and to go in America for a new one.'

We walked through the town being wantonly extravagant, buying mounds of tagliatelli from the fresh pasta shop and treating ourselves to a huge strawberry tart from the bakery. In the newsagents I even found a highlighting kit; I hadn't had my hair done since Majorca and Clare was horrified by the state of my roots.

Early the next morning Clare had one of her rare humour failures. George had been wanting to chase rabbits the night before, so I'd put both dogs on their leads and, since there was nowhere else, I tethered them to the guy rope. At about half past five Bogey and George hurtled off to chase away a stray dog, taking the tent with them. We suddenly woke to find ourselves lying in the open air in the middle of a green meadow, in full view of half the town. Clare's furious swearing only made my giggles worse and she ended up retreating into her sleeping bag like a snail.

Later that morning I received my one and only kick from Hannibal. We were up in the woods to the east of Sassello and he was being badly pestered by horse flies; they were vicious little bastards and attacked him relentlessly, not giving up until they'd drawn blood. They centred on his eyes, his neck and his willy, the last seeming to be the most painful. I wished I could give him a tail extension for he couldn't reach them; instead he tried, unsuccessfully, to kick them away. I tried to swat them and found it quite easy. I was aiming at a particularly large bugger, however, when Hannibal suddenly kicked up with his hind left leg and caught me straight on the jaw. For a while I thought he'd broken it, but miraculously it didn't even leave a bruise – I was almost disappointed.

We treated ourselves to a huge Sunday lunch at the hotel in Palo, washed down with a litre of strong red wine which rendered us totally incapable of walking anywhere in the afternoon. Instead, we found a field with a stream and Clare highlighted my hair. It was a terrifying experience, for I had no mirror and I had to put myself entirely in Clare's hands. I wish we'd taken a picture as she pulled increasingly large tufts of hair through the plastic cap with her crochet hook and slopped blue peroxide all over my head, while the dogs sat watching us in utter astonishment, wrinkling their noses at the horrible smell. My faith in my friend's hairdressing abilities wasn't improved when she pulled away the cap after we'd rinsed it all off and collapsed into helpless laughter. In fact, after it had dried and I'd brushed it, it looked OK – I checked in the wing mirror of a parked car.

The next morning we climbed up the stunningly beautiful Orba valley, through thick forest and past the glimmering turquoise blue lake that was frustratingly far below us as we sweated under the burning sun. In the afternoon the trees disappeared and the country suddenly flattened out into closely shorn, grassy moorland. As we approached the top of the pass, the weather changed dramatically; an hour earlier we'd been longing for ice-creams, but suddenly a light damp mist descended and we needed jumpers.

We reached the Paso del Faiallo and the abrupt change of gradient frightened me: before us was an enormous, steep-sided basin that dropped over 1000 metres to the sea below. We'd planned to camp here but it was too cold and exposed, so we set off along the road that circles the Cerusa valley.

We were up in the clouds, walking along the steep green ridge of the Costa Cerusa, and it felt strange and unworldly. Hannibal suddenly became very excited, pricking his ears up and trying to stop, as a strange, ghostly noise drifted up from the valley below. It was another donkey, who must have heard the echo of Hannibal's shoes. He kept stopping to bray every few minutes and whatever they were saying to each other must have been very emotive because Hannibal grew more and more determined to charge straight down the almost vertical valley. Clare and I began a very noisy singing session in the hope of drowning the communication between them. Poor Hannibal was furious.

The mist had turned to fog and was growing so thick that it was dangerous for us to continue on the road. We were on a narrow ledge with an almost vertical drop to our right and sudden blind bends every few yards, but in true Italian style cars were hurtling along without a thought for possible pedestrians. It was a bank holiday weekend and the traffic was relatively heavy, so we donned our bright waterproofs and Clare shone the torch behind us to let approaching cars know of our existence.

After one very near miss, I decided it was too risky to continue in this way, so I hailed the next car. Inside were an elderly couple who agreed to follow behind us with their hazard lights on to act as a shield. We walked on for about five minutes until more cars had begun to collect behind us, then thanked them and let them all pass, before lying in wait for the next unsuspecting motorist. He was a young man in an Alfa who didn't seem to mind a bit and trailed us patiently for about half an hour, waving on any cars who came behind him, chatting to us out of the window as if he couldn't have thought of a better way to spend a Monday afternoon.

It was growing late and we still had about eight kilometres to go before the next village, so when I saw a relatively flat area of land to our left I decided we should make camp. The young man offered to bring us a pizza from the village, which was tempting, but I suspected he might bring a carload of his mates along too, so we declined and bade him good night.

Thinking of that evening makes me realize how accustomed I had become to the rubbish that lies all over the European country-side. Although I tried not to add to it, it no longer bothered me; Coke cans and dirty nappies had become part of my normal surroundings and I only really noticed rubbish if there was something unusual amongst it. When I went to the loo that evening I came across a (used) pregnancy testing kit and I found it both fascinating and terribly sad that some poor girl had been so in need of privacy that she'd come to this isolated spot.

Luck was on our side that evening, for our pasta had just cooked when the Calor gas ran out. It was a night that reminded me of Spain – I hadn't been so cold, damp and hungry for months, and I found something nostalgically cheering about huddling up to the dogs inside the tiny little tent and swigging Sambuca as Clare and I chatted into the small hours.

The fog had disappeared by the next morning and we safely made our way down the ridge of the Bric del Busa. Bogey was ill again, however; it was the same as before – her head was swollen and she had a temperature, so we had to find a vet as soon as possible. The town of Masone was about twelve kilometres away, but since we were out of food and starving we stopped first at the beautiful village of La Cappelletta. It was a tiny place dominated by the white-fronted church from which it took its name. There were crowds of people around, picnicking and making merry, celebrating what we later learned was the public holiday of Feragosto and everyone was here for the church mass that afternoon. All the shops in Masone were closed so we had no option but to eat at the restaurant here.

Later we decided to make this village the place for our rendezvous with Mum and Dad. They were due to arrive in the area the following evening, so I rang Dad's secretary to explain where we were.

Finding a vet proved impossible; we phoned every one in the phone book, but they were all on holiday. In the end we went to the emergency *farmacia* in Masone – in Italy pharmacists can sell antibiotics without prescriptions – and when I described Bogey's symptoms, I was given a course of antibiotics and vitamin supplements. They checked her fever and stopped the swelling almost immediately.

Apart from the worry of Bogey's illness, we had a lovely few days at La Cappelletta. We camped on one of the terraces to the east of the village and waited, increasingly impatiently, for my parents to arrive. By Thursday the whole village was looking out for their campervan; La Cappelletta didn't usually attract foreigners, and we were treated like celebrities.

Around seven o'clock the next evening Clare and I were pondering whether to cook our supper or not when a sudden shout for 'Sofia' came across the square. I ran outside and there it was – a huge white campervan driving towards us. Mum and Dad were here! I ran towards them, waving my arms in the air and shrieking in delight.

Chapter 26
Home Comforts

It was wonderful to see my parents, and they seemed relieved to have finally found us. Hannibal got off to a very bad start by immediately biting one of the foam padding arm rests off Stevie's wheelchair. Luckily Stevie found it hilarious, but Mum didn't, and Clare's tales of his recent bad behaviour didn't help. Georgie almost passed out with excitement as she leapt over all the familiar faces, but Bogey was confused by all the hugging and kissing and needed to be introduced to everyone slowly before she was convinced that I wasn't in need of protection.

The motorhome could just as well have landed from Mars for all it fitted in with its surroundings. If it had been anyone else's, it would have made me cringe, but it held such unfamiliar luxuries that I didn't mind: a loo, a shower, an oven, a sink; there were our own kitchen mugs, familiar duvet covers, rugs, towels – little things that made that ugly vehicle a beautiful slice of home. Mum had been busy cooking and had brought out three big fruit cakes, plus a huge container of Alpen and over 50 lb of Pedigree Chum for which I couldn't thank her enough; my constant worries about finding food for the dogs disappeared completely.

Stevie had grown a good two inches since I'd last seen him and his voice had broken – suddenly he was a young man and not a little boy any more. He'd been talking about this holiday since Christmas and was thrilled to be here at last; he liked his donkey and he took a particular interest in Bogey, saying her name over and over again. He loved it when Hannibal rolled, saying he wanted to have baths like that too.

We all ate in the restaurant that night. People kept coming to talk to Dad and I had to act as interpreter; I wished I could tell them all to get lost, that he was *my* father and I wanted him all to myself, but these people had been so kind to us over the past few days that I couldn't.

I'd sometimes worried that it might be difficult seeing my parents like this, that I'd changed, that I wouldn't know what to tell them. But there was nothing awkward at all; I wanted to tell them everything. I was so happy that they could actually take part in what I was doing, and hoped they'd come to understand why I loved it.

The next morning, 18 August, TV cameras invaded the village. Luigi, the man who owned the land where we were camping, was big in one of the Italian charities for the handicapped and was very interested in what we were doing. He'd invited the local television station to come and interview us. The film still makes me laugh, for I was wearing a spotlessly white, beautifully ironed shirt that Mum had brought out, and Mum's new white shoes; my hair was brushed and tied back, I looked so unlike the normal me I doubted that anyone would recognize me. We found an interpreter for Mum and Dad, and between us we gave MENCAP some pretty good publicity.

After seeing Clare off from Genova airport at midday, we spent the afternoon sightseeing. It is a beautiful old city, but far from ideal to visit in a wheelchair, for it is built on terraces rising up from the sea. We were exhausted when we finally returned to La Cappelletta. It was late, but of course that didn't matter any more. I cooked supper and it was bliss – a chopping board! a sink! a fridge! and a table to eat it from!

I packed up all my redundant camping gear and Dad tied it on to the motorhome roof, along with Hannibal's pack saddle. I slept on a bed up over the driver's seat and I felt gloriously safe. The mornings were the best, for Dad would pass a cup of tea up to me as I lay there luxuriating in my laziness, waiting for the bathroom, idly chatting as the family came to life. We'd have a proper breakfast round the table, with real butter and homemade jam, and I suddenly had to improve my table manners as I remembered what plates and bowls were for.

For the next week I followed the Alta Via, the old Roman track along the top of the Ligurian mountains. Apparently it was still used commercially until about twenty years ago by mule trains supplying the isolated villages along its route. Now it is largely overgrown and sometimes very difficult to find, as sections have fallen away. With Hannibal free of the pack saddle, we were able to tackle even the most challenging paths and I had the best walking of the whole trip.

That first morning was relatively easy. Dad came with me for the first half hour, although we didn't get very far because the blackberries were so good. I climbed up above the trees of the Paso del Turchino to the bare ridgetops above the Stura basin. The soil was peaty and soft, with outcrops of rock constantly breaking through, and herringbone ridges stretched off in all directions. Hannibal was surprisingly nimble without his packs and we progressed much more quickly than I'd expected.

I reached the village of Praglia by one, and half an hour later Mum, Dad and Stevie arrived by road with lunch. In the afternoon Mum joined me, pushing Stevie in his wheelchair down the road into the next huge basin, while Dad terrified us all by whizzing past at top speed on his bike.

Finding good camping grounds flat enough for the motorhome in such a mountainous region proved difficult. That evening we decided on a rough field at the edge of the small village of Caffarello, not in itself very picturesque but with marvellous westward views to the mountains I'd just crossed. The friendly owner let us camp on his land and introduced us to a couple from Rome who could speak English and gave us a tray of the best peaches we'd ever tasted. Giovanna, his wife, insisted on putting two loads of our clothes and sheets through her washing-machine and saved Mum the chore of having to go into Genova to find a launderette.

Sunday's walk was something of an endurance test. We had to cross the Rico valley, Genova's main artery to Milan, which contains a motorway, railway line and all the attendant equine hurdles – modern bridges, noisy tunnels, heavy traffic, zebra crossings . . . We had a few dicey moments but Hannibal must have been growing braver for we got through without any major hold-ups and by late afternoon we were climbing up into the safety of the woods of il Pizzo, east of Pedemonte.

It was Dad's birthday the next day, so I surreptitiously searched the village of Casella for something resembling a birthday cake. In the end I had to resort to a trayful of delicious shortbreads and miniature meringues. I found some figs and bought an enormous quantity of Parma ham to go with them, plus various other goodies for our evening meal. Rejoining Dad at the post office, I found him going crazy with frustration over the Italian public telephone system; he needed fifty *gettone* coins for a five-minute call to his secretary, which didn't make for a very worthwhile conversation. Politics and isolated Apennine villages weren't mixing very well.

My walk that afternoon included the steepest climb of the trip. Dad and Stevie accompanied me to the Crocetta d'Orera, then I walked up a small road to the beautiful little village of Tiggia, busily being decorated for its summer beanfeast, before setting off up the path to Monte Sella. I found it hard to believe that mule trains ever coped with this gradient – neither of my donkeys could have done it with a laden pack saddle, and I had to join the animals on all fours for some of the way. Two kilometres took about three hours as we climbed across the sheer face of the mountain, but the village we found at the top was well worth the effort. Sella sits at the peak of yet another huge basin, the southern side of which I was to cross the next day. The view was astounding; to the west we could just make out yesterday's camping ground, and to the east was a vast wilderness of wooded mountains that seemed to stretch on forever.

We camped by the tiny white church above the village, built as a memorial to all the young resistance fighters killed in the area during the war. It was a beautiful building, with a huge marble engraving above the entrance depicting three men and a woman in the mountains fighting off the approaching German Army. Nearby were the graves of two villagers, killed at twenty and twenty-one; the words on the stones were surprisingly strong, referring to the 'rabid Germans spreading their plague across Italy'.

People were very friendly as we walked down to look at the beautiful red-roofed houses of the village, and some of them walked back with us as they told us about the place. They showed us the pulley and wire stretching nearly 1000 feet to the valley below, the old lifeline for supplies before the road was built; they talked about the terraces on the flatter upper slopes of the mountains that used to be the sole source of wealth for the village but so many of which now stand neglected. Very few people live there permanently now; all those we spoke to came from Genova and were there just for the summer (although, as usual, their roots were local).

When they heard it was Dad's birthday they brought presents – a delicious fruit loaf, one of Genova's specialities, more fruit and some lovely coffee. I put on my best dress and we had a great evening.

Tuesday was the most physically demanding day of the whole summer. It was brilliant, exhilarating stuff and I experienced almost everything nature had to offer: thick woods, smooth meadowland, thin, frightening ridges, intense midday heat and a sudden storm. If Hannibal had been laden it would have taken at least three days; as it was, we still had one terrible moment while walking along the ridge between Monte Cornua and Monte Alpesina when Hannibal lost his footing and slipped off the path. I held on to his halter and pulled harder than ever in my life as he scrambled madly with his hind legs for some grip and eventually heaved himself back up. If he'd been carrying my stuff, I would have lost the lot down the ridge, and maybe Hanny as well. The experience shook us both and for the next few hours he was very nervous on all the narrower sections of track.

Later I had my first glimpse of Liguria's hidden mountain villages – Canate, Scandolaro, Campovene, Feto . . . – accessible only by vertiginous tracks. Half of me longed to climb down to them to investigate, but since we were having enough trouble coping with the contours on my ridge-top route, it seemed crazy to attempt any more.

I stood on no fewer than seven mountain peaks, all over 3000 feet high, and felt literally on top of the world. By late afternoon we finally reached the last, Monte Spina, and the steep descent to Scoffera lay before us. As Hannibal charged down at top speed I saw a party of people coming up the narrow path towards us. Miraculously my yell of warning reached them just in time and they scattered in all directions as we ploughed through – a huge brown donkey running gleefully down the mountainside, a girl slipping and skidding as she tried frantically to keep up, and two dogs joyfully joining in the chase. (George and Bogey always thought these downhill death-runs were a fantastic game.)

In Scoffera Mum and Dad were nowhere to be seen, so we sat waiting for them by the church while tourists took photos of us and locals stared. This was the first evening that I began to worry about not finding my parents. There was no real reason for my fears, but during the next hour I convinced myself that I was waiting by the wrong church in the wrong place; so many of these Ligurian villages had the same names – there were three Sellas within twenty miles of each other – and I was sure I must have got it wrong. Of course, they turned up in the end, and I pushed my fears to the back of my mind.

Wednesday's mountains were even higher, but I wasn't as ambitious with the distance so we could take it more slowly. As we approached Montaldo we were hit by a ferocious storm, so we ran for shelter into a beech wood. Nevertheless, we were all soaked and freezing within minutes.

That night we camped at Barbagelata (it means 'frozen beard', and when we saw photographs of the place in winter, we understood why). It sits at the head of the Bocco valley at over 4000 feet and the centre of the village was beautifully unspoilt, with tiny archways leading under the stone houses. The little restaurant opened up specially for us when we knocked at the door and the owner sat down with us and talked non-stop while his wife cooked our meal next door – *spaghetti al pesto* and roast meat. We wondered how on earth they could make any money in such a place, but when Dad was presented with the bill we decided that this evening's takings alone would keep them going for a good few weeks; it was one of the most expensive meals we'd ever eaten.

I decided that evening to leave the Alta Via. I loved the remoteness of my ridge-top path, but I was seeing very little of my family;

199

it was impossible for them to accompany me with a wheelchair and in the evenings I was too tired to do anything but sleep. So I decided to head for the coast, where I hoped we would all be able to walk together.

The walk from Barbagelata down the Aveto valley sticks in my memory as being very special. Stevie came with me the whole way, pushed in the morning by Mum and in the afternoon by Dad. It was a shame it was so difficult for us all to walk together at once – we needed a chauffeur.

Although the mountains had been magnificent, I realized that the valleys provided the best insight to Italian life. Villages like Calzagatta, Brugnoni, Priosa and Parazzuolo were ancient farming communities where hay was still cut by hand and old ladies sat with their small herds of cows. We saw goats, chickens, ducks, geese and turkeys, and for the first time since Spain I saw working mules, beautiful animals that sent Hanny into paroxysms of bellowing delight. Wire pulleys extended up and down the hillsides – the lifelines that made existence possible in these remote settlements. We watched as huge loads of wood and hay came hurtling down across the valleys; to my myopic eyes they appeared to be flying.

The villagers were much more interested in my animals than they were in us. In every single village we entered that day, the first question asked was whether my donkey was castrated.

'*Sumaro, e entiero?*' the old men would call, and all were disappointed by my reply; they would have bought him if he'd been a stallion, they said.

We camped that night on a small patch of land beside the twisting road that crosses the steep southern slopes of Monte Cavallo. I asked the farmers nearby for permission out of courtesy really, since we were on little more than a lay-by.

'*No! Andate via!*' they yelled at me. They didn't want a bunch of foreigners on their land. I began trying to explain a bit more about myself in the hope it would change their minds. I laid the charity bit on so thick that eventually they grudgingly agreed to let us stay – but we weren't to disturb the milk churn in the morning, they said, and we were only to stay the one night.

Dad was up soon after six to capture on video the milk churn come clattering down the cable from the tiny farm perched on the hillside above us (it gave Hannibal the shock of his life). The old woman from the farm, who'd been so vile the evening before, came to wait beside us for the milkman. He was giving her a lift into town, she said, since she had to go to the dentist. As she stood there, watching us all slowly come to life, the Thurnham family made its contribution to European harmony: Dad said over and over again the only Italian words he knew – '*Buon giorno*' (perfectly) and '*Multy grarzy*' (not so perfectly), Stevie said '*Ciao*' at least a dozen times, while Mum just nodded and smiled a lot. Slowly the woman's antagonism disappeared and just before the milkman arrived we captured on film what is unmistakably a smile.

Chapter 27
Illegal Alien

Our camp the next night was in what we called Nut Valley – a steep-sided gully full of hazelnut trees. We all gorged ourselves on the nuts, but Hannibal especially adored them, crunching them up as if the shells were nothing but crisps. A picker climbed up into the terraces above us and Dad followed him with his camera as he slowly shook each tree and then transferred all the nuts that had fallen into the nets beneath to a large hessian sack.

I set off early in the morning, alone this time, for I hoped to cross the high range of mountains between us and the sea. I was beginning to grow impatient, and I was also feeling ambitious, for I arranged to meet the others by the church in Bargonasco, a good twenty kilometres to the south.

Discovering that one of the roads on my map didn't exist, I was forced to walk through the little village of Semovigo, but it was so beautiful I almost felt grateful for the extra mileage. On the way down the Paso della Camilla I found a riding holiday camp, where Hannibal insisted on stopping to smell every pile of dung. A little girl showed me a short cut through the woods to the village of Visagna, where a kind restaurant-owner whom I asked for water insisted on feeding us all. It was already three o'clock and I wished there were some way of contacting Mum and Dad to tell them to meet me somewhere closer. But there was still time to make it, so we set off and walked as quickly as possible towards Monte Porcile.

Luck was against us. About a mile before reaching the Paso della Biscia, there was a buzzing in the air and Hannibal stopped dead. Even when the model aeroplane moved further away from us, he refused to move an inch. After twenty minutes of begging and imploring Hannibal to move on, I had to ask the plane enthusiasts if they would bring their models down for ten minutes to give us a chance to walk past. They thought I was absolutely bonkers and in ordinary circumstances I might have found it amusing, but I was so short of time that I just felt angry and frustrated. I had a mountain to cross and only three daylight hours in which to do it.

As darkness fell, I couldn't work out where I'd gone wrong. God, what a time to get lost! We wandered over that mountain for hours, trying every possible track or path; I must have been *so* close to the road I needed to find, but somehow I just couldn't get down to it. The magnificence of the Apennines was now terrifying; at any other time I would have stopped where I was, set up camp and retraced my steps in the morning, but all I could think of were my parents waiting by the church in Bargonasco. I knew Mum wouldn't sleep a wink if I didn't turn up all night.

I could hear church bells ringing in the valleys, but could find no way down to them. The sky filled with black clouds as the sun sank and it grew colder, and I frantically searched for my original track before darkness trapped us – I didn't have my torch with me and knew we'd all end up dead if we were still wandering round on this mountaintop in an hour's time. I tried desperately to think of the sensible thing to do. There was no way we could now walk to Bargonasco, so I'd have to leave the animals and hitch there. I remembered a small shooting lodge I'd passed a few hours before and miraculously managed to find it again. I tethered Hanny outside, then gave the dogs the last of the water and shut them inside, tying the door as securely as I could with twine. I could hear them howling pitifully as I ran as fast as I could towards the road.

I'd gone about a mile when I heard a yelp and turned to see George hurtling towards me; I screamed with frustration, but it was no use telling her to go back, so I called for Bogey too, deciding they might as well both come with me. Bogey, however, was nowhere; I called and called, and grew increasingly worried that she'd fallen and was lying injured in some gully. Eventually I ran all the way back to the hut and found her still stuck inside; they'd only been able to push the door open a little and, unlike George, she hadn't been able to squeeze through the narrow gap. I considered shutting them up in there again, but couldn't bear the look on their faces so called them after me and once more ran as fast as I could towards the road. It was almost pitch dark now, and I dreaded to think how long it would take us to reach Bargonasco, but I was determined to make it somehow.

We had to wait nearly ten minutes before a car appeared, during which time I began to despair. I'd opened my map and from the occasional light of the moon I'd tried to work out the distance to Bargonasco by road. It was at least forty kilometres; direct, it was barely eight. I'd never felt so frustrated. When a car appeared, I gave it no chance of leaving us behind. I stood in the middle of the road to make it stop, then leapt inside saying there was an emergency and would he please take me to somewhere with a taxi as quickly as possible. The driver explained that there was nowhere round here I'd find a taxi, but he'd take me to the bar in the next village where there was a phone.

The village was called Codivara, a tiny place with, I was to discover, an extremely strong sense of community spirit. The next twenty-four hours I can never look back on without a sense of utter disbelief; I don't know how I could have let such a farce occur, but then again, I'm not sure what I could have done to stop it.

I was ushered into a bar where everyone listened in silence as I sobbed out my story. Without Hannibal, it was very difficult to make it sound believable and I'm sure some of them thought I was off my trolley, but they were kind and immediately began to suggest what I should do. I prayed that someone would offer to take me to Bargonasco, but they didn't, so I accepted their advice to ring the local police and ask them to find and inform my parents of my whereabouts. They did the phoning for me and at last I began to relax, sure that everything would now be OK.

Half an hour later two policemen appeared at the door. I leapt up and asked them if they'd found the campervan and was astounded to hear them say that they hadn't been to look for it yet – they wanted to interview me first for more details.

'*Documenti, per favore,*' they asked. I had no form of identification on me whatsoever. I tried to explain that all my belongings were in the van, which was why I so desperately needed to find it, whereupon they informed me that as I was an alien without proof of identity they had the right to arrest me.

Ah.

I tried to persuade them that if they took me to Bargonasco, all this could soon be resolved, but they said they weren't going to look for any vehicle until the morning and meanwhile I would have to stay here. They walked me over to the *pensione* and told the landlady to put me in a single room and make sure I didn't leave. For the next twenty hours she shadowed me as though I were a serious criminal. The policemen left, telling me not to worry, they would find the van in the morning and were sure my story would be verified.

The *pensione* had six other guests, all ladies, who seemed to be permanent residents. They clustered round me as I arrived and were extremely kind, telling the landlady to make me a cup of hot milk and lending me a nightie and a towel.

During the night there was a storm and I worried that Hannibal, exposed to the elements, would have broken free from his makeshift tether and be lost forever on that huge mountain. I hardly slept a wink and was up at the crack of dawn ringing the police station to see if they'd done anything yet. No, they hadn't, and they asked me not to ring again – they would inform *me* if there were any developments.

At nine o'clock I had another visit; there were four of them this time and they informed me that there was no church or main square in Bargonasco; they'd asked the police there to look for a British campervan, but they had found nothing.

I studied the map and suggested that they try further up the valley at the village of Bargone.

'But you said Bargonasco,' said the police, rapidly becoming less friendly.

'I know,' I said, in as apologetic a tone as I could muster, 'but my parents knew my route and when I didn't turn up on time last night would probably have driven further in the direction I was coming from.'

They asked me exactly the same questions as I'd answered the night before, although it was much more like an interrogation this time. I was quite impressed by my remembering four out of the seven characters on the van's number plate, but they weren't – there are thousands of such vans in the area at this time of year, they said. I tried to make them understand that they wouldn't all be on the tiny mountain road in the Bargonasco valley, but they behaved as if I were expecting the impossible. They also wouldn't let me help them look. Whenever I asked, they told me that I was a '*straniera sensa documenti*' and mustn't go anywhere without their permission.

When they left I begged the landlady to let me go and find Hannibal, but she refused absolutely to let me out of her sight. Nor would she let the dogs inside and the poor things were having to shiver out on the porch. It was still pouring with rain and they were in a state as they weren't used to being without me. I felt helpless, furious with myself for letting all this happen. Why hadn't we just slept in that hut till daybreak? We would have reached Bargonasco by now.

The villagers continued their kind, if excessive, interest in me, offering to lend me money for my air fare home, trying to ring the British Consul in Genova to help me (he didn't work on a Sunday) and saying they would look after my animals if I were deported. When I told them how I needed to rescue my donkey from the mountain, a party of about twelve volunteered to go and fetch him for me; they knew of the shooting hut and said I *had* been on the right track at that point. As they set off through the pouring rain, I couldn't help feeling they were all loving it – after all, it hardly took twelve people to rescue one donkey. This was evidently the greatest drama to hit the village for years.

I sat feeling frustrated and worried in the *pensione,* playing cards with the old ladies and wishing there was something I could do. At midday two policemen arrived to tell me that they had been to Bargone and there was no sign of a van there. By now, I realized, Mum and Dad would be out looking for me and retracing yesterday's route. I tried to tell the policemen this, but I detected a distinct lack of sympathy. If your parents are looking for you, they asked, why haven't they contacted the police? I was somewhat perplexed about this one too, but said it was probably because they couldn't speak any Italian.

At about four Hannibal arrived, sodden wet and very hungry but otherwise perfectly OK; at least we were all safe. One of the farmers in the group offered to put him up in his barn and give him hay, and I decided that if we were still here tonight the dogs and I should sleep in the barn rather than pay for another night at the *pensione*.

Two hours later we had another police visit and the village elders tried to persuade them to let me go and search. They walked down to the barn to inspect Hannibal and seemed to conclude from this that my story was more credible than before, so that I could be trusted not to escape. A group of young people offered to drive me to Bargonasco and with sudden hope I ran out of the *pensione* to the car. It was about eight o'clock – over twenty-four hours after our planned rendezvous – when I finally arrived. There was no sign of the van, but some people said they'd noticed one driving around, and had last seen it heading in the direction of Bargone. We drove up the valley to the pretty little mountain village and I prayed that at last this nightmare would be over.

There it was! It was the first thing I saw as we entered the square, parked barely fifty yards from the church. I clambered out of the car and ran over to it; Dad was standing outside talking to someone and turned towards me with a look of utter astonishment on his face. Mum and I hugged each other, almost faint with relief.

Later we swapped our respective stories. Mum and Dad had determined not to panic last night, but had driven up to Bargone, realizing that I was unlikely to reach Bargonasco before darkness fell. They'd stayed by the church, and then this morning, as I suspected, they'd driven up to the mountain passes where I should have been coming from. Mum said this was absolutely terrifying; at one point they'd even had to build up the sides of the road with rocks where it had fallen away down the steep banks. When I failed to show up after a few hours they'd driven back to Nut Valley and retraced my steps from the beginning. Dad had left messages pinned on to trees everywhere; for all I know they're still there – sets of instructions written on House of Commons notepaper all over the Apennines.

When we returned to Codivara the landlady of the *pensione*

presented me with a bill for 68,000 lire (over £30) and I almost wished I'd been arrested properly; at least a police cell would have been free.

Bogey put the crowning glory on the day's events: the combination of being chilled, worried and eating outside her regular mealtimes had affected her stomach, and at two o'clock in the morning her bowels exploded inside the campervan. As I got down on hands and knees with floor cleaner and scrubbing brush, I'm not sure who I felt most sorry for.

On Wednesday morning, 30 August, I climbed down from Monte Guaitarola through pine forests and lavender fields to Levanto and the sea. As we swam from the golden, sandy beach and Mum and Dad explored the shops and treated themselves to new clothes and shoes, I realized that at last we could enjoy something of a normal family holiday. I had a beautiful walk in the evening, round the steep, jagged coastline to Monterosso al Mare, the first of Liguria's Cinque Terre, where we camped in the car park and ate a delicious meal at one of the seafood restaurants on the front.

The Cinque Terre are five villages built along a particularly rugged stretch of coast west of La Spezia. As all available space was filled long ago, there are practically no modern buildings at all and the villages have been able to withstand the onslaught of tourists very well. A railway connects them to each other, but they are extremely difficult to reach by road. According to my guide book, the coastal footpath was suitable for horses, so on Thursday afternoon Dad and I set off with the animals, arranging to meet Mum, Stevie and the campervan in Riomaggiore, the final village, just five miles south.

The slopes behind and between the Cinque Terre, although almost vertical, have been terraced into narrow bands and are covered in vines and olives. Steel tracks run up and down, and farmers tend their crops from electrically controlled seats which whizz along them. It looked more terrifying than any big dipper.

Not surprisingly, considering the gradient, the path was entirely unsuitable for equines – my guide book had lied. Hannibal, however, was magnificent, and coped with the sheer flights of steps, the narrow paths, even the planks connecting the sections that had fallen away. But it took us over three hours to reach the next village, Vernazza, and we realized there was no way we'd get to Riomaggiore before nightfall. Instead, we walked up into the hills and left Hanny happily eating gorse on a hidden slope, then caught the train to Riomaggiore and after an extensive search of the village, we found a very distraught Mother. She'd found nowhere to park, had been continually pestered by the carabinieri for stopping on yellow lines and was ready to murder us by the time we finally turned up three hours behind schedule.

The next two days were much more peaceful. I walked along quiet tracks that followed the contours of the mountains behind La Spezia, through thick chestnut forests that gave no idea of the proximity of a big city. On Saturday I had the morning off, as Dad offered to take Hannibal on his own; it felt very strange, and when, after a couple of hours, we followed in the campervan, I was amazed at how far they had walked.

The relationship between my father and Hannibal was very funny. Dad is not animal-minded at all, but I caught him at odd moments chattering away to my donkey and tickling him behind his ears as though they were old friends. When he was on his mountain bike he would try to get Hanny to pull him uphill by holding on to his back, but Hanny was no fool and always stopped dead until he let go.

Bogey spent most of these weeks travelling in the campervan, at last having the rest she'd needed for months, and she would sit quietly beside Mum for hours. Yet again I cursed the British quarantine laws – she was just the kind of dog that Mum would have liked at home, and I kept thinking how great it would be to bring her back with me.

Mum and I discussed the possibility of bringing Hannibal home and I managed to convince her that it would be wonderful for Stephen; we could train him to pull a little cart and he could keep the gorse under control. She had already found out about import regulations: they were the same as for crossing from France into Italy, so I'd have to find somewhere in Rome to leave Hannibal for a month while he had a blood test. Then we hoped to find him a place on a lorry bringing livestock to England. I felt overjoyed, and very grateful that I'd be spared the misery of leaving another donkey behind.

I told my parents about the way so many people I'd met had presumed I was on a pilgrimage and had asked me to give their love to the Pope. I wondered aloud how anyone manages to meet him and Mum had the idea of writing to Cardinal Hume in London to see if he could arrange anything. It was worth a try, she said, and it *would* make an amazing finale.

On Saturday evening my elder brother, Tim, flew out to Genova for his postponed two-week summer holiday and we met him at the station in La Spezia. On our first day's walk we had what was very nearly a disaster. The bridge I'd planned to cross over the River Magra was being rebuilt and consisted of nothing more than steel rods; to go to the next one up the river would have involved an extra day's walking. As the water was extremely low, I decided we should try wading through it. Tim later told me he thought this was a real adventure, fording rivers and braving rapids, and was disappointed to find that it wasn't an everyday occurrence! Somehow we managed to bribe Hannibal across and I felt very proud of him.

That evening I wanted to kill my father. It was my parents' last night with us and he was trying to finish off the film in his video camera, but his sense of timing couldn't have been worse. We hit yet another storm and I arrived at the beautiful walled village of Caprigliola soaking wet and in desperate need of somewhere sheltered to put Hannibal. I found the bar and the usual group of old men, and I began asking them if they could help. They started discussing possible places and just as they were about to make a suggestion, up drove my father in his thumping great campervan and rushed out with his video camera to capture it all on film. I've rarely felt so embarrassed in my life. When I admitted that I did know this foreigner, he was my father, the old men decided I was not really in any need of help and told me to get lost.

I ordered Dad away – to this day he still doesn't understand why I was so angry – and eventually I persuaded someone to put Hannibal in his barn. This meant we were able to go out for dinner, so we put on our best clothes and drove to Lerici on the coast. It was a lovely evening and my father was soon forgiven; we toasted Emu in her absence on her nineteenth birthday and I wished that she could be here too. It seemed such a shame that she'd been with me only for the worst bit of the trip at the beginning.

Mum and Dad planned to leave early on Monday afternoon, but once again I ruined their plans, this time by finding that one of Hannibal's shoes was loose. In the search for a farrier we were helped by Catherine Anson, an English painter living in Caprigliola. She managed to find a man who was at least able to put fresh nails into the existing shoes and give me the address of a proper farrier a day's walk away, at Luni. I'd been planning to head further inland to the Alpi Apuane, but the detour to Luni put an idea into my head that at the end of the week I was to find irresistible.

It took hours to pack up the saddle bags again; and Hanny took one look at them and tried to bolt in the other direction. I left as much as possible with Mum and forced Tim to discard his trousers and pyjamas; I packed up new supplies of dog food, Alpen and the last fruit cake, then spent ages trying to remember how to put on the pack saddle properly – it seemed like years since I'd last used it. Then we all set off to find a camping ground above the village. It was horrible saying goodbye – I'd felt so safe and happy over the past few weeks. The next time I saw the family my trip would be over, I'd be preparing for Bar school and trying to live a normal life again.

I was dreading going back to London. The thought of sitting in a library swotting up law cases filled me with horror. I couldn't conceive of life without the animals; the thought of sending Georgie off to quarantine and leaving Bogey behind was enough to set off my tears in an instant. I hate the word 'cherish', but it's the only word to describe how I felt about the dogs as we slowly approached Rome during September; I savoured every moment with them, knowing that it would soon be the last.

Chapter 28
A Handsome Man at my Side

Tim and I got on better than ever before in our lives. My elder brother is one of the kindest people I know and he put up with me extremely well. After six months I'd become very set in my ways of travelling and I would have driven most people potty. He was horrified by my low standards of hygiene, and made me remember how much I'd craved for a bath back at the beginning of the trip. Now as long as I was able to wash my face and my bottom once every few days, I didn't really care.

We were in the foothills of the Alpi Apuane, with peaks rising up like a great jagged saw to our left and the sea way down below us on our right. On that first Tuesday we found what was to be one of my all-time favourite villages – Fosdinovo, just inside the Tuscan border. It had the most beautiful church, made almost entirely of marble. Never before had I realized how colourful marble can be, nor how it can be turned and carved into every shape under the sun. There were marble statues dressed in real clothes with real hair, like giant china dolls, and I was mesmerized.

We found a perfect camping ground next to a restaurant up in the forest of La Foce, where the owner knew a farrier from Massa and arranged for him to come and see Hannibal in the morning. Franco il ferrero was an unforgettable character, a large, bearded man who measured Hanny's feet with blades of grass which he took with him to prepare the right sized shoes.

We spent the next night at a hotel in the hills above Massa at San Carlo Terme, for the sky had turned black with cloud and Tim was being wet. 'Hotel' is perhaps too generous a description, since the building was little more than a concrete shell, like a multi-storey car park. From what we could make out, they had run out of money halfway through construction.

Franco met us in the morning in the hotel car park with the shoes he'd made for Hannibal. They were entirely different from the previous ones – much thicker and with high heels which Franco promised would stop Hanny slipping downhill. He also trimmed the hooves back much more than the others had done; it was

213

fascinating how styles could vary so much. He refused to accept anything in payment – it was his contribution to MENCAP, he said, and I was very touched, for it must have taken him hours to make them.

Hanny tottered along that morning like an eight-year-old wearing stilettos, but the heels did seem to help a little with the slipping and I felt relieved that never again would I have to worry about finding a blacksmith; these shoes should last till long after we'd reached Rome.

The beautiful scenery was not the only factor influencing my route through this part of Italy. We were approaching the small town of Camaiore in the hills above Viareggio, which for the past few days had been drawing me like a magnet. It was near here that I had worked the summer before in a hotel above Pieve, and this was where Giovanni lived. He was the man who had made those months so enjoyable, and now I could hardly stop thinking about him – I was craving for a taste of romance. I don't know if I would so blatantly have sought a resumption of intimate relations if I'd been on my own, but having Tim with me boosted my confidence with the opposite sex. Having a tall, handsome man at my side meant that I'd suddenly become invisible, and it made me feel wonderfully free to do as I pleased. I walked round in a swimming costume during most of this time and hardly attracted a second glance – it was great.

Tim said he wouldn't mind baby-sitting the animals if I wanted a night on the tiles, so I summoned up the courage to ring Giovanni's number. We hadn't been in touch since we'd kissed goodbye at Pisa airport last October and as far as he knew I was cooking on a boat in the Caribbean. I think my call surprised him somewhat, but he sounded pleased to hear me and we arranged to meet in Camaiore in two days' time.

Our impending reunion made me very nervous. I suppose it was coupled with anxiety about returning to London and I kept wondering whether I'd changed, whether I was still capable of enjoying a normal relationship with a man. On Friday morning I borrowed Tim's razor and shaved my legs – Clare would have been proud of me – and I stopped in Pietra Santa to buy some make-up. We had an exhausting day and as we approached Camaiore from Monte Gabberi, I feared I'd never stay awake past my usual ten o'clock bedtime. However, so much adrenalin was pumping round my body as I prepared for my evening out that sleep was the last thing on my mind.

We found a derelict house to camp in and I stood in a corner with a bucket of water and scrubbed at my body, suddenly concerned for the first time in months about whether I smelt and wishing I had some perfume. I put on my red dress and tried to stop my hand shaking as I did my make-up. It began raining so I had to put on my waterproof jacket, which rather spoilt the sophisticated image I was trying to create; Giovanni was very concerned about looking good and I prayed that he wouldn't take one look at me and run off in the other direction. My heart was pounding as I left Tim eating his supper at the pizzeria with the dogs and walked down the familiar main street to Bar Nini, our appointed meeting place.

There he was, leaning against the bar, looking as tall and handsome as ever. I needn't have worried – he grinned at me, grabbed my hand and we ran out through the rain to his car and zoomed off to more glamorous watering-holes on the coast. All my fears disappeared, for we couldn't stop talking and got along as well as ever; the sense of humour that had attracted me in the first place hadn't changed a bit and he thought what I was doing was absolutely hilarious. In fact, he didn't believe me till I showed him the press cuttings that I kept in my purse. (I took it as a compliment that I'd convincingly managed to change my usual tramp-like appearance.)

The evening was a real trip down memory lane, for we drove to all my favourite bars and nightclubs in Viareggio, Lido and Forte dei Marmi. We danced the night away, and I can't describe how good it felt, flirting and laughing, being entirely open with someone, never having to worry about leading him on because there was nothing he might want to do to me that I didn't want to do to him too.

I remembered the magic of the summer I'd spent with him. As a permanent boyfriend I'd probably find Giovanni intolerably chauvinistic, but for a few months I'd revelled in the way, when he took me out, he never let me out of his sight, never let me pay for anything, talked to me and only me, and showed me off in public like a prized possession. He evidently still thought I was worth showing off, and he made me feel feminine, sexy and confident, completely on top of the world.

We finally drove back to Camaiore at about half past four in the morning and he dropped me off outside our derelict house. I'd always thought of Giovanni as being rather macho and brave, so it was terribly funny to see the look of horror on his face as Bogey leapt out of the darkness and charged towards us. Giovanni jumped straight back into his car and refused to come out, even when Bogey had calmed down, so I had to kiss him goodbye through the window. I reminded myself never to rely on him in a crisis.

The next morning I had the worst hangover in the history of the world. I could hardly move without wanting to be sick and my head was in agony. It was still drizzling outside, so we decided to have a day off so that I could recover in comfort. I spent the day sleeping and reading John Mortimer's Rumpole books that Tim had brought out to try to revive my interest in law, while he explored the town.

Camaiore marked the end of the Alpi Apuane and I never again came across any mountain range offering equal terrors – where I could fall off a cliff and not be found for years. We were now entering the Tuscany of the tourist books, whose beauty was very different from the harsh and striking surroundings I had grown used to since entering Italy. I had to adjust my eye to appreciate the softness of the landscapes, the gentle, olive-covered hills and the faded pink farmhouses. The colours of the region are what I remember best – hazy muted shades that blended together so well. I could understand why so many artists were drawn here.

Lucca, which we reached on 11 September, was a disappointment. After the charm of the unspoilt mountain villages it seemed touristy and commercial – even the Duomo San Martino didn't seem as magnificent as when I'd last seen it. The suburbs went on much further than my map suggested and Hannibal refused to walk over the level crossing that would lead to open country, so we ended up spending the night on a damp and smelly piece of waste ground between two houses. When we left the next morning, I swore never again to go near a large town.

Tim was a good walking partner and I didn't feel guilty about insisting that we covered large distances before setting up camp – it made up for all those times I'd never been able to keep up with him on fell walks at home. His kite drove me nutty; although it was beautiful when flying perfectly above us, we wasted hours disentangling it from trees or searching for its landing point in the middle of huge fields of sunflowers.

During this time Tim sparked off a habit that I couldn't give up even when he left – of never being able to pass a bar or café without buying a huge tub of ice cream. We soon became experts and Hannibal also decided that Italian ice-cream was the most scrumptious stuff he'd ever tasted. It started off with his licking out the tubs after we'd finished, but he began demanding more and more, and soon we were buying him his own helping; lemon and strawberry were his favourite flavours and he'd eat from a spoon like a child. It was a hilarious sight and attracted huge crowds of spectators. I soon regretted having started it, though, for during the last few weeks of my walk I couldn't stay in a bar for more than two minutes without him braying until I'd brought him his ice-cream – it cost me a fortune.

We had some memorable camps during that second week as we ambled down from Lucca to San Gimignano. On Wednesday, after an exhausting day crossing the Arno and coping with all Hannibal's usual hang-ups about bridges and main roads, we climbed up into the hills southeast of Pontedera and made camp at the edge of the pretty walled village of Monte Castello. A family we met outside the village shop said we could stay in their wooden shed on the olive terraces to the south of the village, so we enjoyed an evening of relative luxury, with a bench to sit on and a huge tank of water to wash in. At the shop we splashed out on *tiramisu* and almond biscuits to dunk into our *amaretto*. Between us Tim and I consumed vast quantities of *amaretto*, our excuse being that it helped us to sleep. Both of us jammed into my tent was an unforgettable experience; I'm still not sure how we did it. Tim is well over six foot, much bigger than Emu or Clare, and the tent had been squashed to what I thought were its limits even then.

During that night in Monte Castello we were suddenly woken at three o'clock in the morning by the fierce hammering of rain on the shed's corrugated iron roof. It proved to be more than just a passing shower, so after five minutes I ran out to rescue Hannibal, who was standing under an olive tree, looking miserable. I led him into the shed and we moved our beds to the far end to give him room to lie down, whereupon he pawed at the dusty floor and rolled, flinging mud all over our sleeping bags and clothes and forcing us out into the rain to escape his lethal flying hooves. When he finally settled down, we ventured back and huddled into the corner, praying that he wouldn't be tempted to roll again while we were asleep.

Hannibal then began another activity, however, which took our minds off his feet and ensured that we hardly slept a wink. Whenever we were on the point of dozing off, he let out resounding and protracted farts which smelt so bad even the dogs tried to cover their noses in disgust. There was nothing we could do but put up with it, for the rain continued all night, but I can't say I loved him very much during those long hours before dawn.

We were exhausted the next day and declared an afternoon off when we reached the village of Palaia. It's a beautiful medieval stronghold, with a strange, walled folly in its midst and a smart restaurant where they wouldn't let us in because Tim was wearing shorts. We were staying in a field beside a farm just outside the village, and when the farmer's wife heard about this she brought out eggs, pasta and wine for us, saying her food was much better than the restaurant's anyway.

The next day we entered a flatter, dryer landscape that reminded me of southern Spain, especially when we found the sad village of Toiano. Save for an ancient couple who gave us water, it was entirely deserted, a ghost town of ruined cottages and cobbled streets. I couldn't understand why this should be, for it was in one of the most sought-after areas in Italy, just twenty kilometres from San Gimignano and in a stunning position.

That evening we took a detour to visit the monastery of San Vivaldo, where we were welcomed with open arms and were delighted to find a highly esteemed restaurant. The abbot, who was dressed in civvies rather than a habit and spoke very good English, said we were welcome to stay under the huge cedar tree outside, and would we like some of his honey?

The restaurant was in the southern wing of the monastery in what looked like the old vaults. It had a huge, arched roof and variously sized tables to sit at, while a busy kitchen at the back served a constant stream of eaters with traditional local dishes. The mixture of clientele was extraordinary; on one side of us sat a monk, on the other a very smart German couple, and down at the far end were a rowdy group of Italian boys celebrating a twentieth birthday, singing and smoking pot. The food was delicious; we had homemade tortelloni stuffed with wild mushrooms in a cream sauce, and a rich wild boar stew which even Tim ate quickly.

On Saturday we reached San Gimignano, which, like Lucca, was too big and developed to be enjoyable. As we fought our way through the busloads of tourists under the high east walls, an American made me realize how near the end of my journey I now was.

'Gee, are you travelling round Europe like that?' he asked as he zoomed up to us with his video camera.

'We're on our way to Rome,' I said, feeling rather proud, utterly unprepared for his reply.

'Only to Rome, huh?'

I was so flabbergasted that my rejoinder was rather pathetic. 'But we've come all the way from Spain.'

He still wasn't very impressed.

We spent most of Tim's last evening doing a massive laundry session in the shower block of the camp site at Santa Lucia – I even washed Hannibal's rug, to my lasting regret since it took days to dry and I was terrified it would give him pneumonia. We cooked up all the food we had left and ate a delicious last supper, but Tim ruined the evening by giving me a pep talk about Bogey. He sat me down and told me that I must not even think of trying to bring Bogey home. He reminded me that I had no income, no house, and had caused enough hassles by having George. I must not rely on

Mum, he said, always to pick up the pieces of my selfish sentimentality. Struggling barristers do not have Dobermann dogs.

I knew that what he was saying was true, but I hated him for it. I longed with all my heart to ring up the Red Lea Quarantine Kennels and change my booking to two dogs instead of one; I spent hours thinking of a way I could justify taking her home, but I knew that without my family's help it was impossible.

Chapter 29
The Path to Rome

Tim left early the next morning and after a few minutes of feeling pathetically sorry for myself – it was the first time I'd been on my own for weeks – I pulled myself together and made a conscious decision to live my last few weeks to the full. I made a series of calls from the camp telephone to English people I knew living in Italy, asking if they could help find a good home for Bogey. Then I rang my parents, who cheered me up with some excellent news – the Pope wanted to see me! He was holding an outdoor service in St Peter's Square on Wednesday, 4 October, and Cardinal Hume had secured a ticket for me and arranged an introduction afterwards. I felt overwhelmed. It had always been a joke when I'd described myself as a pilgrim, but now when people said, 'Say hello to *Papa* from me' I'd be able to say yes. Rome took on a new importance and gave a focus to the end of my journey.

I realized that I had a race on my hands. Today was the 17th, so I had only two weeks to reach Rome, some 250 kilometres away. I set off with new purpose in my step and to my surprise found that I enjoyed being on my own again. Hannibal evidently thought so too, for he was in the most remarkably good mood and trotted most of the way to Quartaia that afternoon. There was something very comforting about just the four of us being together again and I noticed how much nicer people were to me when I was on my own – more generous when I asked for somewhere to stay, more friendly and talkative when I entered a shop or a bar.

As I walked deeper into the Chianti hills I came across numerous people out in the woods looking for mushrooms. It was a strange sight, as these hunters – dressed in green, with sticks and spaniel dogs to sniff out their prey – took their 'sport' desperately seriously. The mushrooms they picked looked terrifying to me, bizarre-shaped fungi that I would instantly have presumed to be poisonous. Some of the hunters took the trouble to explain which ones were edible and shocked me by telling me their market value – they were worth a fortune. They were extremely hard to find, though, and when I was on my own I never had much luck. The best I tasted was a big goldish-green one that I was given near Montecagnano; sliced, cooked in olive oil with garlic and poured over fresh pasta, the flavour was exquisite.

On Tuesday 19 September I stopped for a drink at a restaurant at Ponte della Spina, near Siena. A very friendly man brought me my beer and, after turning away a group of tourists saying he didn't serve food at lunchtime, he asked me if I'd like a sandwich. He also brought out two bowls of food for the dogs, and sat stroking them while asking me about my walk. He and his wife were a nice couple and took a definite shine to Bogey.

'Would you consider selling her?' he enquired.

I find it difficult to describe my feelings at that moment. Half of me felt that my prayers had been answered, that the search was over and I could stop worrying about Bogey's future. At the same time my heart sank – I was having to face the reality of leaving Bogey behind in Italy. I tried to stay calm and went with Renato to look at the area behind the restaurant where he would keep a dog. He wanted Bogey as a pet rather than a guard dog, because he thought she was beautiful and gentle and he'd like to give her a good home.

I explained that I couldn't make a decision there and then, I wanted to have Bogey with me till the end of my trip, so I asked if I could take his telephone number and call him from Rome. He said that was fine, then put some money in my MENCAP tin and wished me *buon viaggio*.

I spent the afternoon in mental turmoil. Nowhere would ever be good enough, I supposed, but it bothered me that he planned to keep Bogey in a kennel outside, not in the house. I'd hoped to find her a happy family with children who'd fuss over her all day and let her sleep on a bean bag by the fire at night, but realistically I knew that it would be impossible to find such a home for a Dobermann – Italians just don't treat big dogs like that. I decided to wait until I'd heard from the English people I'd asked to make enquiries.

As we climbed up into the next range of hills, I met dozens of mushroom hunters from Bagnaia and Grotti who were so friendly that it was impossible not to be in a good mood. It was late when I arrived at Corsano and I was only just in time for the village shop – as ever, I was out of dog food. I bought some fresh ravioli to eat with the fungi I'd been given and asked the shopkeeper if it would be all right to camp on the football pitch I'd seen below the road. (I'd taken to doing this again now that it was difficult to find good grass.) He said I should ask the captain of the team and went out to the bar next door to find him, returning a few minutes later with a nice-looking chap of about twenty called Marco. He looked very embarrassed but said it would be fine as long as I camped on the grass round the edge and not actually *on* the pitch. He led me down there and brought me a bucket of water while I chose a spot behind the goal posts at the far end. 'That'll be fine,' he said, and disappeared back up to the bar.

I quickly put up the tent as darkness fell and changed into a T-shirt and knickers so that I could have a good wash with the water Marco had brought. As I put my pasta into the pan and poured myself another glass of wine, I felt very happy and peaceful – I couldn't imagine anywhere in the world I'd rather be, and I pushed the question of Bogey's future to the back of my mind.

Suddenly the floodlights came on. My heart missed a beat and I scrambled back into the tent to find my shorts as dozens of young men poured on to the pitch. A match was about to start! I couldn't believe that no one had told me, but as I peered out and saw Marco waving at me, I began to laugh. It was too late now to move, so I decided I may as well enjoy the entertainment and settled down beside my stove and watched.

It was a farcical match, because half the players weren't taking the game seriously at all and kept kicking the ball over to my tent; they took longer and longer to retrieve it, sitting down and talking to me and going to have a look at Hannibal. Some of the others who were wanting a proper game became increasingly angry, and a screaming session ensued when the keeper at my end let in a goal while doing pull-ups over the top bar and winking at me.

After the final whistle five of the players came over and chatted for a while, sharing a mug of my wine and pinching all my cigarettes. They invited me up to the bar for a drink, but I pleaded fatigue and they were perfect gentlemen, leaving without any hassle at all.

I covered a tremendous distance the next day, track-walking across the dusty hills and finding some beautiful little villages – Radi, Barottoli and Murlo – sleepy places with mainly octogenarian inhabitants who gave us water before I'd even had a chance to ask. In the afternoon I was trudging along the track to Bibbiano feeling utterly exhausted when a couple of young men pulled up in a car in a flurry of dust. They began asking the usual questions – '*Dove vae col sumaro?*' – and I held on to Bogey's collar, a gesture that always made her seem more ferocious, for we were miles from anywhere and I felt vulnerable. They were nice guys, however; I discovered that one of them was a German who spoke fluent English and the other was a local who ran an equestrian centre nearby and was much more interested in Hannibal than in me. I asked him if he knew of anywhere nearby where I could camp, whereupon the German one, Boris, insisted I come to the farmhouse where he and his friends were on holiday. I was feeling brave and optimistic, so I accepted and wrote down the directions.

The farmhouse itself was beautiful, down in the Ombrone valley surrounded by flat agricultural land where we had crazy tractor races before supper; ducks and chickens were everywhere round the buildings (I had to put Bogey on a very short tether) and the old farmer came over from his modern house in Bibbiano to show me where I could put Hannibal.

The Germans turned out to be a party of six very whacky thirty-somethings from Berlin, four men and two very beautiful girls, who could all speak English and made me feel wonderfully welcome.

When I woke in the morning, Boris was eating a huge breakfast on the balcony with Gianni, the Italian chap who'd been in the car the day before. He was a gorgeous-looking bloke and I enjoyed talking to him as I drank cup after cup of coffee to try to rid myself of my hangover. He ran a riding holiday centre and knew every track and path for miles around, so I asked him if he could tell me the way to Montalcino, the town I could see up on the hill barely six kilometres away as the crow flies, but about twenty-five by road. He began drawing a map to explain where to cross the river, but it grew more and more complicated and after ten minutes he tore it up and asked me how I liked the idea of spending the day on a horse. He wasn't doing anything today, he said, so he could show me the way himself.

They were lovely horses, big chestnut mares that seemed both very fast and refreshingly biddable after Hannibal. The look on Hanny's face when he saw me get up on to the horse was priceless – 'What? Keep up with *that*?' – and I couldn't help laughing as he trotted along behind us desperately trying to keep up. I didn't even need to lead him, for he was terrified of being left behind and would eeyore pathetically if he got left behind. It felt fantastic to be moving at more than three miles an hour for once. When we reached a big open field Gianni held on to Hanny and let me go off on my own for a canter, which felt so wild and free I decided my next walk would definitely be with something speedier than a donkey.

Crossing the river wasn't easy, but there was no way I could have managed it at all without the horses to persuade Hannibal that it was possible. We transferred his packs on to my mare and let him follow in his own time. I still can't believe he did it, for the water came halfway up his tummy and he was practically swimming – and this was the donkey scared of puddles!

Gianni was excellent company. He came from Rome, but had given up city life about five years ago and moved out here to set up

224

his *agriturismo* centre in an old farm. He was much more knowledgeable and appreciative of the area than those who had always lived there, and as we walked along he constantly pointed out landmarks he thought would interest me. He taught me the Italian names for plants and trees that I didn't even know the English for, and he told me about the Etruscan settlements that had been discovered nearby.

Gianni was one of the very few Italians who seemed to understand my enjoyment of what I was doing. He was very envious, he said, and if I ever decided to do a trip on horseback would I please ask him to join me. When he left us at the foot of Montalcino he gave me a tiny mouth harp, which you twang with your fingers and make notes on with your mouth. He tried to show me how to do it, saying that when he went for long rides on his own he loved it. I wasted many hours trying but I never really managed it; nevertheless, it was a welcome change from singing and provided much amusement for the people I passed.

The climb up to Montalcino was exhausting – the slope is almost sheer on the northern side and Hannibal's good behaviour had disappeared with the horses, so as usual there was much mental and physical effort trying to persuade him uphill faster than two paces a minute. We all collapsed outside a bar at the top and Hanny and I shared a huge tub of chocolate ice-cream while tourists crowded round to stare at us. I had grown so used to being a spectacle that I just shook my MENCAP tin at them, put it down on the ground as a barrier between us and then got on with whatever I was doing while answering their questions and explaining my journey to them.

That day I stripped down to my swimming costume and had a scrub and hairwash in the fountain in the Piazza del Populo; a few in the audience tut-tutted, but the children seemed to think it was brilliant and some of them helped me pour water over my head to wash the shampoo out. Then they persuaded me to go and buy some more ice-cream for Hannibal because they thought it was so funny.

Best of all in Montalcino was the *Brunello* wine. Gianni had given me the names of some good ones that weren't too expensive and I bought six bottles, all red. Over the next week they provided me with an enormous amount of pleasure, as the days grew noticeably shorter, the nights grew colder and my evening meals once again played an important part in my life.

The next day I entered a part of Tuscany that was again different – the mountainous area of steep, wooded slopes around Monte Amiata dotted with fortified medieval towns. My favourite was Seggiano, perched on a remote hillside above the River Vivo. It was well worth the detour to walk through its narrow alleyways that looked as if they'd been made specially for donkeys. Santa Fiora, a small village further south, was another lovely surprise, for as I walked through on Saturday afternoon I discovered that a wedding was taking place at the beautiful Romanesque church. We stopped to watch as they all came out and followed the procession of cars and well-wishers through the steep streets before setting off into the wild and unspoilt Fiora valley. From the ruins of an old castle I found one of the best views in the whole of Tuscany, directly south as far as the Piana del Diavolo and the sea.

I spent the weekend walking non-stop through deserted high moorland. Apart from the sheep, I hardly saw a soul till Sunday evening, 24 September, when I reached the medieval town of Sorano. The northern approach to it took me through dramatic scenery; it marked the beginning of the Volsini range of mountains, whose volcanic history has thrown up strange spurs of irregular rock, on one of which stands Sorano above an incredibly steep gorge. Climbing up from the river, we passed row after row of dovecote tombs cut into the rock; they were unprotected and, to my surprise, unvandalized.

Gradually we entered the town itself, which is built on innumerable different levels; the evening sun was highlighting the warm coral shades of the buildings and it looked the stuff of fairytales. I ate a delicious meal at the old trattoria in the square and we camped that night in the stables of a riding school about a mile to the south of the town.

At exactly midday on 25 September we entered Lazio and embarked on the last stage of our journey. I danced round the sign post and counted the miles on my map – just seventy more to go. I'd already decided that I wasn't going to walk all the way into the centre of Rome with the animals. Ordinary towns were bad enough; to take them through the suburbs of a capital city would not only have been a nightmare, but cruel. I decided I would hit the fifty mile mark and then start looking for a place to leave Hannibal.

Winter seemed to arrive overnight. While walking along the upper rim of the volcanic crater in which lies the Lago di Bolsena, a heavy storm broke; I carried on walking, imagining it would pass, but it didn't and we were all drenched and freezing by the time we reached Piansano, another medieval village like Sorano sitting on the edge of a deep ravine. Our camp was almost washed away in the night, for the rain didn't let up at all, so in the morning I left Hanny sheltering in one of the old tombs carved into the steep rock and struggled up to the village with the dogs, feeling very cold and miserable.

Piansano was a perfect place to be stuck for twenty-four hours;

the old upper part was unspoilt, there wasn't a tourist in sight, and there were numerous cafés and bars to sit in with the dogs and write nostalgic letters home while the rain poured down outside. Old villagers told me that the crater where I'd spent the night used to contain the *Lagaccione* (the Nasty Great Lake) where malaria mosquitoes used to breed in their millions. This made me feel so itchy that I splashed out on a luxury I hadn't treated myself to since Spain – a shampoo and blow-dry at the hairdresser's up the street.

It was late afternoon before the rain stopped and we ventured forth once more, walking along the flat straight road to Tuscania and crossing over the line on my map marking the fifty mile radius I'd drawn around Rome. I was ready to finish now, and wanted to get on with sorting out the animal arrangements. As I entered Tuscania and asked a policeman to take a photo of us beside the signpost to Rome, I felt a sudden rush of pride. I'd done it. I'd walked over 2000 miles. I was suddenly in one of those crazy, happy moods when I can't keep the grin off my face and which always seem to make other people be nice to me. Stopping at the *gelateria* on the main street, I blew 10,000 lire on a scoop of every flavour they had on offer. Hannibal and I gorged ourselves and sparked off much interest from passers-by who stopped to enquire after the cause of my madness. They looked after the animals while I shopped in the supermarket, then I set off again along the road heading south of the town, yelling my head off and practically skipping with joy.

Next morning I crossed the Marta, climbed up on to the road to Vetralla, and decided to begin my search for a place to leave Hannibal for his month's quarantine. I thought it would take a few days at least, but I hoped I'd be able to find somewhere before Saturday, as I wanted to get Georgie on the only flight direct from Rome to Manchester, which was on Saturday afternoon.

At about lunchtime I passed a horse farm – fields full of beautiful black Maremma mares with their foals, surrounding a large house with outbuildings and stable blocks. I liked the look of the place – it was all very clean and well kept, so I decided it was worth a try. I summoned up my courage and walked up the drive, practising what I was going to say and hoping I wouldn't be turned away too harshly; despite my donkey expertise I was still intimidated by horsy people.

I found a woman in one of the outbuildings, who introduced herself as Marta Cesetti and asked if I needed help. I'm not sure why but I trusted her immediately. She said she thought it would be fine to leave Hanny in one of their stables and we went up to the big house to ask her father. He was almost blind and rather frightening, but he seemed to like the idea of a donkey on the farm and said yes.

Marta led the way to a stable block a few fields away and I followed, feeling stunned by my good fortune. I never dreamed that the very first place I asked would welcome us; it had all been too easy, and I felt disorientated as it gradually sank in that my journey had come to an end, that this stony track across a field was the final stage of my grand tour. It was an enormous anticlimax; I'd somehow expected trumpets blaring, crowds cheering and a great sense of achievement like I'd had at the signpost in Tuscania the day before. I thought I'd feel elation, but instead there was nothing but dread, my heart heavy in the knowledge of what I had to do in the next few days.

We arrived at a row of three stables with a yard outside where Hanny could roam free and a small room up above where Marta said I was welcome to stay. I tried to explain to her about the month's quarantine and the need for a blood test, but she stopped me, saying that she could handle everything – she exported horses to France, she said, and presumed that the regulations were the same. Her cousin was a vet and he would be able to do the blood test; we could sit down later and sort out the paperwork. She refused to accept a penny from me, even for Hannibal's food, and over the next few days she showed me more kindness than I could ever have hoped for from a stranger, and at a time when I so desperately needed it.

Chapter 30
Farewell to Georgie and Bogey

I spent the afternoon sitting in the little room above Hannibal's stable as the rain poured down outside, sorting through my belongings and trying to give Bogey enough love to last her a lifetime, and Georgie a good six months' worth.

I find this time at the end of my journey the hardest of all to write about – I can't last for more than a paragraph without crying, and remembering it fills me with an intensely personal kind of sorrow. No one else could know Bogey and George as I did, so no one can possibly understand what it meant saying goodbye to them. I can't help feeling that my descriptions have short-changed the dogs – the donkeys have had far more coverage. But the characteristics of the donkeys would have been much the same whoever had been leading them; I was merely an observer, so I found it easier to describe their individuality.

My relationship with the dogs was much more personal and the bond between us much harder to define. Both had been badly treated when I found them, so both adored me much more than I deserved. Both had gradually built up their confidence and trust, only to have me kick them in the face at the end of it. I'd helped Bogey to change into an affectionate, loving friend, with myself as the sole object of that affection and love, and now I was walking away. It seemed cruel that the person who had given meaning to her life should now shatter it. I'd never believed before that it was possible to love an animal too much, especially one so in need of affection, but I now realized that I'd done something very damaging. By being everything to Bogey, I was leaving her with nothing.

I feel vaguely ashamed that I can get so upset about animals; I'm meant to be a tough traveller, I'm meant to be able to cope with this kind of thing. But I haven't coped at all, and a year later I am still grieving for Bogey. Her memory is still a raw nerve in my heart, and the picture of her trusting face as I turned away for that last time is as clear as ever.

On Thursday I went to a travel agent in Viterbo and booked

Georgie on to the Saturday flight from Rome to Manchester. Then I rang all my English contacts whom I'd asked to look for a home for Bogey; none had had any luck, so I reluctantly pushed aside my dream of the big happy family who'd let her sleep on their beds and lick their faces. I rang Renato at Ponte della Spina, who sounded delighted to hear from me, and arranged to take Bogey to him the next day.

It took over four hours to reach Siena by train, which made me realize how far I'd walked in the last two weeks. I spent the journey sobbing into Bogey's side, wishing I could explain to her why I had to leave her, wishing more than anything that I could keep her. She just sat on my lap and helped Georgie lick the tears from my eyes.

We arrived at the restaurant at about six in the evening. Renato had bought her a wooden kennel, a new collar, a new lead, and he took her out to her yard and gave her a huge bowl of food. I did all I could to convince myself that she would be happy here, that it was the best home I could have found for her in the circumstances. The way she looked at me, adoring, trusting, believing that I'd come back, gave me a physical pain like nothing I've ever known before or since.

Renato gave me a glass of brandy and then drove me and Georgie to Siena station. He wanted to pay for Bogey, but I couldn't accept it – Judas and all that. Instead he gave me some bottles of wine and a cheese, which didn't seem so bad. I sat in the train feeling numb; I couldn't accept that I'd really done it and I think part of me had always believed that somehow I'd be able to keep her. I stared out of the window, hating myself, and the tears didn't stop till I reached Rome and had to get on with the next set of arrangements – Georgie's flight to Manchester.

The plane left at five on Saturday afternoon and I'd been told to be there two hours before take-off. The morning was frantic, scouring Rome for a travelling box big enough for her and obtaining the necessary papers. Even though I had Georgie's rabies vaccination certificate from England, which was still valid, and even though English law, because of the six months' compulsory quarantine, makes no demand that a dog should have been vaccinated against rabies, Italian law insisted that I get an Italian certificate, take it to the Ministry of Agriculture for a permission-to-export certificate, then take the latter to a post office for the necessary rubber stamps. Since all the relevant offices closed at midday and were situated at different ends of a city I'd never been to before, I remember Saturday morning as little more than a blur of desperate running and paying enormous taxi fares. We reached the airport by two o'clock and went to the British Airways information desk to ask where I should take Georgie.

I was in too emotional a state to cope with what happened next and I must have seemed pathetic to everyone I came across that afternoon. I was so tired – only on arriving in Rome the previous evening had I discovered that *nowhere* accepts dogs, so I was forced to sleep with the tramps on the station floor behind the lockers where the guards couldn't find us. I'd felt so emotionally dead that I wasn't even frightened, but I didn't sleep much. I hoped that once I said goodbye to George, I could book into a hotel and spend twenty-fours in bed.

'Who told you that you could send a dog on this plane?' asked a big fat man in BA uniform behind the desk.

I explained that it had been someone at the BA cargo desk whom the travel agent in Viterbo had rung for me on Thursday; she had given me the flight number and even all the specifications for the papers I needed and the type of travelling box required.

'But cargo customs do not work at the weekend,' the fat man said. 'To send your dog on that plane you should have brought her in yesterday afternoon.'

The details of the next two hours now seem farcical, but basically consisted of increasingly important airport officials telling me that there was no way I could send my dog on the plane to Manchester. Since the only planes that fly to Manchester are on a Saturday, and since officialdom grudgingly agreed that with no staff to look after her I could not have left George at the airport for over twenty-four hours in a small cage, there was no way that a dog could ever be sent on that plane. What made the whole thing so crazy was that if I'd been travelling on the plane myself, George would not have been counted as cargo but as excess baggage, which would be handled by ordinary customs and there wouldn't be a problem. But not only were the BA staff unrelenting, they were also rude and offensive and they managed to reduce me to a sobbing wreck.

'But you can't send a dog to England anyway,' one of them told me. 'It's not allowed, they have to spend six months in quarantine.'

I tried to keep calm and told him that yes, I knew that, that was why I had all the paperwork saying which quarantine kennels I had arranged to meet her at Manchester airport.

'Why do you want to send a dog into quarantine? It's cruel, six months locked up in a cage.'

At this I went to the Ladies and gave myself the shot of Valium that I'd bought for George. I returned and tried to organize an alternative. I'd have to return on Monday and send her to Heathrow, then have her transferred to a shuttle flight up to Manchester. I discovered that this would cost me over £100 more, plus a handling fee at Heathrow, and Lord knows how I would know

231

which flight to tell the kennels to meet. I was told it was impossible to book George on any flight before she'd been through customs, so there was nothing more I could do till Monday morning.

I spent the next two nights at a camp site outside Rome – luckily I'd brought my tent with me, just in case. I thanked God for giving me such fantastic parents, for after I rang them from the airport to tell them to cancel the quarantine arrangements for that evening, my father contacted British Airways at Manchester and organized the whole thing from that end. I returned to Rome airport on Monday morning to find the now-open cargo office expecting me, with Georgie's ticket all ready and waiting.

Putting Georgie into her cage, knowing that she would not run free again until April of the next year, was terrible. I'd spent the whole weekend alone with her, playing with her constantly in a vain attempt to make up for the months of deprivation that lay ahead, wondering whether I wasn't being even more cruel than I had been to Bogey. I couldn't stop thinking of all the stories I'd heard about dogs dying in quarantine, or going so crazy from the solitude that they'd had to be put to sleep. The cargo officials looked on calmly as I cried and then wheeled her away. I prayed that the Valium I'd given her would work quickly, and then I went to the airport bar and downed a double Scotch to try to erase the memory of her bewildered eyes that hadn't left me till I was out of sight.

I caught a bus back to Tuscania and spent the rest of the day with Marta, who tried to keep me busy and distracted from my grief. She took me to her house in the medieval section of the town and I played with her dogs, which helped somehow, and found out about her father as I looked at the beautiful paintings covering every wall of the house. Giuseppe Cesetti, I discovered, is a brilliant artist, an eighty-seven-year-old maestro of Italian painting. His most famous work is of the Maremma horses that Marta breeds, but my favourite was a huge painting of a brown, horned cow that covered a whole wall of Marta's dining-room. Marta gave me an enormous book of his life's work, and told me that he still paints, even though he has to undergo regular eye operations to stop him going blind.

She also gave me the numbers of various equine transport companies and I made enquiries about the cost of taking Hannibal back to England. None of them gave me a quote of less than £2000 and I began to wonder whether I was crazy to take him home. But after saying goodbye to George and Bogey I couldn't bear to lose Hannibal too – he was my last link – and because I was actually allowed to take him home, I felt that I wasn't going to let something as unimportant as money stop me. Hanging on to Hannibal somehow

232

made up for my betraying the others; keeping him made me able to live with myself more easily. I knew that Marta would treat him well over the next few weeks, so leaving him was comparatively easy. He was the lucky one – he'd be coming home in a month.

Chapter 31
Papal Finale

After supper on Monday Marta persuaded me to ring Giovanni, and to my astonishment he made what he said was the first romantic gesture of his life and said he'd drive to Rome the next evening and take me out to dinner to celebrate. I felt happy for what seemed like the first time in ages, and my bus journey to Rome the next morning was surprisingly cheerful. I went over and over in my mind what I was going to say to the Pope, realizing that this time tomorrow I'd be with him, and I began to feel very excited about it.

Booking into a little hotel near the Vatican, I set off on a wildly extravagant shopping spree. It felt weird being an ordinary tourist – no one was staring at me, no one was clambering round me asking what I was doing, and I'm rather ashamed to admit that I hated it. I felt like a faded pop star who wasn't recognized any more; being an oddity had been part of my life for so long that I felt almost lost without it.

I loved Rome, which surprised me; I thought I'd feel overwhelmed by such a large city, but the sheer scale and grandeur of the ancient buildings made me an instant devotee. London and Paris paled into insignificance by comparison. Maybe it was the sunshine, or the fact that I was meeting Giovanni later, but Rome struck me as a very romantic city – the bridges over the Tiber, the churches everywhere, the street cafés and the beautiful shops made me long to have someone to share it with.

I spent a fortune on my Pope outfit, as it's always been referred to since. Shops selling cheap clothes seemed thin on the ground, so I ended up in the designer boutiques of the Via Condotti. Since February the only new clothes I'd bought were socks and I think I was trying to make up for lost time. It felt glorious trying on things that were utterly impractical, knowing that it didn't matter any more, and I was drawn like a magnet to flimsy materials, pale colours, tight belts and high heels.

I eventually decided on a flowery chiffon silk shirt with a huge lace collar and a brooch button, and a burgundy crushed velvet skirt with a suede belt to match. I splashed out on some burgundy shoes, with a neat, two-inch heel that made my legs look so elegant I hardly recognized them. Then I went mad at the Elizabeth Arden counter of the huge department store on the Via del Corso, making the most of the 10 per cent discount for foreigners and buying all the beauty aids that I'd only been able to dream of since February – foundation, powder, blusher, lipstick. Back at the hotel that evening I went through the whole rigmarole of preparing for a date. It felt like a dream as I rubbed Je Reviens skin lotion on to my newly shaven legs, combed conditioning wax through my hair. Putting on my make-up took ages – I'd almost forgotten how to do it, and my skin felt weird afterwards, as if covered in a mask. I hardly recognized myself in the mirror – but I liked what I saw, and I felt very happy and confident as I set off towards the Piazza di Spagna to meet Giovanni.

It was a lovely evening. I was determined to stay cheerful and kept the conversation firmly away from the events of the past week; instead we spoke of the future, of how I didn't want to go back to London and do law, of how Giovanni wanted to break away from his home town and the only lifestyle he'd ever known. He'd had his thirtieth birthday the previous week and was feeling he didn't have much time left to chase his dreams. As the wine flowed we planned a huge trek round South America together, raising money for Amnesty and taking at least a year over it. Compared to Bar school, the thought of spending a whole year with this handsome, funny man at my side seemed like heaven, and if there was a way we could have set off the very next day, I would have done it.

Giovanni for some reason found it hilarious that someone like me should be meeting the Pope; he'd better not tell his mother, he said, or she might think I was a nice girl and be after him to marry me. He came up with some priceless suggestions about what I should say to him, as did my mother when I rang her the next morning. ('Talk to him about contraception,' she said, 'and women in the church, and embryo research, and . . .')

Early on Wednesday, I woke up feeling like a five-year-old at Christmas, my heart in my mouth with excitement and so much adrenalin pumping round my body that I found it impossible to stay in bed. The service began at 10.30 and I arrived at St Peter's an hour earlier to find it already thronging with people. I joined a queue at one of the entrances, where security men were checking tickets and searching bags and pockets. As I looked around me I suddenly felt sure that Mum had got it wrong, that all my ticket entitled me to was a place in the audience, like all these other

236

people next to me. Their tickets looked no different from mine. I felt disappointed and overdressed, and I took off my shoes, wishing I hadn't spent so much money on my outfit. My feet were in agony and I kept stumbling; my legs were so unused to high heels that they'd forgotten how to walk in them.

The file slowly moved forward. I wished I'd arrived earlier so that I could have got a good position; now I merely hoped to be able to see the Pope.

When I reached the guard and showed him my ticket, I was startled to hear him say 'Follow me' and start clearing a path through the crowds. We walked right up to the front, past the barriers that kept the ordinary ticket-holders away from the huge stage at the foot of St Peter's steps. Around this stage were neat rows of wooden chairs and I was led to seat nine in the front row on the right-hand side.

Wow! I've rarely felt so privileged. There were fifteen of these numbered chairs and they were quickly filling up; people in the crowd looked across at us enviously and some even took photos. I sat down feeling overwhelmed and suddenly very nervous, wishing I knew the formalities of what was going to happen. Photographers began coming down the line asking for our addresses, then an official checked we were all sitting in the correct places.

I looked upwards to the silvery blue dome and marvelled at the sheer scale of the building, and the care and precision put into every detail. I felt pleased that the sight of this magnificent place would be forever associated with the end of my journey.

Meanwhile, the seats opposite were filling up with purple cardinals, and the ones directly in front of the stage with red cardinals. Behind us were, I think, people from the embassies who appeared accustomed to all the pomp and ceremony.

I tried to make out the other people in my row. To my right was a Spanish family, very expensively dressed; at the end on my left were an American couple. I wondered what they'd all done to be here; then a Canadian lady sat down next to me and made me laugh when she explained to me that she'd just walked to Rome from London to raise money for multiple sclerosis. She'd done the whole journey in six weeks, at about three times the speed of mine, and had raised about £50,000. I suddenly felt rather small.

As the clock ticked round to half past ten the crowd gradually fell silent. The Pope came down the steps with very little fuss – I think I'd expected a drum-roll – flanked by three others, and I wasn't sure at first whether it really was him. He was smaller than I'd expected and looked much older. He climbed the steps on to the stage and began the service, whose theme was a call for peace in the Middle East. Apart from the setting, it was surprisingly like an ordinary service, the Pope just like an ordinary priest. He had a wonderful voice and the sound of the prayers as he read them in Italian was breathtaking.

It was a good service, much more modern and informal than I'd expected. The lessons were read by young people, each one in a different language, and the sermon didn't go on too long. I grew increasingly nervous as I wondered what was going to happen afterwards and what on earth I should say. It was incredibly hot and I tried surreptitiously to fan my skin under my shirt, praying I wouldn't have any damp patches showing at the vital moment.

Suddenly the service was over. The Pope came down the steps and I held my breath, but first he went over to talk to the band. Then he turned towards us and the official beside him began to read our details from a clip board.

He worked down the line quite quickly, shaking hands, talking occasionally, giving everyone a small blessing. I tried to concentrate on how all the women were shaking his hand, bowing their heads and making a brief curtsy, but all I could really think of as he walked down the line in a blaze of camera flashes and cheering from the crowds was how I wished the animals were with me. I wanted them to share in the honour of all this and I wanted everyone to know what we had done together.

Suddenly he was shaking the hand of the girl beside me. It was me next. I felt terrified, with that swooning light-headedness I've only had before when about to walk out on stage and know I'm not going to be able to remember a single line.

He stepped towards me and looked into my eyes, and I felt overwhelmed by the kindness in his face. I can never describe it without sounding foolish, but he looked so good and honest that something tugged at my heart. He stared right into my eyes and smiled as I did all the wrong things, holding both hands out in front of me and not a curtsy in sight. He put his hands round mine and began speaking, saying I must be the girl from England – well done and congratulations. I wish I'd said something worthwhile back, but all I could manage was '*Si*' and '*Grazie*' – I hoped my smiles made up for it.

He gave me a blessing, in Italian, and suddenly he'd moved on to the Canadian lady beside me. I couldn't take my eyes off him till he was out of sight, then as I looked around me I felt puffed up with pride, grinning from ear to ear. I thought how incredible it was that a man whose views I didn't really agree with, whose statements had often made me angry could make me feel so happy just by holding my hands and smiling at me. He gave the impression that the meeting was as memorable for him as it had been for me, which of course couldn't have been so, but still.

I spent the next hour hugging and kissing everyone who gave me a chance. I was on cloud nine, skipping down the Via della Concili-azione, exchanging addresses with the Canadian lady and stopping for a drink with some of the others from my hotel who'd been in the crowd and wanted to know every syllable he'd uttered to me.

Once back at the hotel, I suddenly had a very strong desire to go home, a feeling that to stay would be inviting an awful anticlimax. I didn't want to come down off this incredible high and the way to avoid it was to go on to something even better – home. There would always be another time to explore Rome.

I found a travel agent, said I wouldn't go on a British Airways plane as a matter of principle and booked on to the Alitalia evening flight that reached Heathrow just in time to connect with the last shuttle to Manchester. After a series of phone calls I eventually tracked down my mother at a business meeting in Leicester and she agreed to pick me up from the airport on her way home. I couldn't believe that everything was working out so well, and I still couldn't stop smiling – I even kissed the hotel manager goodbye as I paid my bill and gave a huge tip to the taxi driver who took me to the bus terminal. I was now a familiar face on the airport bus – this was my fifth trip on it – and the driver refused to believe that I was really leaving this time.

For once I wasn't even bothered by my usual fear of planes. I found it strange talking to the other passengers about my trip – it was already in the past tense, the final chapter coming to an end. The baggage terminal seemed to provide everyone with great amusement, as among the designer suitcases my pack saddle appeared on the carousel, followed by six very faded canvas saddle bags.

Mum was waiting for me at Manchester, looking beautiful in her blue business suit, and as we drove north I felt hopelessly excited – the miles couldn't roll by fast enough. At last we were home, and I ran in to see the cats, sitting around the Aga just where I'd left them, and out again to see the sheep. Then I went upstairs to the bathroom, suddenly the most beautiful part of the house; I ran twelve glorious inches of bubbling hot water and spent nearly two hours soaking in my first proper bath since April.

A selection of bestsellers from Headline

FICTION

GASLIGHT IN PAGE STREET	Harry Bowling	£4.99 □
LOVE SONG	Katherine Stone	£4.99 □
WULF	Steve Harris	£4.99 □
COLD FIRE	Dean R Koontz	£4.99 □
ROSE'S GIRLS	Merle Jones	£4.99 □
LIVES OF VALUE	Sharleen Cooper Cohen	£4.99 □
THE STEEL ALBATROSS	Scott Carpenter	£4.99 □
THE OLD FOX DECEIV'D	Martha Grimes	£4.50 □

NON-FICTION

THE SUNDAY TIMES SLIM PLAN	Prue Leith	£5.99 □
MICHAEL JACKSON The Magic and the Madness	J Randy Taraborrelli	£5.99 □

SCIENCE FICTION AND FANTASY

SORCERY IN SHAD	Brian Lumley	£4.50 □
THE EDGE OF VENGEANCE	Jenny Jones	£5.99 □
ENCHANTMENTS END Wells of Ythan 4	Marc Alexander	£4.99 □

All Headline books are available at your local bookshop or newsagent, or can be ordered direct from the publisher. Just tick the titles you want and fill in the form below. Prices and availability subject to change without notice.

Headline Book Publishing PLC, Cash Sales Department, PO Box 11, Falmouth, Cornwall, TR10 9EN, England.

Please enclose a cheque or postal order to the value of the cover price and allow the following for postage and packing:
UK & BFPO: £1.00 for the first book, 50p for the second book and 30p for each additional book ordered up to a maximum charge of £3.00.
OVERSEAS & EIRE: £2.00 for the first book, £1.00 for the second book and 50p for each additional book.

Name ....

Address ....

....

....